The cruelty man

Manchester University Press

Copyright © Sarah-Anne Buckley 2013

The right of Sarah-Anne Buckley be identified as the author of this work has been asserted by her in accordance with the Copyright, Designs and Patents Act 1988.

Published by Manchester University Press
Altrincham Street, Manchester M1 7JA, UK
www.manchesteruniversitypress.co.uk

British Library Cataloguing-in-Publication Data is available

ISBN 978 1 5261 0896 8 *paperback*

First published by Manchester University Press in hardback 2013
This edition first published 2017

The publisher has no responsibility for the persistence or accuracy of URLs for any external or third-party internet websites referred to in this book, and does not guarantee that any content on such websites is, or will remain, accurate or appropriate.

Printed by Lightning Source

The cruelty man

Child welfare, the NSPCC and the State in
Ireland, 1889–1956

Sarah-Anne Buckley

Manchester University Press

For Eva

Contents

	List of tables	*page* viii
	Acknowledgements	xi
	Foreword	xiii
	Terms and abbreviations	xvii
	Note on sources	xix
	Introduction	1
1	The origins of child welfare in Ireland, 1838–1952	10
2	The NSPCC in Ireland, 1889–1921	46
3	The NSPCC 'in transition', 1922–56	70
4	Institutionalisation, the State and the NSPCC	110
5	Incest and immorality	152
6	Gender, familial problems and the NSPCC	171
	Conclusion	200
	Appendices	204
	Select bibliography	208
	Index	219

List of tables

Note: Prior to 1922, tables refer to the thirty-two counties of Ireland, after 1922 they refer to the twenty-six counties, unless otherwise stated.

1.1	Number of persons proceeded against summarily for offences against the Elementary Education Act, 1895–1908	*page* 26
3.1	Number of NSPCC cases in Ireland, 1934–39, by offence	76
3.2	Sample incomes and rents from NSPCC case files, taken from sample cases in the inspector books and the case files	78
3.3	Breakdown of cases in sample of NSPCC files for Wexford District Branch in 1939, by 'nature of allegation' box on inspection forms	83
3.4	Number of families investigated by the NSPCC for living in overcrowded conditions, 1934–39	94
4.1	Number of children in industrial schools in Ireland, England and Wales in 1881	119
4.2	Number of boys and girls committed to reformatories in 1881	120
4.3	Breakdown by sex of those sent to industrial schools and reformatories in 1881	120
4.4	Number of children sent to industrial schools as a result of investigations in Wexford by the NSPCC, 1937–39	135
4.5	Classification of schools to which children were sent as a result of investigations in Wexford by the NSPCC, 1937–39	135

List of tables

5.1	Number of investigations of immoral surroundings or moral danger and other wrongs in NSPCC annual reports, 1933–50	162
6.1	Class 1 offences punishable by trial by jury in 1881: comparison between Ireland, England and Scotland	173
6.2	Number of persons tried at the Assizes and Quarter Sessions for offences against children and nature of indictable offence, 1880–1908	174
6.3	Number of persons proceeded against summarily under the Poor Law Acts for 'neglecting to maintain family', 1880–1908	175
6.4	Number of persons sent to trial at the Assize Courts and the Quarter Sessions for the indictable offence of 'Cruelty to or neglect of children', 1895–1917	176
6.5	Number of persons convicted on indictable offence of cruelty to children, 1924–49	178
6.6	Number of persons committed on conviction for the non-indictable offence of cruelty to or neglect of children, 1927–40	179

Acknowledgements

This book began as a PhD thesis at University College Cork (UCC), and was completed as I embarked on my academic career in National University of Ireland, Galway (NUI Galway). It is therefore the result of many people's time, energy and support for which I am very grateful.

Firstly, I thank Donal Ó Drisceoil, my supervisor at UCC. Throughout my undergraduate and postgraduate career, he encouraged me to look at history critically, to study topics I was passionate about and not to shy away from controversy. He is an excellent scholar, a mentor and a friend. Over the last number of years, the Department of History at UCC has been a central part of my life and has assisted me in many ways to which I am very grateful. In particular, I would like to thank Sandra McAvoy, Liz Steiner-Scott, David Ryan, Geoff Roberts, Charlotte Holland and all the administrative staff. I know that the friendships I have made there will continue to be a constant, and to Ruth Canning, James Ryan, Barbara O'Donoghue, John Borgonovo, Gregory Foley and all the David's 'Sláinte' – I didn't know it was possible to talk history for so many hours until I met you all. To the staff in the Department of History at NUI Galway, you have all made me feel so welcome, I consider myself incredibly lucky to call Galway home now. As there are far too many excellent colleagues to single out, I want to say to them all that I look forward to the coming years and continuing to work in such a warm, vibrant and engaging department.

Thanks are due to the staff of the UCC's Boole Library and the National Archives of Ireland, in particular Dave, Brendan and Robert. Similarly, the staff of the Limerick Office of the Irish Society for the Prevention of Cruelty to Children (ISPCC) let me sit for hours, working my way through reports and files, and I thank in particular Suzanne and Aoife. As always, this would not have been possible without the funding I received as a postgraduate from the Irish Research Council for the Humanities and Social Sciences (IRCHSS). A number of people have guided me in developing this book from a thesis. Maria Luddy and James Ryan read the manuscript in its entirety, for which I am very grateful. At Manchester University Press, Tony Mason, Lianne Slavin and Corinne Orde have been a pleasure to deal with. To Vincent Browne, who kindly agreed to write the foreword, I am very thankful and as always a fan. To Jim Beresford – we'll write the story of child imprisonment in depth one day soon; this book will only touch on the enormity of your and others' experiences.

I am extremely indebted to my family and friends for their support while this work was in progress. To Jason, you believed I'd finish this long before I did, thank you. Ciara Breathnach has encouraged this work and me for the last number of years to which I am, and continue to be very grateful. To Kate, Áine, Alice, Sarah, Gerry, Mary, Graham, Elaine and Séan – you all helped in so many different ways I hope to repay. To Adrian, you listened to me when I complained, took me away from it when I needed to get away, and made me feel loved all the time. Thank you.

Finally, to Mam, Dad, Lynn and Eva, thank you doesn't even begin. I wish I had the words to express how much you have helped and in so many ways. This is as much yours as mine.

Sarah-Anne Buckley

Foreword

Vincent Browne

A hundred years ago, in 1913, William Martin Murphy, the owner of the Dublin United Transport Company, demanded that employees of the company forswear their membership of the Irish Transport and General Workers' Union or face dismissal. The workers refused. William Martin Murphy locked them out of their place of employment, and thus began one of the most celebrated labour disputes in Irish history, involving 20,000 other Dublin workers who came out on strike in support of their transport colleagues.

The scale of poverty at the time among the working class in Dublin was already legendary. The dispute worsened the poverty, and children literally starved. A feminist, Dora Montefiore, instigated the evacuation of some hundreds of these starving children to the homes of sympathetic workers in Liverpool for the duration of the strike and, later, to the homes of Catholic working-class people in Belfast. The Catholic Archbishop of Dublin, William Walsh, stated that he had read of the initiative 'with nothing short of consternation'. To Catholic mothers who were thinking of sending their starving children to Liverpool, he posed the question: 'Have they abandoned their faith?'

In the ultimately successful effort to prevent these working-class children from being sent to Liverpool and Belfast for the duration of the dispute, one of the most prominent organisations was the Ancient Order of Hibernians, a Catholic secret society. One of its leaders was John Nugent. At a public meeting held to celebrate the successful blocking of the evacuation to Belfast, he said: 'We are patient with wrong; we are patient with poverty; we are patient with the violation of rights; but there is one thing that we are not patient with, for patience then would be a crime, not a virtue – we have no patience with them who would deprive the little ones of their faith'.

This book by Sarah-Anne Buckley shows vividly how patient the Irish establishment and the Irish Catholic Church were with poverty, starvation, and cruelty towards and abuse of children and women. That patience became perhaps the most striking feature of the new Irish Independent State and, arguably, remains so. The book's focus is the National Society for the Prevention of Cruelty to Children (NSPCC), which became, in part, an agency for the infliction of cruelty on children, aided and abetted by the Irish State.

The book shows that in the first decades after independence parental rights were seriously eroded. It also traces how legislation on compulsory education, institutional provision, welfare and illegitimacy inflicted terrible hardships on poor parents and children. Children were taken from their parents very often simply because of poverty at a time when the State largely ignored poverty.

The primary concern was not the material welfare of children but the preservation of their 'faith' in Catholicism; and this was the primary concern not just of the Roman Catholic Church and its support organisations, but also of the State.

An enduring concern throughout the nineteenth century and into the twentieth, which led to the establishment of Catholic orphanages and schools, was the fear of proselytism. This, for instance, led to the exclusion of Ireland from the provision of school meals to children under the 1906 School's Meals Act. This exclusion followed a protest by Catholic clergy and others who feared that would take the responsibility from feeding children away from parents, however poverty-stricken they may have been.

Not that the entitlement of parents was of primary concern, for, as this book shows, the first decades of Irish independence saw an erosion of the rights of parents as carers and educators through legislation on compulsory education, institutional provision, welfare and illegitimacy.

The 1920s saw the introduction of censorship, the abolition of legal divorce, a ban on women sitting on juries and the introduction of the civil service marriage bar, all the fruits of Irish independence. These are topics that are covered in this book, as is the issue of birth control, which was driven underground from 1930 to 1970, leading to the importation of illegal contraceptives and backstreet abortions.

The book also catalogues instances of shocking abuse and neglect. For instance, an NSPCC report for 1933–34 recorded: 'The inspector's attention was directed to a family living in one room (in the Dublin slums), in a tenement house. In this one room fourteen persons (seven adults and seven children) [of] mixed sexes, lived, slept and ate. The room was about 17ft by 10ft and contained two beds only. Several members of the family had to sleep on the floor'.

The years of the Second World War (called 'the Emergency' in this southern State) witnessed the imposition of an austerity involving cuts in public expenditure that now seems very familiar. As Sarah-Anne Buckley shows, the areas which received the biggest cuts were the social services – housing grant loans, unemployment payments and employment schemes.

Sarah-Anne Buckley quotes Tony Gray, who became a distinguished *Guardian* journalist, claiming that by the end of the Second World War the Irish 'were doing better than they'd ever done since the state was founded'. Yet one unpublished account into the level of poverty in Cork city during the Emergency estimated that forty-five per cent of households were living in destitution and deprivation by 1944.

James Dillon, who was twice Minister for Agriculture in coalition governments (1948–51 and 1954–57) and later leader of Fine Gael (1959–66), seemed, in the latter role, almost a Victorian character (he was, incidentally, a relative of John Nugent of the Ancient Order of Hibernians). It is surprising then to learn from this book that he was among the few politicians who regularly raised in the Dáil issues to do with the treatment of disadvantaged children and people living in poverty.

In 1939, Dillon spoke in the Dáil about the treatment of children: 'If the conditions surrounding juvenile delinquency in this country were known in Great Britain or in America, we would be scandalised. In the worst and most backward city in America, conditions such as we have in this country would not be tolerated for a house. In no part of England would, such conditions as at obtain here be present for an hour'.

Dillon had already railed in 1937 against the underfunding of programmes to deal with juvenile delinquency and with children with disabilities. He complained about the exclusion of the public from children's courts and he wanted the abolition of reformatories and of borstal institutions.

The book shows that as early as 1935 it was clear that grievous abuse was being perpetrated in Artane Industrial School. A letter from Hannah Sheehy Skeffington recorded: 'A few weeks ago, a boy named John Byrne lost his life in Artane Industrial School following a beating by a teacher named Lynch. This terrible tragedy calls for an investigation. There is every reason to believe that the authorities intend to let the matter pass and take no action. The boy's parents (he was their only son) are endeavouring to take the matter into the Courts and to make a claim for compensation for the death of their son. But this cannot be done without financial help. £5 is needed at once to enable the solicitor to proceed'.

In contrast to the situation that prevailed in Ireland, the British state from the 1930s onwards began to assume responsibility for ensuring a minimum standard of living for all and, following the war, a 'cradle to grave' welfare state. When the Irish State tentatively broached a similar initiative here with the mother-and-child scheme of 1951, the Catholic Church was outraged (again) and the State backed off.

Sarah-Anne Buckley records: 'The [Irish] State ... continued to rely on the services of (voluntary) organisations, instead of trying to develop a proper public welfare system [here]'.

The patience that John Nugent spoke of a hundred years ago – patience with wrongdoing, poverty and the violation of rights – persists. We remain patient with almost one in five children (19.5 per cent) aged between nought and seventeen years who are at risk of poverty, 8.1 per cent of children who are living in consistent poverty and, in 2010, over 200,000 children who were living in households that were experiencing poverty.

This book provides a backdrop to the depressingly shocking revelations of abuse in residential institutions and in Catholic dioceses. It shows that such abuse was not an aberration but was part of a culture of abuse. The book is therefore a hugely valuable resource in our understanding of Irish society.

Terms and abbreviations

CC	Circuit Court
CCC	Central Criminal Court
CICA	Commission to Inquire into Child Abuse
CRF	Convict Reference File
CSWB	Catholic Social Welfare Bureau
DDA	Dublin Diocesan Archives
Ireland	Prior to 1922, Ireland refers to the whole island comprising thirty-two counties. After 1922, the constitutional term 'Ireland' is used to refer to the Irish Free State and later the Republic of Ireland
IRPRS	Irish Catholic Protection Rescue Society
IER	*Irish Ecclesiastical Record*
IHA	Irish Housewives Association
ISPCC	Irish Society for the Prevention of Cruelty to Children
JCWSSW	Joint Committee of Women's Societies and Social Workers
JSSSI	*Journal of the Statistical and Social Society of Ireland*
NAI	National Archives of Ireland
NLI	National Library of Ireland
NSPCC	National Society for the Prevention of Cruelty to Children
NVA	National Vigilance Association
SPCC	Society for the Prevention of Cruelty to Children
SVDP	Society of St Vincent de Paul
WNHA	Women's National Health Association

Note on sources

Archive of the NSPCC

The archive of the NSPCC is held in the offices of the Irish Society for the Prevention of Cruelty to Children (ISPCC) in Limerick. Near the end of research for this study the Society employed an archivist to catalogue the materials. Prior to this, all files were kept in boxes sorted by decade of investigation. Records can be broken down into three categories – the annual reports (limited for the period prior to 1933, but more complete from 1933 to 1955); the inspectors' books (1921 onwards); and the case files. The earliest case file located is from 1919, and there are 247 files available, up to and including 1940. The majority of these relate to the Wexford District branch, with a small number from Mayo and Wicklow. There was fire in 1961 in the central office, and as a result the other branch case files were destroyed. From 1930, a generic form was used (see Appendix A) to document cases; prior to this the files are made up of letters and notes relating to cases. The year 1940 was chosen as the end point for the examination of case files in this study for reasons of privacy. While other researchers have looked at a certain amount of these materials, principally Moira Maguire,[1] this is the first study to utilise all available materials up to 1940 in the case of the files, and up to 1955 for the official reports. The Society in Northern Ireland is not addressed, as even for the period before partition, documentation was not available to this researcher.

Due to the sensitive nature of the files, a confidentiality agreement was signed, wherein it was agreed that all names used would be fictional, and all record numbers would differ from the agency case numbers. Original case file numbers were replaced with a coding system unique to this study (for example CF #203). As previously mentioned, both qualitative and quantitative analysis was employed in the research. While the quantitative evidence is imperative, the qualitative evidence adds essential and colourful detail about the situations for children and families.

Case files in the NSPCC archive

Of the 247 case files available from 1919 to 1940, the majority are from the Wexford branch, with a small number from the Cork and Waterford branches. The quality of these files varies greatly. Prior to 1930, most were handwritten letters from families, neighbours, parish priests, gardaí, other NSPCC inspectors and members of religious orders working in institutions. From 1930, a generic case file template was used. This recorded details such as age, gender, offence, comments on parents, number of supervisory visits and actions taken by the inspector. In *Discipline and Punishment*, Michel Foucault demonstrates the move to individualisation in social work from the beginning of the twentieth century, as characterised organisationally by the use of the case file by reformers.[2] The Society in Ireland appears to have been late in instigating this procedure, but its use of the case file does highlight its professionalisation as a social work agency.

The earliest case file located relates to an investigation of neglect and starvation as a result of desertion. In the report the wife states, 'his people were not satisfied to keep me and our children without payment and I came back to Wexford to live and reported my case to the inspector of the NSPCC Society who has since been endeavouring to trace my husband ... I hope you can get my husband arrested and dealt with for his cruel neglect.' The inspector describes the man as 'fond of drink and an alleged immoral man'. It was not until 1921, two years after the initial letter, that the payment of outdoor relief was provided to the woman. What the case demonstrates is both the need to plead destitution to receive any welfare and the use of the Society by women to gain this small financial assistance. The remaining cases in the 1920s are primarily from 1929 and relate to instances of desertion, the committal of children to industrial schools and girls who had deserted babies in the County Home. Because of a lack of documentation, it is not known whether a professional case record was used. In the 1930s, the case files are more complete, particularly from 1938 to 1940. Prior to the late 1930s, most of the files consist of letters regarding children in institutions. These are addressed to the inspector from religious orders, families, the Boards of Health, government departments and charitable organisations such as the Society of the St Vincent de Paul (ISPCC, Limerick). Generally, the limitations of the files lie in their inconsistency and small quantity. However, for 1939, one half of the case files for Wexford District branch have survived, providing a case study of the Society which will be discussed in Chapter 2. Also, when supplemented with the annual reports and inspector books, the files provide detail on situations that would be difficult to document otherwise. While many were written by inspectors whose bias towards clients is apparent, many also contain statements from the families involved.

Annual reports of the NSPCC

From the foundation of the Dublin Aid Committee in 1889, the annual reports of the NSPCC provide rich detail on the work of the Society. Statistical evidence was, and still is, a huge part of the reports, as are sample cases. While statistics provided the Society with the opportunity to showcase its work, sample cases allowed it to highlight issues of concern at that time – from intemperance to desertion. Both must be investigated with these biases in mind. Aside from quantitative evidence, the reports contain the names of subscribers, the sums they donated and the names of all inspectors and members of each branch committee. They demonstrate the connection between the British and Irish branches and, crucially, in the post-independence era all financial accounts are recorded. This is particularly useful when examining inspectors' wages, contributions from the local boards of health, money spent on travel and contributions to families. Many of the reports up to 1933 have been destroyed. From 1933 to 1955 they are more complete. Appendix A is a record of all reports utilised.

The courts

Court records on incest

Appeal Court files contain transcripts of evidence and information on legal arguments. Circuit and Central Criminal Court files tend to contain the depositions of children, parents, doctors, gardaí and other witnesses in cases. Some provide information on how individual prosecutions arose, the relationship of the child involved to the accused, and other details about the family situation. In the absence of discussion of incest, the depositions of victims, gardaí and witnesses provide a valuable source of information, as do judges' comments on cases.

Court records on wife-beating

While the records for cases prosecuted in the petty sessions for wife-beating prior to 1921 have been utilised in this study, after independence, as the files were not transferred to the district court, they are unavailable to researchers. This lends even greater weight to the importance of the NSPCC files relating to instances of domestic violence.

Convict reference files

The convict reference files are utilised for the period 1880–1920. Although prisoner petitions after this date exist, I was unable to see these files during research. The files consist of prisoner petitions to the Crown for release, and so have an inherent bias as a source. With regard to the offences investigated, they are utilised in the case studies of cruelty to children/child neglect, incest and wife-beating.

Other official sources

Official sources can be broken into three main categories: figures for prosecutions taken from the House of Commons Papers prior to 1917;

Oireachtas Debates; and official reports that demonstrate the State's role in child welfare reform. These comprise in particular the *Report of the Commission on the Relief of the Sick and Destitute Poor, including the Insane Poor* (Dublin, 1928); the *Report of the Committee to Inquire into the Reformatory and Industrial School System* (Dublin, 1936); the *Report of the Committee of Inquiry into Widows' and Orphans' Pensions* (Dublin, 1933); the *Report of the Interdepartmental Committee of Inquiry regarding Venereal Disease* (Dublin, 1926); the *Report of the Criminal Law Amendment Acts (1880–85) and Juvenile Prostitution* (Dublin, 1935); the minutes of the Carrigan Committee; the NAI files on Family Allowances (1939, 1944) and Adoption (1939–52); the Kennedy Report (1970–71) and the Cussen Report (1934–36); and the Ryan Report (2009).

Notes

1 Moira Maguire, *Precarious Childhood in Post-independence Ireland* (Manchester University Press, 2009). In her introduction, Maguire discusses the importance of the NSPCC case files and also the limitations of the source.
2 Michel Foucault, *Discipline and Punish: The Birth of the Prison*, transl. Alan Sheridan (Knopf Doubleday Publishing Group, 1977), p. 191. This concept of the policing of families, particularly working-class families in Britain is examined by Linda Mahood in her work *Policing Gender, Class and Family: Britain 1850–1940* (University College London Press, 1995).

Introduction

The family, childhood, parenthood and the issue of children's rights are at the centre of many public controversies in Ireland today. Social work has been critiqued, the Catholic Church has been exposed for its mistreatment of generations of vulnerable children, and the negligence of the State and its agencies has been shown with regard to children in their care. Debates surrounding child abuse and child neglect, welfare, children's rights, foster care, and the lines between State, voluntary and family care of children continue to rage. There have been controversies surrounding abuse in Ireland's industrial schools (and later its residential homes); issues emanating from cases of incest and abortion; scandals and complete disregard for women in Ireland's Madgalene laundries; and fears of 'unruly teens', being oversexualised and undereducated. The children's rights amendment has been lauded as a cure of all ills, while welfare is again being assessed outside the context of a nuanced discussion of poverty and distribution of wealth. Reports have followed more reports, yet the history of child welfare in Ireland remains to be told comprehensively. Excellent work has been conducted by those outside the discipline of history – most notably Caroline Skehill, Eoin O'Sullivan and Mary Raftery. Among the historians are Caitríona Clear, Moira Maguire and Lindsey Earner-Byrne, whose work this book will build upon. Perhaps this slow development is due in part to the proximity of the various scandals in the public mind, or the slow development of social history in Ireland. What is clear is that many of the contemporary fears mentioned echo those highlighted during the period treated in this book – a period when topics such as cruelty to children, child neglect, child labour, child sexual abuse, juvenile delinquency, poverty and the issue of single parenthood were the focus of numerous campaigners and philanthropists. Today's debates concern issues that are rooted in the historical record, debates that emerged from the mid-nineteenth century when the State became actively involved in the family unit, initially through the Poor Law, and subsequently through legislative measures pursued under the banner of child protection. By examining the social problems addressed by philanthropists and child protection workers, and the efforts they made to combat these problems, we can begin to understand more about the treatment of children and the family today.

'Cruelty Man' or 'Children's Man'?: The NSPCC in Ireland

> The Society differs in its aim from all other Societies seeking the welfare of unhappy children, in that, whilst others seek to house and provide for the wanderer, homeless, destitute, it seeks to punish those worthless parents who make children wanderers, homeless and destitute, and to render other provision than their own home less necessary.[1]

This statement is taken from the first report of the first branch of the National Society for the Prevention of Cruelty to Children (NSPCC) in Ireland. It is apparent from the quote that the Society was primarily concerned with the welfare of children in poverty, as were other SPCCs internationally. This was, however, a difficult task as the effects of poverty cannot always be addressed through punitive measures. How successful the Society was in helping children and punishing parents will be addressed in this book.

In nineteenth-century Ireland, philanthropists, social reformers, religious orders and the State focused much attention on children and childhood experience. Over the last sixty years or so, scholars have done the same. In 1960, Phillipe Aries set the bar with his seminal work *L'enfant et la vie familiale sous l'Ancien Régime*, focused on childhood and the family in France. With regard to childhood in Ireland, Maria Luddy's book on women and philanthropy, as well as Joseph Robin's work on children and charity work in the nineteenth century, are important early contributions. In Britain, Hugh Cunningham posed the question 'what is a child or to be a child?', while Harry Hendrick asked 'can the history of children (childhood) ever be more than that of what adults have done to children and how they conceptualised childhood?' Central to all these works are conceptions of childhood and philanthropic measures directed at children. In both Britain and Ireland, the NSPCC was at the forefront of the child protection movement. However, aside from work by Harry Ferguson and Maria Luddy, the history of the Society in Ireland has not been fully addressed. This book aims to fill this vacuum, charting the history of the Society from its foundations in 1889, to the passing of responsibilities to the Irish Society for the Prevention of Cruelty to Children (ISPCC) in 1956. It provides a study of the Society, while also utilising it as a vehicle to examine the treatment of poverty-stricken children and families by the State. It addresses issues surrounding institutionalisation, welfare, family violence, compulsory education, child abuse and the role of charity in the provision of welfare. Based on research of the available records in the NSPCC archive, and court records held in the National Archives of Ireland, the text addresses issues hitherto neglected by historians, by exploring the concept of childhood and the development of child protection while also probing the treatment of families by the Roman Catholic Church and the State. Although the Society was the first child protection agency operating in Ireland during the period of examination, and as such the Society's inspectors could crudely be considered to be Ireland's first social workers, the book is not a history of social work in Ireland but a history of the NSPCC and what this organisation tells us about child welfare and welfare generally.[2] As mentioned previously, work by Caroline Skehill in particular has problematised and explored the critical issues surrounding the development of social work in Ireland. In her work on Ireland and Northern Ireland after its foundation, she has used a 'history of the present' approach to explore issues of culpability, State involvement, parental rights and the problems surrounding the development of the profession in Ireland. Similarly, Harry Ferguson's work on the NSPCC and on child protection practices in Britain and Ireland is noteworthy.

Ironically, one of the major strengths of this book, the case studies from the NSPCC archive, also represents a major weakness. During a fire in 1961 in the NSPCC offices, many of the files were destroyed. For this reason, the majority of the cases are from the east of the country – County Wexford primarily. While a comprehensive study of the court records has allowed the author to examine other parts of the country, it is accepted that the study is focused primarily on the urban districts and acknowledges that poverty and living conditions in the west of Ireland were very different.

Over the last thirty years, the lacunae in Irish social history have been slowly filled, most notably by practitioners of women's and labour history. While the history of the family and childhood has begun to receive much needed attention, there remains much work to be done in relation to Ireland, particularly in the areas of welfare and institutionalisation. Notable exceptions are the 2009 *Éire-Ireland Special Edition on Childhood*, principally Maria Luddy's article on the NSPCC, Virginia Crossman's examination of children under the Poor Law, Crossman and Peter Gray's edited collection on poverty and welfare, and Mary Daly's examination of parental rights and education from the 1950s. Lindsey Earner-Byrne's excellent work *Mother and Child: Maternity and Child Welfare in Dublin, 1922–60* (2007) and Moira Maguire's *Precarious Childhood in Post-independence Ireland* (2009) cover a number of topics addressed in this book, but neither deal with the pre-independence period to any great extent. In Britain, the literature on child welfare is more extensive and developed. George K. Behlmer's *Child Abuse and Moral Reform in England, 1870–1908* (1982) was one of the first works to look at the issues of child abuse and child neglect in England, focusing in particular on the actions of the NSPCC.[3] This book was a landmark in the historiography of child protection, but Behlmer's assessment of the Society as 'classless' and his interpretation of the Society's shift in focus from cruelty to children to child neglect have since been challenged, most notably by Harry Hendrick. In his recent work, *Child Welfare: Historical Dimensions, Contemporary Debate* (2003), Hendrick considers the use of the concept of child welfare by successive British governments from the 1880s and the role of the NSPCC and other child protection agencies in establishing the discourse on child welfare.[4] Hendrick states his aim to be 'to bring children closer to the forefront of *historical* understanding'.[5] Highlighting the issue of age, in conjunction with class, gender and ethnicity,

Hendrick's work sheds new light on the history of child protection and childhood in Britain, and his binary theory of children as both 'victims and threats' is applied throughout this book.

In assessing the actions of the NSPCC and the State in the area of child welfare, a number of questions are addressed in this book: how and why did child protection agencies emphasise cruelty to children and child neglect in the late nineteenth century? How were these offences related to, or a result of, poverty, alcoholism, domestic violence or differing attitudes to childhood? How influential was the NSPCC in Ireland? Did it conflict with the State and other charitable or welfare organisations? What legislative reforms were implemented both before and after independence in the area of child welfare? Why was institutionalisation repeatedly chosen to deal with children perceived to be social threats? Was Ireland unique in its treatment of children after 1922, and in particular in its policy of punitive measures as opposed to welfare? How did child protection work affect the 'discovery' of incest, wife-beating and desertion, and their visibility in the twentieth century?

Outline

The book is broadly chronological in structure, with the themes covered emanating from the official concerns of the Society. Chapter 1 addresses the origins of welfare in Ireland from 1838 to 1952, looking at general trends, legislation, ideology, religion and society, in order to establish the broad context in which the child protection movement emerged. It provides an outline history of the Poor Law in Ireland, issues surrounding boarding-out and nurse children, the establishment of reformatory and industrial schools, the introduction of free education at primary level and the growth of nationalism in the late nineteenth century. It discusses the changing social, economic and political environments in post-famine Ireland, the increasing influence of the Catholic Church and the middle class, the importance of religion to all aspects of society and the conflict between Catholic and Protestant agencies. In essence, it sets the scene for the remainder of the book, highlighting issues that are developed in later chapters.

The second section of the chapter deals specifically with legislation introduced by the Irish Free State after independence. The fundamental argument is that the first decades after independence witnessed a weakening of parental rights. Legislation on compulsory education, institutional provision, welfare and illegitimacy placed poor parents and children in impossible situations. From the introduction of measures that increased the situations in which children could be removed from the home, to the State's inability to tackle the poverty that separated families, working-class families suffered most from Church and State action. Although the sanctity of the family was being espoused from the pulpit and the parliamentary chamber, in reality the family, or specifically the working-class family, was not supported by the State. This demonstrates the inherent contradiction in State provision of welfare to families – an attitude of apathy and fear of State interference in child welfare, mixed with the continuation of a policy of institutionalisation and intervention.

As with many historical examinations of Ireland from the mid-nineteenth to the mid-twentieth centuries, the study of the NSPCC as an organisation is a tale of two parts. In Chapter 2, the period 1889–1921 is addressed, focusing on the NSPCC's foundation, expansion and increasing influences, and the Irish branches' connections with the British Society. The year 1921 marked the transition to independence, which coincided with changes internationally in child protection work due to the effects of the First World War and shifting attitudes to childhood.[6] The chapter begins by looking at the international emergence of Societies for the Prevention of Cruelty to Children (SPCCs) from 1874. Of particular significance is that the NSPCC in Ireland was part of an international movement to intervene in families and erode parental rights, and that Ireland was one of fifteen countries to embrace the ideals of the movement. As will be shown, the expansion of the Society in Ireland was rapid, as was the support for the Society in parliament and in the press. The moral attitudes of those involved in the setting up can also be seen in the Society's reports. Although poverty was acknowledged to be a major concern, the Society, through its work, differentiated between the deserving and undeserving poor. Intemperance and particularly 'intemperate mothers' were at the crux of this differentiation. By placing the foundation of the NSPCC in the context of earlier philanthropic and charitable work directed at children in Ireland, the Society's interventionist and punitive approach is demonstrated. This chapter not only sets the scene for the establishment of the Society in Ireland and internationally, it provides a comparative dimension to the third chapter which looks at the Society in the Irish Free State after independence.

Chapter 3 addresses the period from 1922 to the setting up of the ISPCC in 1956. From 1922, the Society had to adjust its focus to survive in independent Ireland. This notion of 'crisis and change' was not unique to the Irish Society, as Christine Anne Sherrington's examination of the NSPCC in Britain has shown, but Irish circumstances exacerbated the need for changing foci. In the aftermath of the First World War, many states had engaged in a discourse on the rights of children, the role of the State in child welfare and interventions in the family. For the Irish NSPCC, the challenges to its existence were significantly increased due to the Catholic Church's increasing influence in child welfare; a loss in the earlier financial support provided by the Anglo-Irish; and increasing numbers of families approaching it for material assistance. As Chapter 3 demonstrates, the Society's response was to redefine its role: it now provided advice and material assistance instead of solely threatening and prosecuting parents. The expansion and recategorisation of child neglect was central to this, as was the Society's efforts in highlighting issues of overcrowding, children's courts, widows' pensions, poor relief, illegitimacy and desertion. Although these were pertinent issues, the issues the Society chose to ignore demonstrate its continuing collaboration with the State, most significantly in its involvement in prosecuting parents and sending children to industrial schools. One of the most significant elements of the chapter is the investigation of Catholic social work agencies, and in particular that of St Vincent de Paul. The relationship between the secular NSPCC and religious social work agencies is crucial to the history of child welfare in Ireland, particularly in this period. By illuminating the situation for individual families investigated through the use of case files, the chapter gives readers an insight into the horrific conditions in which many families in poverty lived.

Chapter 4 looks specifically at the use of institutionalisation by the State and the NSPCC to 'deal' with children and families in poverty. It will show that, although industrial schools, reformatories and borstals were established in the nineteenth century in many countries, the continuation from the 1920s of a policy of institutionalising poor children for long periods was a particularly Irish phenomenon. Financial and religious concerns superseded the welfare of those children committed to industrial schools and reformatories, and the NSPCC was prominent in many of these committals. As discussions in parliament, in official reports, and by dissenting voices demonstrate, there was an acknowledgement of the problems in industrial schools, but they continued to be effectively unregulated by the State. The relationship between the NSPCC inspectors, the courts, the gardaí and the religious orders shows the web of bureaucracy that maintained punitive, regimented institutions so akin to prisons in the public mind. Since the airing of the *States of Fear* documentary series on Irish television in April 1999, and the publication of Mary Raftery and Eoin O'Sullivan's *Suffer the Little Children*, public attention has been focused on the industrial school system in Ireland. More recently, the Report of the Commission to Inquire into Child Abuse in Ireland (the Ryan Report) increased the media and public interest. This chapter demonstrates not only that the NSPCC was involved in placing children in schools, but also that monetary gain was at the heart of many inspectors' and managers' actions.

Chapter 5 looks at 'hidden' Ireland, in particular the issue of incest and sexual immorality. In 1908, the Punishment of Incest Act was passed by the British parliament, and incest became a criminal offence in Britain and Ireland. Credit for the passing of the act was given to the NSPCC and the National Vigilance Association (NVA) in Britain, both of which had been campaigning for legislative change from the mid-1880s. In 1922, British legislation was amended, following intense debate in three separate committees on sexual offences over the previous five years. This was followed swiftly by legislative change in Northern Ireland. Yet in the southern State, these changes would not occur until 1995, with incest remaining a misdemeanour and cases continuing to be heard *in camera* up to this time. The reasoning behind this seventy-year lag is addressed in this chapter, particularly with regard to the treatment of sexuality and sexual 'morality' after independence. As will be demonstrated, attitudes to sexuality and gender would have a knock-on effect on the reluctance of the State to deal with issues such as sexual crime, and especially sexual crime within the family. The need to protect the sanctity of the family in the Irish Free State, and the moral power of the Catholic Church in society, would act as bulwarks against any interference in the family unit that would cause disruption. Revelations of incest would surely have done just this. As the Church and State focused on 'morality' and 'immorality' within certain parameters, incest remained outside of the discourse, even though cases featured regularly in the courts. For the NSPCC, allegations of incest or 'immorality' had always been a rationale for institutionalising girls, and for victims, recourse was limited and problematic. By utilising testimonies from the court records, this chapter demonstrates the absolute bind for victims of incest in Ireland, and the lack of alternatives and resistance available to them. While both Moira Maguire and Diarmaid Ferriter address this issue, here over sixty court cases are utilised, providing a more in-depth examination of the topic.[7]

As with incestuous abuse, recourse was limited for women in situations of domestic violence and desertion in Ireland. The NSPCC was, however, a port of call where wives who were also mothers could turn to for advice. Chapter 6 addresses this topic, and in particular the treatment of women in their social role as mothers and wives. While the help they received was restricted, the Society did utilise its connections with branches in Britain and the United States to track husbands who had deserted their families and attempted to procure maintenance. The chapter also demonstrates that gender bias was inherent in child protection work and the development of welfare in Ireland. Changing discourse on the role of mothers and fathers can be observed in legislation, but also in prosecutions for cruelty to children in the courts. This is of interest to the debate on child protection, and also to debates on changing attitudes to motherhood and fatherhood; gender in the Irish Free State; and the role of the family in Irish society.

Notes

1   Annual Report of the Dublin Aid Committee (hereafter AR Dublin Aid Committee), 1889–90 (Dublin, 1890), p. 9. The Dublin Aid Committee was the first branch of the NSPCC set up in Ireland. For a discussion of the committee, see Maria Luddy, 'The early years of the NSPCC in Ireland', *Éire-Ireland*, 44:1–2 (Spring/Summer 2009), 62–90. This book draws on research and findings from my PhD thesis; Sarah-Anne Buckley, 'Protecting "the family cell"? Child welfare, the NSPCC and the State in Ireland, 1880–1944', Unpublished PhD thesis (University College Cork, 2010). For further discussion of the NSPCC in Ireland, see Sarah-Anne Buckley, 'Child neglect, poverty and class: the NSPCC in Ireland, 1889–1938 – a case study', *Saothar: Journal of Irish Labour History*, 33 (2008), 57–72; Luddy, 'The early years of the NSPCC

in Ireland'; Maria Luddy, *Women and Philanthropy in Nineteenth-Century Ireland* (Cambridge University Press, 1995), chapter 3, 'Saving the child', pp. 68–96. For a discussion of the NSPCC in Britain, see George K. Behlmer, *Child Abuse and Moral Reform in England, 1870–1908* (Stanford University Press, 1982); Tom Cockburn, 'Child abuse and protection: The Manchester boys' and girls' refuges and the NSPCC, 1884–1894', *Manchester Sociology Occasional Papers* (Jessica Kingsley Publishers, 1995); Susan Creighton, *Trends in Child Abuse* (NSPCC 1984); Gary Clapton, '"Yesterday's men': The inspectors of the Royal Scottish Society for the Prevention of Cruelty to Children (RSSPCC), 1888–1968", *British Journal of Social Work Online*, DOI 10.1093/bjsw/bcn031 (March 2008); Harry Hendrick, *Child Welfare: Historical Dimensions, Contemporary Debate* (Policy Press, 2003); Sue Wise, *Child Abuse: The NSPCC Version* (Feminist Praxis, 1991); NSPCC, *NSPCC: The First Hundred Years* (NSPCC, 1984); Christine Anne Sherrington, 'The NSPCC in transition, 1884–1983: a study of organisational survival' (unpublished PhD thesis, University of London, 1984).

2   For a discussion of the history of social work in Ireland, see Caroline Skehill, *History of the Present: Child Protection and Welfare Social Work in Ireland* (Edwin Mellen Press, 2004); 'Child protection and welfare social work in the Republic of Ireland: Continuities and discontinuities between the past and the present', in N. Kearney and C. Skehill (eds), *Social Work in Ireland: Historical Perspectives* (Institute of Public Administration, Dublin, 2005); Harry Ferguson, *Protecting Children in Time: Child Abuse, Child Protection and the Consequences of Modernity* (Palgrave Macmillan, 2004). For a discussion of child welfare in Ireland, see Caitríona Clear, *Women of the House: Women's Household Work in Ireland 1922–1961: Discourses, Experiences, Memories* (Irish Academic Press, 2000); Lindsey Earner-Byrne, *Mother and Child: Maternity and Child Welfare in Dublin 1922–60* (Manchester University Press, 2007); Luddy, *Women and Philanthropy*; Moira Maguire, *Precarious Childhood in Post-independence Ireland* (Manchester University Press, 2009); Joseph Robins, *The Lost Children: A Study of Charity Children in Ireland 1700–1900* (Institute of Public Administration, 1980). For a discussion of England, see George K. Behlmer, *Friends of the Family: The English Home and Its Guardians, 1850–1940* (Stanford University Press, 1998); Anna Davin, 'Imperialism and motherhood', *History Workshop Journal* 5 (1978), 9–65; Anna Davin, *Growing Up Poor: Home, School and Street in London 1870–1914* (Rivers Oram Press, 1996); Deborah Dwork, *War is Good for Babies and Other Young Children: A History of the Infant and Child Welfare Movement in England 1898–1914* (Tavistock Publications, 1987); Harry Hendrick, *Child Welfare in England 1872–1989* (Routledge, 1994); Carolyn Steedman, *Strange Dislocations: Childhood and the Idea of Human Interiority, 1780–1930* (Harvard University Press, 1995); John Stewart, 'Children, parents and the State: The Children Act, 1908', *Children & Society*, 9:1 (1995), 90–9. On the history of child protection in Scotland, see Lynn Abrams, *The Orphan Country: Children of Scotland's Broken Homes from 1845 to the Present Day* (John Donald, 1998).

3   George K. Behlmer, *Child Abuse and Moral Reform in England, 1870–1908* (Stanford University Press, 1982).

4   Hendrick, *Child Welfare: Historical Dimensions*. Social control is a phrase

usually attributed to sociologist E.A. Ross. He used the phrase as the title of a collection of essays in 1901, referring to the widest range of influence and regulation societies imposed upon individuals. E.A. Ross, *Social Control* (New York Macmillan, 1901). From the 1940s and 1950s, Talcott Parson's writings have been associated with the view that intervention into the family had increased and become a characteristic of modern society. Parsons proposed the 'transfer of functions' thesis and the notion that professionals had taken over many family functions such as education, childcare and medical care. In contrast, in the same period, there was a more pessimistic view emerging from the Frankfurt School of German Marxists who condemned the decline in family autonomy and even attributed it to, in part, the horrors of totalitarianism.

5   Hendrick, *Child Welfare: Historical Dimensions*, preface.
6   Harry Hendrick sees the year 1918 as a marker in the history of child protection, but due to the upheaval caused by the War of Independence and the Civil War, 1921 is a more appropriate marker for Ireland. See Hendrick, *Child Welfare: Historical Dimensions*, preface.
7   Maguire, *Precarious Childhood;* Diarmaid Ferriter, *Occasions of Sin: Sex and Society in Modern Ireland* (Profile Books, 2009).

1

The origins of child welfare in Ireland, 1838–1952

Introduction

This chapter will set the scene for the remainder of the text by tracing the origins of child welfare, from the introduction of the Poor Law (Ireland) Act in 1838 to the introduction of adoption legislation in 1952. Both of these dates are significant markers in the history of child protection – and while developments up to publication of the Kennedy Report in 1970 will be mentioned, they represent the core of the discussion.[1] Overall, the chapter will assess the role of the State, the Catholic Church and voluntary organisations in the development of child welfare, through an examination of legislation implemented to 'protect' children. After an initial analysis of the Poor Law, it will address the issue of boarding-out and children placed at nurse. This is followed by an examination of the impact of compulsory education on families, as well as issues relating to childhood, nationalism and socialism. In the second half of the chapter, the development of child welfare after independence is discussed, with particular reference to motherhood and gender, public assistance for poor families, adoption, the impact of the Emergency and the introduction of children's allowances. While legislative reforms up to 1970 are mentioned, the bulk of the chapter addresses the period of the NSPCC's existence, with the conclusion focusing on developments and changes after this time.

Child welfare before independence, 1838–1921

Throughout the nineteenth century, children, and in particular poor children, had come to the attention of religious organisations and the State under the auspices of education, health and welfare. Much of this attention was related to fears of proselytising, the nationalist movement's recognition of the usefulness of children in its struggle and the worries prevalent in Britain surrounding the health and success of the British Empire. Childhood had been redefined and children had become a principal focus of State and voluntary efforts – for example, the introduction of compulsory schooling, changes to child labour laws, the development of child protection legislation and the focus on infant mortality. In Britain, continued emphasis on children as 'assets' and the 'children of the nation' related directly to fears for the Empire and population. Religion and proselytising were crucial to the manner in which many educational and punitive institutions developed and expanded, as the battle to 'save the souls' of children caused divisions in philanthropic societies and political movements. These divisions would affect the development of feminism and, more crucially, the actual care of children, as Maria Luddy's work has shown.[2] The speed with which institutions and schools for children opened can be attributed to religious concerns as well as social need, as Catholic orders established orphanages and schools to counteract what they saw as the proselytising fervour of Protestant institutions. The fear of proselytism could be seen in many areas, such as the debates on the setting up of reformatories for young offenders in 1858, during which the Catholic hierarchy demanded that all boys and girls be sent to schools of their own denomination. Yet the fears worked both ways, as during debates on the formation of industrial schools, Ulster Protestants expressed fears that working-class Protestant children could be ill-treated or stigmatised if they were ever placed in Catholic industrial schools. Throughout the century, orphanages, 'ragged schools', industrial schools and reformatories were set up to cater for orphaned and deserted children, and, later, for neglected children.

Legislatively, reforms demonstrate the areas in which children had become the focus. These included the 1838 Poor Law (Ireland) Act, the 1858 Reformatory Schools (Ireland) Act, the 1862 Irish Poor Law Amendment Act providing for boarding-out for workhouse children up to the age of eight years, the 1868 Industrials Schools (Ireland) Act, the 1884 Summary Jurisdiction over Children Act, the 1898 Pauper Children Act and extension of boarding-out, the 1907 Probation of Offenders Act (which resulted in the inception of the present probation service) and the 1908 Children Act. Lindsey Earner-Byrne has shown that, in the context of child welfare generally, many of the issues that would be intensified after independence with regard to State interference in family welfare, non-Catholic assistance of families and the role of voluntarism and activist groups would be played out prior to independence. While nationalist groups consistently argued that child and family welfare would be improved under Irish rule, the development of activist groups such as the Women's National Health Association (WNHA) attracted the attention of the Catholic Church which remained uncomfortable with any measures vaguely resembling socialism.[3] With regard to institutions catering for children, by 1900 there were approximately 104 industrial schools, reformatories and voluntary orphanages operating throughout the country.[4] Although many moral reformers were motivated by genuine concerns for children in poverty, in the workhouse and those suffering from parental neglect, what must be addressed in this chapter is the extent to which their methods in dealing with families were successful. Before looking at this, the options available before the 1880s must be addressed, in particular the workhouse, boarding-out and placing children at nurse.

The Poor Law

Prior to the setting up of industrial schools, reformatories and other charitable homes and institutions, the Poor Law and the workhouses represented the primary option for those in destitution. Following on from the English Act in 1834, the Poor Law (Ireland) Act was passed in 1838, and workhouses were built throughout the country. The workhouse system was developed not as a permanent solution but as a measure to tackle the poverty within the country. Although this discussion will not deal with the history of the Poor Law, it is worth noting the effects that the famine had on the system, the opposition to its introduction in Ireland and the reluctance of Poor Law guardians to provide assistance that would encourage dependence in families. This was particularly evident in the reluctance of guardians to grant outdoor relief, as the section on boarding-out will show. More recently, scholars have questioned the use of the workhouses as a temporary relief measure, demonstrating how many people learned to use the system for their own ends. With regard to children, despite concerted efforts from philanthropists, the majority of children under the care of the Poor Law were kept in the workhouse as opposed to being boarded-out. As the system was designed to 'reform as well as relieve', the need to mould workhouse children into valuable citizens remained throughout the nineteenth century in Ireland and may explain the reluctance of Poor Law guardians to opt for alternative measures. Not only were children not boarded-out, but most were separated from their families inside the workhouse and sent to schools or work as early as possible. Children were separated from parents at the age of two years, and most parents did not apply for formal visitation. Looking at the conditions and structures of the workhouse, it is not difficult to decipher why many philanthropists focused on the need to develop other options for destitute children. As Virginia Crossman's work has demonstrated, it is also understandable that they would focus on the family in a period of rapid change, as it represented a unit that could be influenced and moulded. Similarly, Anna Clark argues that many Irish nationalists, the Catholic Church and philanthropic women 'used the issue of poor infant children as leverage in their confrontation with the British state'.[5] What is certain is that the workhouse was not a suitable place for children, and that whatever the objections, alternatives needed to be pursued. One such alternative was fostering or boarding-out, as will now be discussed.

Boarding-out

The boarding-out system was first introduced under the Irish Poor Law Amendment Act (1862) which allowed Poor Law guardians to board-out with local families children that would otherwise be placed in the workhouse. The system was re-affirmed in 1924 under the County Boards of Health (Assistance) Order and the Public Assistance Act (1939). From

1922, responsibility for the system fell to the Department of Local Government and Public Health, but this section will deal primarily with the period before 1922. Although boarding-out became an option from 1862, as will be illustrated, the policy was not followed uniformly. In her 2009 article on children under the Poor Law, Virginia Crossman traces the history of the boarding-out system, through the prism of efforts by campaigners in Ireland in the mid-nineteenth century to remove children from workhouses.[6] The work highlights the enormous diversity of boarding-out experiences, particularly with regard to class and regionalism. Generally, in contrast to Scotland, the majority of Poor Law children in Ireland and England remained in some form of institutional care throughout the nineteenth century.[7] Integral to Crossman's examination are conflicting views from Poor Law guardians, the Poor Law commissioners and the Catholic Church regarding nurse children placed in the workhouse, or those needing to be boarded-out. While Catholic critics of the system denounced the workhouse as an unsuitable environment for pauper, orphaned, deserted or illegitimate children, they were not against their own institutional provision. Similarly, variations in the application of boarding-out practices in different Poor Law unions were the result of individual boards of guardians, as opposed to the Poor Law commissioners.[8] In the 1850s, Poor Law commissioners had accepted the need for boarding-out deserted children, before the campaign for boarding-out had been introduced. In 1862, the Poor Law Amendment Act gave boards of guardians the power to place orphan and deserted children out to nurse up to the age of five years, with the proviso that guardians could extend this to children aged up to eight years with the consent of the Poor Law commissioners if they believed it necessary for the child's health.

Speaking before the Statistical and Social Inquiry Society of Ireland in 1876, academic John K. Ingram stated that boarding-out was 'the best means of developing [children's] moral natures, cultivating their practical intelligence, training them for real life, and incorporating them with the honest and industrious mass of the labouring population'.[9] In 1873, the Annual Report of the Local Government Board stated that the introduction of boarding-out was a result of 'the necessity which existed for remedying the mortality incidental to infant children reared without mothers in workhouses'. Whatever the ultimate reasoning for its introduction, boarding-out was a very limited system in the early years. One of the reasons for the guardians' reticence was the fear that pursuing an interventionist approach to poverty alleviation would encourage parents to be irresponsible in having children and abandoning them. With regard to conflicting views on the upper age limit, the disagreement reflected the inherent debate over the merits of industrial over domestic care.[10] However, increased pressure from philanthropists and awareness of the horrors of the workhouse convinced government, albeit slowly, to improve the system. In 1898 they increased the age to fifteen years and bestowed more control on the Board of Guardians to implement boarding-out.

Two issues were critical to the success of boarding-out – the choice of foster parent and the quality and frequency of inspections. Examination of both issues demonstrates problems with the system. Most foster parents were found through the efforts of members of boarding-out committees, philanthropists devoted to the cause and other interested persons. Occasionally, advertisements were placed in the local press promoting the need for more adoptive parents. In 1877, the Local Government Board for Ireland issued a contract of conditions which prospective foster parents had to satisfy in order to ensure the wellbeing of children. The legal criteria concerned their moral character, religion, health, housing and economic status. One stipulation stated: 'no child shall be permitted to continue with any foster-parent who ... shall keep any pig, cow, donkey or other such animal in the dwelling house.'[11] Most unions also made use of references or testimonials signed by a local clergyman, magistrate or medical officer who could attest for the good conduct and respectability of the foster parents. However, because there was no legal requirement to follow this type of assessment, unsuitable parents were often found, and in her 1904 report on boarding-out, inspector Marie Dickie confirmed that there were cases where 'the desire to help some person in circumstances of poverty ... led to children being placed in surroundings which were altogether unsuitable'.[12] With regard to inspections, inspectors, or relieving officers, were to oversee and monitor the supervision and wellbeing of children in foster homes, provide regular reports to the Local Government Board on the workings of the system and make recommendations in relation to particular cases. As with the selection of foster parents, inspections were haphazard and varied between each union. As Chapter 4 will address, this would reflect the treatment of inspections of industrial schools and reformatories. When carried out regularly, inspection results proved to be very favourable. In 1873, the inspector for the Galway region noted: 'children are in good hands and well cared for. I inspected them on Saturday last, and found them well housed, comfortably clothed and presenting a clean and healthy appearance', while also stating that there seemed to 'exist some degree of kinship' between the children and family.[13] In contrast, Dr Roughan of the Sligo district wrote that in the Cooloony region, one house was 'a damp hovel, with filthy surroundings. It consisted of one apartment, containing 2 beds, each occupied by four persons. A cow, a calf and a pig occupy or share a portion of it.'[14] His report continued with another case of ill-treatment in the area.

> The baby, aged six months, lay in a wooden cradle, without a bed of any kind, not even a particle of straw between the board and the emaciated body. An empty feeding bottle lay near the little one, from which in vain it endeavoured to draw sustenance, it was in a state of squalor and emaciated to the last degree – so much so that I believe, unless it is promptly supplied with proper nutriment, a few days will terminate its existence.[15]

The report ends with a side note stating that the baby, Mary Green, was confirmed dead three days later. The cases demonstrate the variety of experiences in the boarding-out system.

How many children were actually boarded-out during the period? In their 1870 report on administering poor relief in Ireland, the Commissioners calculated that 1,207 children had been fostered. This was a marked increase on the 689 children of the previous year, an outcome which was largely attributed to 'the extension of the age to which this class of children may be relieved out of the workhouse' and also 'to the further adoption of the system by Boards of Guardians.'[16] Nevertheless, when this is compared with the 15,000 children still living in workhouses during the same year, it emphasises how pervasive this institutional method of pauper relief was in Ireland. In 1907, the Local Government Board stated: 'the aim of all Boards of Guardians should be, if possible, to keep every pauper child outside the workhouse.' In 1920 there were still 2,920 children living in the workhouse, which suggests that many of the authorities in Ireland continued to be apprehensive about the system, even when official opinion had turned in favour of it.[17] With Ireland's predominantly rural population, it could be argued that there was a multitude of potential foster parents available. Not only did boarding-out provide a family-care model but it was also significantly cheaper than the workhouse, costing only half the price, at £6 on average per child per year. In reality, however, local authorities preferred to spend the extra money on institutional care; what they lost in financial terms they recouped in human resources and energy as it was easier to send children into workhouses (and later industrial schools) than to expend the time necessary to solicit applications and inspections. Boarding-out was a time-consuming scheme that required dedication on the part of inspectors and guardians to secure and maintain children in appropriate homes. These official positions, however, were 'usually filled by very busy men compelled by the demands of their own affairs'.[18] The children suffered as a result of this, as Marie Dickie pointed out – 'philanthropy [was] not so widespread as to provide an open door for one orphan after another from the local workhouse.'[19] Whether this situation could have been improved by local authorities or the State is extremely difficult to assess. What is certain is that after independence, the continued reluctance of the State to implement fostering and boarding-out would differentiate Ireland from many other countries. The following section will address another group of children who could have benefited from further protection – nurse children.

Nurse children

The situation for nurse children in Ireland has received limited attention by historians.[20] In this discussion, children placed at nurse were predominantly illegitimate children who, due to economic necessity and the shame of illegitimacy, needed to be kept for a number of months or years by someone other than a relative. The women who cared for these infants were known as nurses and usually took responsibility for care in return for financial reward. This does not mean that women did not become emotionally attached to the children they nursed, but the primary reason for the undertaking would have been financial. In many instances, children in the workhouse would be placed at nurse, as even after the setting up of the industrial schools, they would have been too young to be placed in the schools. Most importantly though, placing children at nurse provided a temporary option for mothers and parents.

One of the big issues surrounding nurse children is the distinction between a 'nurse' and a 'baby-farmer'. From 1867, the term 'baby-farmer' began to be used in Britain and other countries to describe nurses who had taken more than one child to nurse – usually six or more – and been neglectful in their care. The *British Medical Journal* (*BMJ*) had been the first to use the term to describe a situation in which a woman's four children died sequentially in the care of the same nurse.[21] An article entitled "'Baby-Farming' insinuated that the mother had turned her children over to the 'baby farmer'" with the implicit understanding that they would be neglected until they died. In a series of sensationalist pieces published the following year, the *BMJ*'s editor Ernest Hart argued that many baby-farmers committed serial infanticide. His articles attracted a great deal of attention and brought the term 'baby-farming' into widespread use. At this point, the term described the practice of adopting children or 'taking them to nurse' in exchange for payment. It could refer to sincere foster mothers as well as to women who neglected or abused the infants that they were paid to rear. 'Baby-farming' was an accusation, and would not have been the term nurses would have applied to themselves. In Ireland, the press and the courts were very reluctant to use the term 'baby-farming', and very few did so during the period under examination. This appears to have been related to attitudes surrounding childhood, Irish women and the image of Ireland as a place where cruelty to children did not occur. In 1872 for example, writing in reference to the Infant Life Protection (ILP) Act, an editorial in the *Irish Times* stated:

> The Act applies to Ireland, although baby farming, in the English meaning of the term, is unknown in this country … whoever included Ireland within the field of operation under the Act, either know nothing of this country or designed to save the reputation of the baby farmers of England by including Irish nurses in the same category as them.[22]

In the courts, while a handful of cases were prosecuted under the ILP Act for baby-farming, the term was not utilised to the same extent as in other countries.[23] In fact, the first case was not prosecuted under the ILP Act until 1894. The question is, did this reflect the actual situation and demonstrate that baby-farming was not a problem in Ireland? Due to a lack of urbanisation in Ireland, arrangements involving one or two children being looked after by one nurse appear to have been more common than large-scale baby-farms. This does not mean that illegitimate children needing care was not an issue; on the contrary, it would remain an issue in Ireland far longer than in Britain, but many arrangements were smaller in scale. Similarly, Ireland's high level of institutionalisation of illegitimate children may have contributed to less need for large-scale baby-farming. Finally, as will be demonstrated by cases from the courts, baby-farmers and nurses could be charged with a whole range of offences against the person, including murder, manslaughter, infringements of the various ILP Acts or the 1908 Children Act, cruelty and neglect, etc. 'Baby-farming' was never a specific offence in its own right, but a depreciatory label. It also related directly to the topic of adoption.

The question of who cared for illegitimate children is at the heart of any examination of nurse children. Without nurses, single mothers who lacked the support of family and friends would have found it difficult to keep themselves and their infants out of the workhouse. Few private charities extended their help to unmarried mothers before 1920, and the Poor Law Amendment Act (1834) prohibited guardians from giving outdoor relief to unmarried mothers. When they could find work, usually in domestic service, single mothers either paid nurses to board and care for their children or gave a lump sum payment (known as a 'premium') to women who thereby 'adopted' their babies. This afforded unmarried mothers a way to cope financially with illegitimacy, and also offered other poor women an opportunity to profit from it. However, illegitimate infants at nurse were usually deprived of breast milk because their mothers had to work, and they were therefore more susceptible than breast-fed babies to illness and the digestive complications that accompanied artificial feeding. This contributed to the high mortality rate for illegitimate infants. Another issue that must be discussed when addressing illegitimacy is the prevalence of infanticide and suspected infanticide as a response to unwanted pregnancies. Elaine Farrell's work on infanticide in the latter half of the nineteenth-century addresses a sample of 4,635 cases of suspected infanticide, attempted infant murder and concealment of birth. This is a startling figure, and unquestionably demonstrates the high incidence of infanticide in the period. Although placing children at nurse appears to have been the most desperate option for women wishing to maintain their children, infanticide cases surely demonstrate the absolute desperation women must have felt, for a variety of reasons.[24]

The 1872 ILP Act and the 1908 Children Act

> In this country, happily, we have no need for a law to protect infant lives. The foster-mother loves the nurse-child fully as tenderly as she loves her own, and the woman who treated a nurse-child unfairly would suffer at the hands of her own sex penalties more severe than the law could convict.[25]

As the above quote demonstrates, the 1872 ILP Act was not seen by many in Ireland as a necessity. Yet the act had been the result of years of campaigning by middle-class philanthropists in Britain particularly. It represented an early attempt to make some provision for the protection of neglected or 'deprived' children outside the ambit of the Poor Law or the judiciary. It required those receiving more than one infant for maintenance in return for money payments to register their houses with the local authority. The Infant Life Protection Amendment Act (1897) made it the duty of the local authority to enforce the act. Relatives and guardians of children, hospitals, convalescent homes or institutions 'established for the protection and care of infants and conducted in good faith' were exempted from the provisions of both acts, as well as persons maintaining children under any act for the relief of the poor. In 1908, the Children Act again changed the law with regard to nurse children. Now all foster homes, even those with only one child, were included under the act. It also specifically set out that if a carer or parent could not afford doctors' fees themselves, they could access a physician using the Poor Laws. Indeed, this proviso within the act had in large part been the result of an ongoing controversy between 1868 and 1908 over the extent to which parents were obliged to provide medical care for their children. The act stated that those accepting children into their care would have to register the child with the local authorities within forty-eight hours. Failure to do so could result in prosecution. The act also compelled local authorities to inspect the situations of children at nurse once a month, up to the age of seven years.[26] The forty-eight-hour period extended to other provisions. For example, the carer had to notify the local authority in writing of a change of address or residence and if an infant died or was removed. If a person violated any of the above provisions, not only would they be guilty of an offence under Part 1 of the 1908 act, they would be liable to forfeit the whole or part sum of money received for the child.

Part 2 of the 1908 Children Act dealt specifically with inspection of nurse children, responsibility for which lay with local authorities. It stated that the authorities in an area had to appoint one or two persons 'of either sex' to be infant protection visitors. It is interesting and notable that the inspections included women, as at this stage women were excluded from the inspection duties of many other societies such as the NSPCC. The infant protection visitors were to visit the homes in which children had been placed at nurse 'from time to time', in order to check the premises and the care of the children. They were also encouraged to provide advice or direction as to the nursing and maintenance of children where necessary. Interestingly, with regard to the NSPCC and other philanthropic societies, the act stated that infant protection visitors could pass responsibility to philanthropic societies and 'so authorise the society to exercise those powers as respects those infants, subject, however, to the obligation to furnish periodical reports to the local authority'.[27] Also of interest was the provision that a local authority could exempt from visitation or inspection those premises that they believed or deemed to be well conducted. Finally, the local authority could also fix the number of children under the age of seven years that any one premises or person could nurse. If premises were found to be overcrowded, dangerous or insanitary, or if the person in charge was regarded to be unfit due to 'negligence, ignorance, inebriety, immorality, criminal conduct, or other similar cause', they could be charged. Anyone previously convicted of an offence under the 1897 Act or the 1904 Prevention of Cruelty to Children Act could not keep an infant or child at nurse. In the case of the death of an infant, aside from notifying the local authority, the person who had the care of the infant was obliged to notify the coroner within twenty-four hours in order that an inquest could be held and the cause of death ascertained. Finally, if any person was found to have caused the death or allowed the death of a child to occur for the purpose of claiming life insurance, they would be prosecuted under the act. Again, the issue of life insurance was one that could be found in the discourse of the NSPCC, particularly in Britain, and the court records show a number of cases in which parents were prosecuted for suspected insurance fraud.

In 1894, the *Irish Times* reported on the first case in Ireland prosecuted under the ILP Act of 1872, stating that 'since the passing of the act in that year it had remained a dead letter'. The case was quite shocking, as it involved the deaths of fifteen children in the charge of one woman, a Mrs Coffey. The article claims that the woman was responsible for a previous four deaths of infant, but that no steps were taken in these cases. It goes on to state: 'the whole question of infant life protection deserves more attention from the public than it has hitherto received'. The woman in this case received a £5 fine for non-registration of her home under Clause 2 of the 1872 ILP Act.[28] The NSPCC was also publicly praised for its work on bringing the case before the courts. While a charge of manslaughter would have been a more severe deterrent than a fine of £5, the woman was not charged with the most severe crimes because cases could not be prosecuted any more than six months after the alleged offences occurred.[29]

The involvement of voluntary institutions in providing nurses with children is an interesting aspect of the history. In 1905, a case emerged in the papers which involved not only the deaths of three nurse children but also the participation of the Cottage Home in Dun Laoghaire in their transferral to the nurse accused. The nurse, Sarah Tennant, was accused of the manslaughter of three babies, two of which had been transferred into her care by the home. These were baby Henry Tomlinson and baby O'Brien. In the third case, involving baby Kathleen Redding, the mother had approached Sarah Tennant herself after obtaining her name from the matron of the home. The coroner stated, in the case involving Henry Tomlinson and Kathleen Redding, that the matron of the Cottage Home could not be exempted from blame, because the parents and relatives involved had trusted that the home would not send the children to an unreliable nurse. The matron was found guilty of negligence in giving a child to be nursed by an unregistered person. In the second case prosecuted, involving Kathleen Redding, it emerged that the mother of the child had agreed to pay five shillings per week for Tennant to look after the child. Although the mother had not been able to pay for the first four weeks, in written communication with the mother, Sarah Jane Redding, Tennant stated that the child was doing well. When the mother visited the child she found her in an emaciated condition and upon calling the doctor was told that the baby was 'in a dying condition'. At this point, although two months old, the child weighed only 6lbs 7ozs. When the baby was born, the hospital recorded a weight of 7lbs 4ozs and noted that she was in good health. The third child, baby O'Brien, was found in a similar condition. Yet the Cottage Home had been happy to send children to this woman without checking her premises or character. It was not only institutions like the Cottage Home that were involved in providing nurse children. In 1890, there was a serious case involving a verdict of neglect of a nurse child by a Mrs O'Dea in Dublin. It emerged during the trial that the case was more complicated than some involving nurse children, because a nurse in the lying-in ward of the Coombe Hospital was also involved. It was suggested that one particular nurse was receiving money for giving children out to nurse. In this instance, the child was severely neglected, and although Mrs O'Dea took the charge of neglect, both the jury and the judge acknowledged that there were other actors involved and hoped that the press would include this in the record, as they did.[30]

In 1879, the Dublin City Coroner commented on his dissatisfaction with the registration clause which was an integral part of the 1872 ILP Act. He referred to a case involving the death of one young infant while in the care of an unregistered nurse working in the locality. Newspaper reports suggest that the case produced a mixture of shock and amazement from both the neighbours and the judge, the latter of whom stated that in over twelve years he had seen no more than twelve cases of infanticide, and never a case of baby-farming. Although the report of the case was entitled 'baby-farming in Dublin' in the *Irish Times*, the court was very reluctant to utilise the term throughout the proceedings.[31] At this stage, the term was too emotive for those in court, if not in the press.

In 'an alleged case of baby-farming' in 1893, in which a number of children had died during the care of a Mrs Lynch, a trained nurse, it was revealed that the NSPCC had been negligent in its investigations. In the Coroner's Court in Dublin, the jury stated:

> We think that the Society for the Prevention of Cruelty to Children should have taken earlier action, and not have allowed thirteen people to live in an unsanitary house, the living room of which was only twelve feet square; and we are of the opinion that baby-farming places should be registered and regularly inspected.

In fact, the Society had sent a number of the children to Mrs Lynch, whom they felt was a suitable nurse.[32]

After the introduction of the 1908 Children Act, many of the cases that directly related to nurse children involved non-registration. In a case in 1928 for example, a woman was prosecuted for failing to notify the reception of a nurse child, as well as failing to inform the coroner of the child's death. The judge in the case stated: 'the life of one child was more important than the supervision of all other material things put together'.[33] The case is interesting, as a secretary from the Board of Health was present at the hearing. The judge asked the representative whether the Board had sent someone to visit the foster home to check if the child was sufficiently cared for, to which he replied in the negative. In response, the judge stated:

> it was an appalling state of affairs that the required supervision of infants did not exist. He was sure the fault did not lie with the capable secretary of the Board of Health; but it seemed extraordinary that so much attention was given to the supervision of dairy stock and other such matters and that the provision of infants in such cases had been overlooked.[34]

Again, the issue of inspection, or lack thereof, is one that reverberates throughout investigations of nurse children, both those in foster care and those in institutions.

Legislating for child protection before independence

In 1889, the Prevention of Cruelty to Children Act was passed in Britain and Ireland. Credit for the passing of the Act is given to the London SPCC, as well as to leaders of the Child Study Movement. It was a landmark act in its enormity and in the number of separate acts and issues it drew together. Prior to this, the Poor Law represented the primary means by which parents could be punished for 'wilful neglect', and for the first time 'moral neglect' was referred to as an offence. With reference to the Poor Law guardians and the act's implementation, Harry Hendrick cites the reluctance of the guardians to punish parents for 'wilful neglect' as a significant factor in the legislative success. The NSPCC had made many people aware through publicity and meetings that there were problems with the care of children, and that it was the group that could address them and keep children in the home. The 1889 act represented the first significant piece of legislation lobbied for by the Society and the beginning of a child welfare legislative marathon. From 1889 to 1910, fifty-two acts relating to child welfare and child protection were passed in Britain.[35] Not every legislative measure passed in Britain was extended to Ireland. In some instances, for example the British 1907 Notification of Births Act, Ireland was not included in the legislative district.

What significant acts were passed in Ireland as a result of lobbying by Irish activists? In 1910, the Notification of Births Act (1907) was extended to Ireland after lobbying by groups such as the WNHA. Although in principle it was an act for all classes, as Lindsey Earner-Byrne states, 'Dublin Corporation viewed the act's primary purpose as infant protection through the targeting of the poorer classes.'[36] In 1915, the Notification of Births (Ireland) Act made the 1907 act compulsory and provided funding for the work of public nurses. Fifty per cent of the spending of the scheme (to a maximum of £5,000) could be recouped by local authorities.[37] However, it only applied to urban districts. This issue of a divide in urban and rural services and experiences for maternity and child welfare is a significant one, and one that resonates throughout this work. Aside from the benefits of the act for the women affected, one of the significant results was that local authority committees were now allowed to include women. Margaret Ó hÓgartaigh's examination of Kathleen Lynn also focuses on this issue, as Lynn and other women in the medical profession, recognising the potential for women in public health, became very involved in initiatives such as the Babies' Clubs.[38] In 1918, the Midwives (Ireland) Act was enacted. The act had its roots in the professionalisation of the medical profession, as it was no longer deemed appropriate to allow the 'local handy woman' to act as midwife in the community. It ensured that any mother who did not qualify for free treatment under the medical charities scheme was entitled to free medical aid in case of an emergency. Again, however, it was a measure implemented in urban areas only. The early twentieth century also saw the introduction of a number of liberal social reforms emanating from Britain in other areas. The Old Age Pension Act (1908) and the National Insurance Act (1911) in particular. In 1906, the Provision of School Meals Act was not extended to Ireland after protests by Catholic clergy and others who feared it would take the responsibility of feeding children away from parents. The measure would have ensured that school-going children would receive at least one substantial meal per day. In response, Maud Gonne set up the Ladies' School Dinner Committee. In 1914 a compromise act, the Education (Provision of Meals) (Ireland) Act was introduced. It allowed Urban District Councils to take over the responsibility of feeding starving children.

In 1894, an extension of the 1889 act made intentional ill-treatment or neglect an offence punishable by up to six months' imprisonment. The act also empowered police officers to take a suspected child from the home without a court order; courts could impose fines of up to twenty shillings; and drunkenness was now cited as a reason for children to be placed in alternative home situations. Further 'NSPCC inspired legislation'[39] came in 1904 and 1908. The 1908 Children Act was particularly significant. This aimed to

> consolidate and amend the law relating to the protection of children and young persons, reformatory and industrial schools, and juvenile offenders and otherwise to amend the law with respect to children and young persons.[40]

The six parts of the 1908 act's legislation covered infant life protection; the prevention of cruelty to children and young persons; juvenile smoking; reformatory and industrial schools; juvenile offenders; and miscellaneous and general. These broad areas alone demonstrate the direction in which the NSPCC and the State were heading – a direction in which parents, children, delinquents and industrial and reformatory school children were clearly defined. Part 2 strengthened the law to prevent cruelty to children, and extended the legislation of 1904 by adding the crime of 'wilful cruelty' to that of 'negligence'. Cruelty included the failure 'to provide adequate food, clothing, medical aid or lodging' or, if parents were unable to do so, failure to 'to take such steps to procure the same to be provided under the Acts relating to the relief of the Poor'. It was also an offence to allow a child to beg, or to be in a brothel, and courts were given the power to remove children from prostitute mothers or drunken parents, partners or guardians. (Section 26 on the powers used to deal with habitual drunkards will be covered in Chapter 2.) With regard to the religious persuasion of those guardians with whom children were placed following their removal from parents, section 23 ensured that if this religious guidance was not adhered to, the child could be removed. Part 4 dealt with industrial and reformatory schools, and consolidated nineteen statutes. It dealt with certification of schools, inspection of schools, boarding-out of children, and the mode with which children could be sent to schools. It also dealt with the expenses of schools, offences which would result in transferral and other details pertaining to industrial schools and reformatory schools. Sections 77 to 83 dealt with certified day industrial schools – although this did not apply to Ireland hereafter. In 1909, the Dublin branch of the NSPCC described the importance of the act: 'Not only has it made the Society a far greater power for good in the cause of children, but it has made its work, hitherto but partially known, to be now and "epistle known and read of all men".'[41] What is dominant in the act is the idea that parents were responsible to the State and its agencies for the care of their children, and punishment of both parents and children would be how this responsibility would be enforced. In Ireland the act would remain one of the primary pieces of legislation dealing with child welfare until the 1991 Children Act.

1913 strike and lockout

> [T]he religion which could not stand a fortnight's holiday in England had not much bottom or very much to support it.[42]

Nationalism and child welfare were significant issues during this period also, and there are a number of incidents which will be mentioned briefly. In 1900, Queen Victoria's visit to Ireland and subsequent children's party (which 40,000 children attended as there were free buns and sweets) angered many nationalists.[43] In response, Maud Gonne and other nationalists set up a similar party in Phoenix Park, this time involving cultural events such as Irish dancing, singing and, yet again, the mandatory bag of sweets and buns. Children's support for each cause was now at play. While there are many similar incidents, the history of the Gaelic Athletic Association and other nationalist groups demonstrate the importance of children's participation. They will not be addressed here but are worthy of much further examination.

One of the common arguments of nationalist groups before independence was that Ireland would be better off as an independent nation with regard to infant mortality, child welfare and public health. Many of these issues, as well as fears surrounding socialism, proselytising and radicalism, can be seen in the events surrounding the 1913 strike and lockout in Dublin. In particular, this section will address the treatment of children during the lockout – not only by the press but by all groups involved. Specifically, it will look at the 'Kiddies Scheme', an idea proposed by Dora Montefiore and backed by James Larkin at a meeting in Dublin in 1913.[44] The scheme proposed by Montefiore would involve the Irish children of the lockout families travelling to England for a break. Montefiore envisioned that the scheme would help the children but also unite workers in Ireland and England. However, it would become one of the most controversial events during the lockout – as children became central figures in the dispute. The Archbishop of Dublin, William Walsh, responded angrily, claiming that Irish children should not be sent to homes where proselytising agents could be at work. Walsh's opposition and the subsequent backing by parents were enough to ensure that the scheme did not go ahead, and fears of socialism and proselytism again had triumphed over the welfare of children.

The press were central to the feud. At the time of the lockout, both *The Irish Worker* and the *Irish Independent* were engaged in a propaganda war – the *Irish Worker* emphasising the employers cruelty and injustice, the *Irish Independent* emphasising the position of the Catholic Church and business interests. Children were used by both sides to gain support. In 1913, Larkin stated, 'he could forgive them any crime in the calendar … but he could not forgive them when they denied the hungry child food.'[45] In his eyes, the denial of the visit to these children was unforgivable. Similarly, Ben Tillet wrote that the strike was 'the fight for the God-given right of life and freedom'.[46] In opposition, W. E. L. argued, 'surely if we have to barter the souls of our own children for foreign charity, better they were never born!'[47] The reference to the souls of children was very common during the entire period of this book. The *Freeman's Journal* also covered the events extensively, stating: 'a number of mothers said that though their children were homeless and had not a roof to cover them, they would not part with them, and that they would rather see them dead in their arms than give them to strangers.'[48] The *Irish Independent* similarly argued that Larkin was supporting the 'forcible deportation of Dublin children',[49] the children sent to Liverpool being referred to as 'vile traffic' being 'lured away'.[50]

Children were not passive actors in the dispute either, being involved in the Easons and Sons Schoolboys' Strike (a result of children refusing to use the school textbooks that were supplied by the firm with which their parents were currently engaged in a strike)[51] and the strike of a number of schoolboys in protest against a school's decision to remove its principal.[52] While the topic of children and striking cannot be addressed here, it is a rich area and one that often led directly to the following section – the introduction of compulsory education and the effects on both conceptions of childhood and actual family situations.

The introduction of compulsory schooling

In the last quarter of the nineteenth century, the experience and conceptualisation of childhood underwent a major transformation as children were moved from the labour force to the school. The shift occurred in many Western societies, but the effects varied depending on the class, gender and location of the children. The 1892 Irish Education Act ordered that all children under the age of twelve attend primary school for at least seventy-five days a year, or parents would face a summary conviction. There were many positive impacts from the introduction of compulsory schooling, most notably in the education of girls and boys who previously did not have the option of attending school, particularly past the age of ten years. These positives must, however, be set against the speed with which families were expected to adapt from a situation where children contributed financially to the home to one where they did not, which should not be underestimated. The effects of the introduction of compulsory education for families reliant on children's contributions have been addressed by a number of British scholars, although work remains to be done in the Irish context. Anna Davin examines this issue of 'home versus school' in London, concentrating on the 'usefulness' of children from the age of five or six in working-class homes.[53] Not only were children needed to contribute financially, but older children, particularly girls, were relied upon to care for younger siblings while mothers did the numerous jobs needed to maintain a home in extremely difficult conditions. With the introduction and enforcement of compulsory schooling, the State was directly influencing relations within families. Schools expected children to behave in a certain way, and corporal punishment was used to inculcate obedience. In general, from the State's perspective, compulsory schooling allowed surveillance of children and working-class families beyond anything envisioned previously. With regard to the running of schools, in Ireland the Protestant and Catholic religious orders took the mantle of responsibility, and although education was a contentious issue between the Church and the State in nineteenth-century Ireland, by the end of the century these issues were largely resolved.

Mary Daly argues that the 1892 act was 'poorly enforced, only applied to county boroughs and to a limited number of local authorities ... and did not apply in rural Ireland'.[54] This meant that while children in urban working-class areas could come to the attention of the NSPCC inspector or the police, many other children's absence went unnoticed. The experience of families in rural and urban areas was again very different. However, Table 1.1 demonstrates that parents were increasingly being prosecuted under the act from its introduction, and by 1917 (the last year for which figures from the parliamentary papers are available), 7,074 persons were proceeded against for offences against the Elementary Education Acts. This was fifteen times more than in 1895, and this figure would continue to rise following the introduction of the 1926 School Attendance Act, as will be addressed in the next section.

Table 1.1 Number of persons proceeded against summarily for offences against the Elementary Education Act, 1895–1908

Year	Number of persons
1895	461
1896	695
1897	1,063
1898	1,617
1899	2,315
1900	3,287
1901	3,477
1902	4,143
1903	4,547
1904	4,409
1905	4,544
1906	5,157
1907	5,859
1908	6,779

Figures taken from the *Criminal and Judicial Statistics for Ireland*, House of Commons Parliamentary Papers, 1895–1908.

But what do the increasing prosecutions represent? Were fewer children attending school, or did the State and its agencies became more focused on prosecuting parents? While these questions can only be speculated on in this examination, it is probable the NSPCC's increasing surveillance of families and the State's increasing involvement in child welfare were paramount. Also, as children found to be working became a more prevalent issue due to unemployment and growing awareness of child labour as an issue, police, NSPCC inspectors and concerned citizens may have become more active in reporting. What the table also demonstrates is that, even with the threat of fines and prison, the economic necessity to keep children at home was great enough to risk discovery. The industrial schools will be addressed in more detail in Chapter 4, but they figure prominently in this debate. While children whose parents were deemed unsuitable by the courts could be removed to industrial schools in the late nineteenth century, in 1908 the Children Act increased the instances in which children could be removed from the home, and the 1929 Children's Act would further extend the grounds to include non-attendance at school specifically.

Gender is another factor in this debate. As Davin points out with regard to London, 'Girls ... were more likely to miss attendances than boys',[55] which could be a factor in the consistently higher number of girls being sent to industrial schools on court orders. Similarly, Davin discusses the pressures placed on mothers not only to sacrifice children's help in the home but to send children to school clean, clothed and sufficiently equipped. So, not only were mothers and fathers expected to do without children's help, they were also expected to present them in a way most could not afford to do. The issue was addressed in the Irish suffrage paper the *Irish Citizen* in 1915:

> 'Stay at home and mind the children' is the stock rule of the anti-suffragist. But one cannot mind the children at home when our male Government has decreed that the said children are to be out of the home for the best part of the day. In country places, the long walk to school – often meaning damp boots and clothes, is a cause of consumption according to some experts ... We believe that with the spread of the women's movement, the idea will become known, even to our masculine protectors, who have hitherto failed so lamentably to do their chosen work of looking after the children outside the home.[56]

With children now attending school until the age of twelve (fourteen after 1926) notions of childhood were also being altered and extended, and a new category, adolescence, was emerging. Overall, compulsory schooling offered a variety of benefits to the State. It created an educated workforce, kept children off the streets and dealt with child unemployment. For children, it provided an opportunity to learn and play, although with the continuation of corporal punishment the experience of schooling may varied greatly. However, viewed another way, compulsory education was another mechanism to control poor families and bring working-class children into line with middle-class behaviour. Hendrick's dualism of children as victims and threats can be applied to this discussion. If children were in schools, they were perceived to be less of a threat than when they played, worked and lived on the streets and in the fields. School offered structure, discipline and an opportunity to invest in the nation's future through educating its citizens. This leads to the question – in other aspects of child protection and State intervention – as to how far policies directed at the 'protection' of children were actually child-centred. It appears that, in matters of education, work and infant mortality, the future role of working-class children as citizens often drove the reform.

Child welfare after Irish independence, 1922–52

> In exceptional cases, where the parents for physical or moral reasons, fail in their duty towards their children, the State as guardian of the common good, by appropriate means shall endeavour to supply the place of the parents, but always with due regard for the natural and imprescriptible rights of the child. (Article 42, *Bunreacht na hÉireann*, 1937)

The first decades of Irish independence were typified by an erosion of the rights of parents as carers and educators. In legislation relating to compulsory education, institutional provision, welfare and illegitimacy, parents and children in poverty were the focus of repressive legislation that removed children from the home, or were victims of the State's inability to tackle the poverty that separated families. Working-class families suffered most from Church and State action, as the sanctity of the family espoused in Catholic doctrine and political rhetoric was far from the reality. Integral to this discussion is the State's lack of planning and initiative in reducing the poverty that so many families faced. Unemployment and poverty contributed to the need of many parents to send their children to industrial schools or to nurse, to give them up for adoption, or to have them boarded-out. Had this been addressed, situations for many children could have been improved.

With regard to legislation and services, the first significant change in child welfare legislation after independence was in 1924, with the transfer of responsibilities for the reformatory and industrial schools from the Prison Service to the Minister for Education. It also signalled the introduction of the Courts of Justice Act, which proposed to set up children's courts in the four larger cities. From 1925 to 1927, the Commission on the Relief of the Sick and Destitute Poor, including the Insane Poor dealt with the issue of children in care, while 1926 saw the introduction of the School Attendance Act. This act would raise the age of compulsory education from twelve to fourteen years. In 1934, the Children Act was passed, amending the 1908 act in minor ways. From 1934 to 1936, the Commission of Inquiry into the Reformatory and Industrial School System (or Cussen Commission) would be held, while 1943–51 represented the period of collecting information surrounding the Commission on Youth Unemployment. From 1950 to 1970, there were a number of significant changes in child welfare reform, some of which are outside the remit of this book but very worthy of note. In 1952, adoption was legalised, while the Health Act of 1953 saw changes again to the situation for boarded-out children. The year 1962 saw the inception of the Juvenile Liaison Officer Scheme. In 1966, the Tuairim Report into the situation in Ireland's industrial schools (*Some of Our Children*) was published, which was a contributing factor in the setting up of the Committee on Reformatory and Industrial Schools under District Justice Eileen Kennedy. This section will deal with 1922 to 1952.

Politically, socially and economically, the 1920s and 1930s would see the introduction of censorship, the abolition of legal divorce, a ban on women sitting on juries and the introduction of the civil service marriage bar. With Cumann na nGaedheal in power for the first ten years of the Irish Free State's existence, they would attempt to balance the books and balance the demands of the Catholic Church – which was filling the vacuum left by the British government. Although in reality very little changed, aside from the investment in the Irish language (whose success lay on the shoulders of children mostly), and the introduction of Catholic-influenced legislation, this was enough to impact on families. In 1932, Fianna Fáil emerged from its excommunication and began a sixteen-year reign. That year also saw the Eucharistic Congress showcase an extremely Catholic Ireland, with Eamon de Valera embracing the hierarchy and they him. In 1937, the new Constitution *Bunreacht na hÉireann* reflected this in law with the special position of the Catholic Church being enshrined. Women's special place in the home was also enshrined, although there are a number of interesting points in this regard. Firstly, the proportion of mothers to women was the lowest in Europe thanks to emigration and low marriage rates. Secondly, the reality of motherhood in Irish homes was far from de Valera's ideal of comely maidens dancing at the crossroads, due in many cases to the social and economic collapse of rural Ireland. There were no policies to help women, men earned more and women did a restricted range of jobs. Which poses the question, if a woman's place was officially now in the home, why not reward her financially? Mothers' payments had been introduced in many countries in the aftermath of the First World War to encourage women back to the home (and open up more expensive positions for men); why not introduce such proposals here? Unfortunately, this was not an issue addressed in Ireland at the time.

The issue of birth control was also driven underground from 1930 to 1970, leading to the importation of illegal contraceptives, back-street abortions and prosecutions for those that broke the law. The only area of debate accessible was in the context of social morality and censorship. Also, the issue of birth control and maternal health copper-fastened the emerging alliance between the Catholic members of the medical profession and the Catholic hierarchy. Opponents used *Casti Connubii* to defend positions – going so far as writing to the League of Nations against the principle of anti-conception in cases where the mother had serious health conditions. Motherhood had become a focus of State and voluntary effort from the 1900s, yet as scholars have highlighted, unmarried mothers often suffered the most from the focus on female sexuality in the Irish Free State. Socially and economically, they were signalled as a deviant group, and as a group they were over-represented in cases of infanticide, abortion and forced emigration. As Maryann Valiulis states, 'Irish ecclesiastical discourse about the ideal woman had very direct and very real consequences for women in the Irish Free State'.[57] Encompassed in this debate is the notion that the focus on women's supposed 'immorality' offered a welcome distraction from the realities of poverty, unemployment, poor housing and high infant mortality[58] and the question of the State's responsibilities in this regard. The focus on female sexuality was not new. During the First World War, fears were vocalised by the clergy, the medical profession and the government about the danger to the morals of Irish girls travelling to Britain to work. These fears were echoed in the press, which regularly featured letters from those interested in 'the welfare of young Irish girls'. The 'white-slave trader' was placed at the centre of these fears, and Irish girls were warned of the attractions of well-paid posts in England. In 1915 the *Irish Citizen* noted:

> It is time that Irish parents should be warned, and Irish parents, and the Irish public generally need educating on this point. All girls should be warned of the perils and pitfalls of life, and hitherto, unfortunately Irish parents have been deplorably slack in this respect ... Irish parents still live in the happy days of Brian Boru. Irish girls, whether they live at home or abroad for their living, need to be better instructed to face the dangers, especially rife in a world at war.[59]

After independence, these fears became exacerbated, and in particular, young working-class women became a focus of institutions, laws and philanthropic practices. From the 1927 *Report of the Commission on the Relief of the Sick and Destitute Poor, Including the Insane Poor*, to the 1935 Criminal Law Amendment Act, enquiries that could have resulted in the provision of welfare for single mothers, greater protection of children from abuse, and other child welfare reforms that were being implemented internationally, instead resulted in draconian measures. The establishment of the Carrigan Committee in 1931, to examine the 1880 and 1885 Criminal Law Amendment Acts and the 'problem of juvenile prostitution', was, according to Máire Leane, 'a victory for the Catholic moral reformers who had sought to have issues of public morality placed on the political agenda'.[60] From the mid-nineteenth century onwards, issues of sexuality, motherhood and reproduction were constructed in Britain as issues of public concern which required both legislative and philanthropic regulation. Internationally, clerical writings from the first two decades of the twentieth century demonstrate the challenges which women's movements were posing to the Catholic doctrine. In 1930 in his Papal Encyclical, Pope Pius XI rejected calls for female emancipation as 'debasing of the womanly character and the dignity of motherhood and indeed of the whole family'.[61] In Ireland these challenges to female emancipation were further imbued with fears of materialism and working-class frivolity. Motherhood became the principal focus, with women being held as 'moral agents who had responsibility not only for themselves but also for men'.[62]

Public assistance for poor families

One of the first initiatives of the Irish Free State was the reorganisation of the Poor Law system. Under the Local Government (Temporary Provision) Act (1923), the powers of boards of guardians were transferred to county boards of health and public assistance; those workhouses that were not closed were renamed 'county homes'. The act also provided for the provision of outdoor relief (home assistance), a measure that had been rejected by Poor Law guardians prior to independence.[63] Yet decisions on who should receive relief and how much were left to the judgment of individual county boards. This represented a major flaw in the system, as authorities had no obligation to grant relief. If, as was the case with many unmarried mothers, committees did not want to be seen to endorse illegitimacy, they could reject individual claims. As various newspaper articles demonstrate, boards could be incredibly harsh to those that were forced to come beg for assistance, and while financial concerns were paramount, 'moral' concerns were also significant.

In 1925, the government appointed a commission to investigate the administration and law affecting the relief of the destitute classes, principally, widows and their children, children without parents, unmarried mothers and deserted children. Published in 1927, the *Report of the Commission on the Relief of the Sick and Destitute Poor* found that while public assistance was better than the previous system under the British administration, the amount of relief offered was too small. This is a point that can be seen repeatedly in the NSPCC case files, as the Society continued to campaign for increased assistance up to the 1950s. In particular, the report criticised the small amount given to widows with children, and able-bodied men with families. Both of these cases represented the 'deserving' poor, as opposed to unmarried mothers and deserted wives who were not encouraged to seek relief. The report also addressed the problem with county homes, which were now institutions catering for all those in destitution and completely unsuitable to the needs of children. Yet aside from mother-and-baby homes, the county homes were the principal 'dumping grounds'[64] for illegitimate children who could not be provided for by other means. While the homes were supposed to represent temporary stopgaps for women and children, many remained there for long periods as they were not provided with alternative arrangements. There were only a handful of mother-and-baby homes operating during the 1930s and 1940s, most privately run and therefore inaccessible to poor women, with Bessboro House in Cork city and Pelletstown in Dublin representing two exceptions. While both homes would allow poor 'respectable' women to have their babies in secrecy, without money they could not keep them. In these situations the homes would usually organise illegal overseas adoptions, as will be addressed later in the chapter. As late as 1942, the Department of Local Government and Public Health informed the Taoiseach's office of maladministration within the Dublin Board of Assistance. With regard 'the disposal of illegitimate children', the letter stated:

> There was no settled policy. Due, we think, to inaction, institutional treatment has become the rule, that is to say, when the children become too big for Pelletstown or when Pelletstown becomes too crowded, it is the custom to send them to Institutional Schools. The mothers lose touch with them and whatever contribution the mothers have been making to their maintenance ceases altogether. The mothers of the children, the majority unmarried, come for the most part from the country and have only been a short time in Dublin – from one night to a few months.[65]

For unmarried mothers there were three principal options besides emigration and institutionalisation in mother-and-baby homes known as Magdalene laundries – boarding-out, placing children at nurse and overseas adoptions. Adoption will now be addressed.

Adoption

From the 1940s to the 1970s numerous Irish children, mostly illegitimate, were sent to the United States in illegal adoptions organised by Catholic agencies. Yet due to opposition from the Catholic hierarchy (among others), adoption was not legalised in Ireland until 1952. The issue, therefore, epitomises the Church and State's complete lack of concern for the welfare of poor children, or more specifically, the handing over of any meagre assistance when issues of religion, proselytism or morality were involved. Yet in this instance, the Church and State officials were not the only ones colluding. Civil servants, parents and American adoption agencies were all complicit, and the legality of the situation was rarely questioned. The only issue was that children would not be sent to Northern Ireland or England for fear that they would be adopted by Protestant families. What is surprising is that there are media articles detailing the fact that children were being adopted by American couples despite the fact that there was no adoption legislation in the Republic of Ireland. Official documents also show that the issue of adoption was discussed by both politicians and the Catholic hierarchy in Ireland at the time.

What underpinned the policy of Catholic agencies and institutions was the idea that unmarried mothers were unfit to care for their children. With limited places in mother-and-baby homes such as Bessboro House, foreign adoption was viewed as an acceptable solution. Although numbers cannot be ascertained, hundreds if not thousands of Irish children were sent out of Ireland to America up to the 1970s. Yet adoption was still illegal in Ireland. By 1952, when adoption legislation was finally introduced, Ireland lagged behind most European states. That the issue of adoption had been discussed in various forums as early as the 1930s demonstrates the importance of the Catholic Church in the legislation of child welfare. The fear that Catholic children could not be protected from being adopted by non-Catholic families was paramount. That there were practical advantages to introducing adoption legislation was ignored by Irish legislators. When legislation was finally passed it was a result of concern for Ireland's reputation abroad after a number of highly publicised cases in the American and British press. Illegal adoptions continued, but this fact was denied. In this instance, the rights of unmarried mothers and their offspring were of the least concern.

A number of scholars have illuminated the debates on adoption.[66] While the importance of the Adoption Society of Ireland in the passing of legislation was pinpointed as critical in early accounts, Moira Maguire has demonstrated that the act was also a result of Ireland's image internationally.[67] With regard to opposition, the Catholic hierarchy had prevented reform on numerous occasions from the 1930s. In the 1940s, Miss Litster, an inspector of boarded-out children, was again in conflict with the hierarchy, this time on the issues of adoption and mother-and-baby homes. The Bishop of Ferns, J. Staunton, argued that as she and the head inspector of boarded-out children were both Protestants, they represented a significant threat to vulnerable Catholic children: 'they have plenty of money and powerful influence ... They use deceitful explanations ... The number of unmarried mothers of the better class is increasing and their secrecy, impossible to a Catholic Organisation where Catholics are concerned, is exploited by the Birds' Nests.'[68] He continued by listing the threats that the Protestant mother-and-baby homes posed to Ireland and Catholicism, highlighting the fact that children sent to institutions were not obliged to go to one of the same religious persuasion – 'I think that according to our present law and its administration, a Mohammedan could open up an institution, take destitute children, bring them up as Mohammedans, without suffering any inference from the public authority.' Finally, he pointed to the need for 'a maternity home in which the children of Catholic unmarried mothers could be born in the same secrecy as in the "Church Missions Homes"', as well as a home for children up to two years of age, "the age of adoption" with 60 or 100 cots'.

In many respects, the fight for adoption legislation represented a preamble to the mother and child scheme in 1951. By 1952 there were just eight Christian countries that had not yet legislated for adoption – Haiti, Honduras, Ireland, the Netherlands, Nicaragua, Paraguay, Portugal and El Salvador. The issue of legal adoption had been addressed by many states in the aftermath of the Second World War, given the high number of orphans and illegitimate children. In the late 1940s several articles appeared in newspapers about the ease with which Americans had 'adopted' Irish children.[69] This negative publicity and the fear that Irish children may be brought up in non-Catholic homes forced Archbishop John Charles McQuaid to put a halt to the overseas adoption of children from the mother-and-baby homes in his Dublin dioceses. He began negotiations with Catholic charities in the United States about how best to safeguard the faith of Irish children after their adoption. A set of guidelines was established which allowed for the continued export of children as long as their prospective parents could prove their devotion to Catholicism. Parents would have to submit their baptismal and marriage certificates, recommendations from their parish priests and medical certificates stating that they were not deliberately shirking natural parenthood. They would also have to swear an affidavit guaranteeing that they would raise their child as a Roman Catholic.

Jane Russell and the introduction of the Adoption Act 1952

Despite the founding of the Adoption Society of Ireland in 1948, it appeared that the government was in no rush to introduce the legislation that many were calling for. In fact the Attorney General at the time, Charles Casey, defended the government's decision not to introduce legislation in the late 1940s, stating that it may not have withstood a constitutional challenge.[70] In spite of his position as Attorney General, he also defended the non-introduction of legislation on the ground that it would conflict with Catholic teachings, stating – 'This country is predominantly a Catholic country. This does not mean that Parliament should penalize any other creed, but it does mean, that Parliament cannot surely be asked to introduce legislation contrary to the teachings of that great Church.'[71] However, by late 1951 the government could no longer shy away from the fact that adoption legislation would have to be drawn up, most notably in the wake of the Jane Russell scandal and pressure from middle-class parents who had previously adopted children in Ireland illegally and wanted their identity and family name recognised – often for inheritance issues. Jane Russell, a Protestant American actress, had come to Europe in 1951 to adopt a child with her husband. Her religion, and the fact that she was over forty, prevented her from adopting an Italian child, while English law prevented her from taking an English child out of the country. She was advised to travel to Ireland as there was no legislation regulating adoption. In the end Ireland came to Russell. She was approached by Florrie Kavanagh, an Irish woman living in London with her Irish husband and three children. Florrie and Michael Kavanagh discussed giving their youngest son, Tommy, to Jane Russell for adoption.

Despite the fact that British law prohibited the adoption of children who were citizens of the Republic of Ireland but resident in Britain, Tommy Kavanagh was able to leave England on an Irish passport with Jane Russell. Russell was an international star, and her intention to adopt a child while in Europe was well documented prior to her meeting with Florrie Kavanagh.[72] This brought Ireland more negative publicity. The Department of Foreign Affairs responded to the Russell controversy by circulating the following memorandum to Irish consulates abroad:

> As from the receipt of this minute, we would be glad if you would refer to the Department any application for a passport made to you by or on behalf of a person of either sex under the age of 18 years ... You may have noticed in the Irish papers of the beginning of last week a reference to a case in which the Embassy at London granted a passport to an infant, on the application by the father, and that the child was subsequently brought to the United States by an American film actress. The whole business received a great amount of undesirable publicity in the Press (particularly the English Sunday papers of the 11th inst.) and the reason for this instruction is that we wish to ensure that an Irish passport will not again be issued in such circumstances.[73]

The German newspaper *8 Uhr Blatt* carried on article in December 1951, under the headline '1,000 children disappear from Ireland'.[74] This article claimed that almost one thousand children had been sent to the United States with no organisation set up to ensure their safety once they had landed there. In early 1952 the Episcopal Committee issued a statement in favour of legal adoption provided that certain safeguards were enshrined in legislation. The most important safeguard was contained in Section 12(2) which states: 'The applicant or applicants shall be of the same religion as the child and his parents or, if the child is illegitimate, his mother'.[75]

The Church played a central role in the drafting of the Adoption Act, with McQuaid later admitting that he and Fr Cecil Barrett had gone 'over every clause'[76] in the act. Prior to the publication of the act, many believed that it would prohibit non-nationals from adopting Irish children, thus stopping the flow of Irish children to the United States. Even the mother-and-baby homes feared this, and in 1952, one hundred and ninety-two children were sent abroad for adoption, an increase of sixty per cent on the previous year.[77] However, under Section 40 of the act, it became illegal to send legitimate children abroad to be adopted, but it was still legal to send illegitimate children. It was these illegitimate children that the Church was concerned with. The only other restrictions in the act concerned the child's age and permission from the mother or official guardian to have the child adopted. The act did make it an offence to charge for arranging an adoption, but it was not illegal to donate money to an organisation that may have helped you during the adoption process. Only Catholic couples could adopt Catholic children. Couples in mixed marriages were not allowed to adopt, and the children from mixed marriages were not allowed to be put up for adoption. This act was introduced to establish legal adoption within the twenty-six counties of the Republic of Ireland and as a result did not help to stem the flow of Irish babies across the Atlantic. While many may have hoped that the introduction of long-awaited legislation would have put an end to the export of babies, it was in reality more concerned with keeping Irish babies out of the hands of Protestant couples.

'The sanctity of the family' and the international image of moral Ireland

A major feature of the post-independence period was the gap between Catholic rhetoric and practice with regard to children and the family. From the 1920s, 'the family' was repeatedly put forward as the basis of society by different institutions – the State, the NSPCC and above all the Catholic Church. The State was at pains to put forward an image of Ireland as pure, moral and traditional. Censorship was vital to this endeavour, and it appears to have reached as far as League of Nation reports and questionnaires. The following question was addressed in questionnaire form to all members of the League from the 1930s:

> Please give as full information as possible of all cases during the year in which persons have been discovered procuring, enticing or leading away women, or children of either sex, for immoral purposes in order to gratify the passions of another person, or attempting to commit these offences.

In every report bar one in the 1930s, the Irish response was 'nothing to report'. Yet numerous cases of child sexual abuse and prostitution reached the courts. For example, in January 1936 Bernard Rooney was prosecuted 'for living wholly or in part on the earnings of the prostitution of Susan Dunne'.[78] In June of the same year, Rose McBreen Smith was charged with two counts of procuration, for procuring Mary McBreen and Rose McBreen to become prostitutes.[79]

In the report from the United Kingdom in 1936, four cases were cited. As with the Irish report, the Union of South Africa stated: 'No cases reported. Report states that traffic in women and children is non-existent and its development in the near future is unlikely. There are no foreign prostitutes nor any foreign procurers.' In contrast, Austria reported 220 cases, an example of one being a case in which a foster father had made an indecent assault on a girl of thirteen and had introduced her to other men. The United States cited 4,758 cases of rape known to the Police Departments of 1,658 cities; and 42,236 persons charged for prostitution and commercialised vice. While there is an obvious discrepancy in what countries were viewed as relevant, in retrospect, the Irish report must have appeared farcical. In 1934, with regard to the question on children and adoption, the Irish report stated:

> The System of adopting or bartering children does not exist and no special measures are considered necessary. The Catholic Protection and Rescue Society, other philanthropic Societies and the Clergy of all denominations take a very active interest in infant welfare and protection, and their activities are to a great extent responsible for the absence of juvenile bartering in An Saorstat.

As will be further addressed in Chapter 3, from the 1930s to the 1970s, many of the Catholic societies discussed in this response facilitated the transfer of hundreds of Irish children to the United States for illegal foreign adoptions, many in exchange for financial contributions. The disparity between the actual situation and the image being portrayed by the Departments of Justice and External Affairs shows them to be highly hypocritical. Similarly, as will be addressed in Chapter 4, Catholic religious orders were using children in the industrial schools and reformatories as unpaid labour, both within the schools and afterwards. That these children and their parents were not seen as significant to the discussion is revealing, as is the fact that the illegality of adoption was not mentioned.

The Emergency

In 1939, Eamon de Valera stated, 'the Emergency could be a blessing in disguise for the Irish if it forced them to find answers for problems which would never have arisen in peacetime.'[80] While some partial truths can be observed in the notion that liberal Ireland today 'had its genesis during the dark days of the Emergency',[81] for those who experienced the mass emigration, poverty and bleakness of Ireland during and after the war, there were very few 'answers' found to problems that were most certainly not 'new'. Ireland's dependence on Britain economically meant that the war represented 'the ultimate national emergency',[82] and the acceptance of the Emergency Powers Act (EPA) effectively resulted in the severe restriction of democracy for the duration of the war, as the Government provided itself with dictatorial powers over almost every aspect of the life of the country. Neutrality was viewed as 'the least divisive policy',[83] and as the war progressed State survival would become synonymous with the survival of this policy of neutrality. With regard to working-class children and families, the Emergency witnessed an exacerbation of the poverty they had experienced throughout the 1920s and 1930s, highlighting the appalling social conditions in which many Irish citizens lived. The result was a return to the use of soup kitchens in response to starvation, the introduction of children's allowances and a re-examination of the role of charity versus state responsibility for family welfare. Before addressing these issues, the government response to the social conditions will be addressed, as will the actuality of emergency conditions for working-class families.

In 1938–40, the Department of Finance would exercise the greatest influence on pre-war policy in Ireland, and would continue this influence throughout the war period. Unlike in 1914–18, higher taxation would be imposed to prevent a rise in the cost of living, and all unnecessary imports would be prohibited. In 1939, the Wartime Economy Committee proposed cutting government expenditure by more than £8.25 million, out of a total of roughly £28 million.[84] Unfortunately, for the Irish people in most need of assistance, the areas which would receive the biggest cuts would be in the social services. The larger of these cuts included local loans (£2.5 million), housing grant loans (£1.25 million), unemployment payments (£1.16 million), employment schemes (£1.15 million), and a possible reversion to the 1925 level of the agricultural grant, saving about £1.3 million. However, some of the minor reductions would, for many, 'cut closer to the bone',[85] with such social services as the Free State Mill Grant and medical treatment of school children being completely suspended if the committee's recommendations were to be adopted. The committee also proposed that unemployment assistance benefits would be stopped immediately in rural areas to entice 50,000 persons back into agriculture for an intensive tillage campaign. Ultimately, some aspects of the report were attempts at 'indirect social engineering'.[86] It was the committee's belief that the withdrawal of unemployment assistance from the western areas of Ireland would result in migration from west to east. Not surprisingly, the government chose not to publish the committee's report, and also rejected a number of its proposals while offsetting most of its recommendations. Nevertheless, the committee had highlighted the severity of the economic challenge for the government in the pre-war period. Shortages of materials had direct employment consequences in certain industries and indirect ones on certain services. Emigrants' remittances would decrease and hospital sweepstakes were already under threat. Most alarmingly, the government was anticipating the return of thousands of Irish emigrants from Britain, which would further exacerbate the unemployment situation.

While one author has claimed that by the end of the war the Irish 'were doing better than they had ever done since the state was founded',[87] much of the statistical evidence available indicates the contrary. In one unpublished account of the level of poverty in Cork City during the Emergency, it is ascertained that forty-five per cent of households were living in destitution and deprivation by 1944. This figure, obtained by applying Rowntree's classic 'human needs standard' test, demonstrates the severe effect of the wartime period on so many of the nation's families.[88] Patterns of internal migration also characterised this era, as the population growth in Dublin city and its surrounding county areas increased by 49,000 persons between 1936 and 1946. In an article in the left-wing paper *Workers' Action* in 1942, the author describes the deprivation and abject poverty of many of the nation's families: 'Hunger and want, and even starvation, intensified immensely since the outbreak of the present war, haunt many of the homes of Southern Ireland.'[89]

In 1941, the President of the Dublin Chamber of Commerce, A.A. Brunker, told a meeting of the Chamber that 'despite unemployment and other problems, life in Eire was probably happier than in any other country in the old world at the present time'.[90] In order to accept this assertion, one must assume that Mr Brunker had not at that time experienced the tenements and slums in his native city. Four years later, T. W. Dillon would proclaim: 'never in the history of the slums have the worst landlords had a gayer time'.[91] However, whatever critique is to be placed on the morality of the Dublin landlords, in historical retrospect, the government's obvious failure to provide decent housing for the poor is indefensible. Amid an abundance of sailing regattas and ballroom dances, and a blooming cultural scene in wartime Dublin, over half of the population was living in 'multitudinous fever nests and death traps'.[92] Life in the Dublin tenements was a battle for financial survival, which usually did not include steady employment, and if you did not work, you starved. While the Emergency is not being cited as the *raison d'être* for this situation, the already pitiful conditions present before the wartime period were exacerbated, and this trend would continue throughout the 1950s.

Poverty

[I]f poverty were eliminated from the life of the people, the expenditure on Social Services would fall to an infinitesimal figure. (Labour Party Report on Social Services, 1943)

In November 1939, the cost of living in Ireland had already increased by 11 per cent. By March 1944, this would peak at 71 per cent above the pre-war level. Neither of these figures factor in the price of goods on the black market. In an article in *Workers' Action* in May 1942, the author claimed that by 1942, while theoretically the cost of living had increased by 'only' 37 per cent, this was a result of the fact that 'government theory leaves out a lot of things which the housewife in practice must buy'.[93] Between 1939 and 1942, the price of corned beef increased by 71 per cent; in many cases fish prices increased by 200 per cent; potatoes by 50–60 per cent and fruit by 200–50 per cent. In broad economic terms, real wages dropped by 30 per cent, the share of wages and salaries in net manufacturing output fell by almost 4 per cent, and labour's share of domestically generated national income dropped from 51 per cent in 1938 to 44.3 per cent in 1944.[94] While workers' wages and social welfare payments were stabilised, profits for manufacturers and traders continued to soar. The poor suffered most, as is to be expected, as those with a disposable income were obviously better placed to avail of the produce on the black market. In 1942, the Minister for Finance revealed that for the previous year, the total expenditure on the social services was slightly in excess of £12,600,000. Of that sum only £6,343,059 was provided from State funds.[95]

The introduction of children's allowances

From 1939, the issue of family allowances was addressed by the Fianna Fáil government and in the houses of the Oireachtas. The debates on the allowances were contentious, as has been demonstrated by Mel Cousins, Finola Kennedy, Fred Powell, J.J. Lee, Caitríona Clear and other scholars.[96] Lee argues that the debates were couched in concerns about British initiatives, with the Beveridge Report in Britain involved in discussions, while Cousins highlights that the major concern was the alleviation of poverty and provision of a supplement for large families. In contrast, Powell argues that pronatalist views were intrinsic in the allowances introduction. While this is true to an extent, it appears from the files that the alleviation of poverty in larger families was the primary concern, as opposed to social engineering.[97] The concerns about the social and health conditions of poor families had been raised by voluntary and charitable organisations during the Emergency period, forcing the State to take a more interventionist role in child protection.[98] In 1942, the Inter-departmental Committee, set up to investigate the allowances, acknowledged that there was significant poverty in large families to which the allowances could offer some assistance. Yet the proposals, driven in the Dáil by Seán Lemass and Eamon de Valera, did receive much opposition. Seán MacEntee was the most vocal opponent, claiming that the allowances would undermine the role of the father as the provider in the family, and therefore amount to State interference in the family unit. The Department of Local Government had a number of concerns, most surrounding the interference of the State in the family; while the Department of Finance pointed to the 'numerous charitable institutions and organisations which through voluntary effort and subscription of money cater most efficiently for the poor and the sick'.[99] Even those who were in favour of the allowances were hesitant about the sum that would be paid, and the parent to which it would be administered. Clear, Cousins and Kennedy have all addressed the issue of payment, concurring that the payment to fathers was a result of anxiety over the sanctity of the family and of the need to protect preconceived gender roles within the family. The decision to give the payment to fathers reflects this concern. That this was the case until 1974 is also significant.

Although the debates from 1939 to 1944 are significant, a study of the provisions of the 1944 act reveals the principal concerns most explicitly. That the father would receive payment is significant – both in its continuation of gender inequality in welfare provision, and its endorsement of the male breadwinner family model. Clear has noted that while many fathers nominated mothers as recipients of the allowances, this does not take away from the State's choice to award the allowances to the father. The naming of the allowances in this instance is also significant, as 'children's allowances' did not signify a replacement of the family wage in the way that 'family allowances' did. That the payments were a 'paltry sum'[100] shows that the government was careful not to make it appear that the allowances would supplant family initiative, particularly in the face of possible criticism from the Catholic hierarchy. Finally, that the allowances were initially given only from the third child onwards demonstrates an official endorsement of larger families, but most importantly, the existence and recognition of poverty in large families. Although the provisions in the 1944 act did balance the Church/State boat sufficiently, the introduction of the allowances also signalled the beginning of the Irish welfare state. While there would be numerous battles fought between the Church, the State and groups campaigning for welfare for poor families and children over the coming decades, the State had finally begun to realign the dependency on charity with regard to the care of vulnerable families.

Conclusion

This chapter has attempted to explore critical aspects of the origins of child welfare in Ireland, from the introduction of the Poor Law (Ireland) Act in 1838, to the introduction of adoption legislation in 1952. It has discussed the role of the State, the Catholic Church and voluntary organisations, while also touching on topics of critical importance in Irish history – primarily nationalism, welfare and poverty. Prior to independence, child welfare legislation focused on 'protection' while also increasing the use of institutionalisation by the State to maintain vulnerable and neglected children. Although legislation emanating from Britain brought about an increase in institutional care, the zeal with which the Catholic Church and to a lesser extent the Protestant Churches in Ireland adopted this measure is notable.

Institutionalisation would also become a feature of Irish society far longer than was needed.

In the first three decades after independence, Church and State action in the area of child welfare left much to be desired for families in poverty. In legislation relating to compulsory education, welfare, illegitimacy and institutional provision, the protection of 'the family cell' as espoused in the 1937 Constitution was visible in Church and State rhetoric only. For unmarried mothers, options continued to be limited, and in the case of placing children at nurse, extremely hazardous. As local authorities continued their complacency in the boarding-out of children and the inspection of homes to which children had already been boarded-out, the most vulnerable children remained the least significant concern. As the introduction of adoption legislation in 1952 demonstrates, the international image of independent Ireland remained a State priority. That children's allowances were introduced in the light of changes in Britain resulting from the Beveridge Report supports this assertion. Acknowledging the importance of the allowances in the alleviation of poverty in large families, and the affect they would have on the role of charity in the provision of welfare over the coming decades, the provisions in the act demonstrated that the Church was still a prominent bulwark in the move towards a welfare state.

Notes

1 For an excellent discussion of developments after the Kennedy Report in 1970, see Eoin O'Sullivan's contribution to the Commission to Inquire into Child Abuse, chapter 4, 'Residential child welfare in Ireland, 1965–2008: An outline of policy, legislation and practice: a paper prepared for the Commission to Inquire into Child Abuse', pp. 245–430.
2 Luddy, *Women and Philanthropy*. Also Oonagh Walsh, *Anglican Women in Dublin: Philanthropy, Politics and Education in the Early Twentieth Century* (UCD Press, 2005).
3 The WNHA was a pioneering public health organisation founded by Countess Aberdeen, the wife of the Lord Lieutenant of Ireland in 1907, in response to the conditions she observed in Dublin. By 1911, the WNHA had 155 branches and 18,000 members. Its activism was focused on issues affecting the poor, from hygiene to maternal and child welfare. Earner-Byrne, *Mother and Child*, p. 15. The Women's Cooperative Guild was another group working to push the needs of working-class mothers to the centre of social policy. See Irvine Loudon, *Death in Childbirth: An International Study of Maternity Care and Maternal Mortality 1800–1950* (Clarendon Press, 1992).
4 Luddy, *Women and Philanthropy*, p.71.
5 Anna Clark, 'Orphans and the Poor Law: Rage against the machine', in Virginia Crossman and Peter Gray (eds), *Poverty and Welfare in Ireland, 1838–1948* (Irish Academic Press, 2011).
6 Virginia Crossman, '"Cribbed, contained and confined?" The care of children under the Irish Poor Law, 1850–1920', *Éire-Ireland*, 44:1–2 (Spring/Summer

2009), 37–61.
7   For a discussion of boarding-out in Scotland, see H. J. MacDonald, 'Boarding-out and the Scottish Poor Law, 1845–1914', *The Scottish Historical Review*, 75 (1996), 197–220.
8   Crossman states, 'the slow take-up of boarding-out was a consequence of the misgivings of local guardians, not the poor law commissioners'. 'Cribbed, contained and confined?', p. 50.
9   John K. Ingram, 'Additional facts and arguments on the boarding-out of pauper children', *Journal of the Statistical and Social Inquiry Society of Ireland*, part 49, February 1876, p. 516.
10 See Caroline Skehill, 'The origins of child welfare under the Poor Law and the emergence of the institutional versus family care debate', in Crossman and Gray (eds), *Poverty and Welfare in Ireland*.
11 *Annual Report of the Local Government Board for Ireland*, 1877, [C1761], p. 44.
12 *Annual Report of the Local Government Board for Ireland*, 1904, [C2320], p. 110.
13 *Annual Report of the Local Government Board for Ireland*, 1873, [C794], pp. 61–2.
14 Ibid., p. 80.
15 Ibid., p. 85.
16 *Annual Report of the Commissioners for Administering the Laws for the Relief of the Poor in Ireland*, 1870, [C156], p. 13.
17 *Annual Report of the Local Government Board for Ireland*, 1907, [Cd3682], p. 35.
18 Florence Davenport-Hill, 'The system of boarding-out pauper children', *The Economic Journal*, 3:9 (March 1893), p. 62.
19 *Annual Report of the Local Government Board for Ireland*, 1910, [C5319], p. 24.
20 See Sarah-Anne Buckley, '"Found in a dying condition": Nurse children in Ireland 1872–1952', in Elaine Farrell (ed.), *'She Said She Was in a Family Way': Pregnancy and Infancy in Modern Ireland* (Institute of Historical Research, 2012).
21 See Ruth Ellen Homrighaus, *Baby Farming: The Care of Illegitimate Children in England, 1860-1943* (Unpublished PhD thesis, University of North Carolina at Chapel Hill, 2003), p. 14.
22 *Irish Times*, 7 November 1872.
23 The *Irish Times* regularly ran features on baby-farming in countries such as Britain, France, Poland and Russia, while continuing to expound its rareness in Ireland.
24 For a discussion of infanticide in Ireland, see Elaine Farrell, '"The fellow said it was not harm and only tricks": The father in suspected cases of infanticide in Ireland, 1850–1900', *Journal of Social History*, 65:3 (2012), 990–1004; '"Infanticide of the ordinary character": An overview of the crime in Ireland, 1850–1900', *Irish Economic and Social History* (November 2012); '"A very immoral establishment": The crime of infanticide and class status in Ireland, 1850–1900', in *'She Said She Was in a Family Way'*.
25 *Irish Times*, 21 December 1874.
26 1908 Children Act, also known as the Children and Young Persons Act.

27 Ibid.
28 *Irish Times*, 21 September 1894.
29 It was not the first case to use the term baby farming, as a case in 1879 had referred to the term and again in 1893, but it was the first to utilise the ILP legislation.
30 *Irish Times*, 18 June 1890. In 1905 there was another case involving a child sent to nurse from the Coombe Hospital. See *Irish Times*, 5 October 1905. See also, *Irish Times*, 23 April 1897; 7 August 1926; 16 July 1926; and 'Baby-farming charge: Woman sent to prison: Failure to notify authorities', *Irish Times*, 16 October 1935.
31 *Irish Times*, 13 September 1879.
32 *Irish Times*, 3, 5, 9 August 1893.
33 *Irish Times*, 21 June 1928.
34 Ibid.
35 Ireland would not benefit from many of the acts passed in Britain, particularly with regard to maternity and child welfare. For a discussion, see Earner-Byrne, *Mother and Child*, chapter 1, pp. 8–23.
36 Ibid., p. 10.
37 Ibid.
38 Margaret Ó hÓgartaigh, *Kathleen Lynn, Irishwoman, Patriot, Doctor* (Irish Academic Press, 2006).
39 Ibid., p. 29.
40 Hendrick, *Child Welfare: Historical Dimensions*, p. 79.
41 AR Dublin Branch, 1908–9 (ISPCC, Limerick), p. 14.
42 James Larkin, leader of the Irish Transport and General Workers' Union, 1913. *Irish Independent*, 24 October 1913.
43 For a discussion, see Janette Condon, 'The patriotic children's treat: Irish nationalism and children's culture at the twilight of the Empire', *Irish Studies Review*, 8:2 (2000), 167–78.
44 Donal Nevin, *James Larkin Lion of the Fold* (Gill and Macmillan, 1998), p. 223.
45 *Irish Worker*, 31 May 1913.
46 *Irish Worker*, 1 November 1913.
47 *Irish Independent*, 25 October 1913.
48 *Freeman's Journal*, 21 October 1913.
49 *Irish Independent*, 24 October 1913.
50 *Irish Independent*, 24 October 1913.
51 *Irish Worker*, 27 October 1913.
52 *Freeman's Journal*, 18 September 1913.
53 Ibid.
54 Daly, '"The primary and natural educator"? The role of parents in the education of their children in independent Ireland', *Éire-Ireland*, 44:1–2 (Spring/Summer, 2009), 194–217, pp. 196.
55 Anna Davin, *Growing Up Poor: Home, School and Street in London 1870–1914* (Rivers Oram Press, 1996), p. 101. In the Irish context, for a discussion of the focus on domestic education, see Joanna Bourke, '"The health caravan": Domestic education and female labour in rural Ireland, 1890–1914', *Éire-Ireland*, 24:4 (Winter 1989), 21–38.
56 *Irish Citizen*, 28 August 1915.

57 Maryann Valiulis, 'Neither feminist nor flapper: The ecclesiastical construction of the ideal Irish woman', in Mary O'Dowd and Sabine Wichert (eds), *Chattel, Servant or Citizen? Women's Status in Church, State and Society* (Institute of Irish Studies, University of Queens, 1995), pp. 168–78.
58 Louise Ryan, *Gender, Identity and the Irish Press, 1922–1937* (Edwin Mellen Press, 2002), p. 4.
59 *Irish Citizen*, 18 October 1915.
60 Máire Leane, 'Female sexuality in Ireland 1920 to 1940: Construction and regulation', Unpublished PhD thesis (University College Cork, 1999), p. 115.
61 Ibid., p. 71.
62 Ibid., p. 82.
63 See Seamus Ó'Cinnéide, *A Law for the Poor: A Study of Home Assistance in Ireland* (Institute of Public Administration, 1970).
64 Ibid., p. 90.
65 Minutes of the Dublin Board of Assistance, 1942, file s12956 (NAI, Dublin).
66 A number of scholars have examined the issue of adoption. See Maguire, *Precarious Childhood*. For a discussion of foreign adoptions and adoption policy in Ireland, see Maguire, 'Foreign adoptions and the evolution of Irish adoption policy, 1945–52', *Journal of Social History*, 36:2 (2002), 387–404; Mike Milotte, *Banished Babies: The Secret History of Ireland's Baby Export* (New Island Books, 1997).
67 Maguire, *Precarious Childhood*, p. 121.
68 Letter from Bishop J. Staunton to Dr Mackey re. 'Church Mission to Roman Catholics' (NAI, Dublin).
69 'Woman turns tables on husband bringing 2 orphans as 'surprise', *New York Times*, 29 July 1949.
70 The Constitutionality of the Adoption Act 1952 was upheld by the Supreme Court in the case of The State (Nicolaou) v An Bord Uchtála [1966] I.R.567.
71 'Attorney-general criticises the *Irish Times* on legal adoption', *Irish Times*, 14 February 1951.
72 An article had appeared in the *Irish Times* on 30 October 1951, in which Russell stated her intention to travel to Ireland to adopt a boy.
73 DFA345/96/I (NAI, Dublin).
74 '1,000 children disappear from Ireland', *Uhr Blatt*, 13 December 1951.
75 Adoption Act 1952
76 John Whyte, *Church and State in Modern Ireland 1923–1970* (Gill and Macmillan, 1971), p. 276.
77 Figure taken from Milotte, *Banished Babies*.
78 1D-61-1 (NAI, Dublin).
79 Ibid.
80 Speech in the Dáil in 1941 by Eamon De Valera, in Tony Gray, *The Lost Years: The Emergency Years in Ireland, 1939-45* (Little Brown, 1997), p. 59.
81 Ibid., p. 19.
82 Bernard Share, *The Emergency: Neutral Ireland: 1939–1945* (Gill and Macmillan, 1975), p. 5.
83 Donal Ó Drisceoil, '"Whose Emergency is it?": Wartime politics and the Irish working class, 1939–45', in Donal Ó Drisceoil and Fintan Lane (eds), *Politics of the Irish Working-Class, 1830–1945* (Palgrave, 2005) p. 320.
84 Andrew McCarthy, 'Reacting to war: Finance and the economy, 1938–1940',

in Dermot Keogh and Mervyn O'Driscoll (eds), *Ireland in World War Two: Neutrality and Survival* (Mercier Press, 2004), p. 51.
85 Ibid., p. 52.
86 Ibid.
87 Gray, *The Lost Years*, p.223.
88 Liam Ryan, 'Urban poverty', in Stanislaus Kennedy (ed.), *One Million Poor? The Challenge of Irish Inequality* (Turoe Press, 1981), p. 35.
89 *Workers Action*, 'How the National Income is Divided', May 1942.
90 Share, *The Emergency*, p. 112.
91 Kevin C. Kearns, *Dublin Tenement Life: An Oral History* (Gill and Macmillan, 1997, p. 10.
92 Kearns, *Dublin Tenement Life*, p. 31.
93 *Workers Action*, p. 2.
94 Ó Drisceoil, 'Whose Emergency is it?', p. 324.
95 *Tenth Annual Labour Report*, p. 24.
96 Finola Kennedy, *Cottage to Creche: Family Change in Ireland* (Institute of Public Adminstration, 2001); Fred Powell, *The politics of Social Work* (Sage, 2001); Caitríona Clear, *Women of the House: Women's Household Work in Ireland 1922–1961: Discourses, Experiences, Memories* (Irish Academic Press, 2000); Mel Cousins, 'The introduction of children's allowances in Ireland, 1939–1944', *Irish Economic and Social History*, 27 (November 1999), 35–55; J. J. Lee, *Ireland, 1912–1985: Politics and Society* (Cambridge University Press, 1989); Earner-Byrne, *Mother and Child*.
97 *Report of the Inter-departmental Committee on Family* Allowances, file s12117B (NAI, Dublin).
98 Earner-Byrne, *Mother and Child*, p. 108.
99 'Summary of the views of three departments', 5 September 1940, p. 5, cited in Earner-Byrne, *Mother and Child*, p. 110.
100 Earner-Byrne, *Mother and Child*, p. 109.

2

The NSPCC in Ireland, 1889–1921

> The Society differs in its aim from all other Societies seeking the welfare of unhappy children, in that, whilst others seek to house and provide for the wanderer, homeless, destitute, it seeks to punish those worthless parents who make children wanderers, homeless and destitute, and to render other provision than their own home less necessary.[1]

The above quotation, as cited in the introduction and taken from the first report of what was to become the first branch of the NSPCC, the Dublin Aid Committee, is an apt illustration of the Society's focus in its early years. Parental responsibility, the very real vulnerability of children, derogatory and punitive language – these themes marked the early years as parents became the focus of the NSPCC and the State. This chapter will look at the period from 1889 to 1921, to assess the early years of the Society, from its alumni and supporters to the number of branches opened. It will address the formation of the SPCCs internationally and the origins of the NSPCC in Ireland. It will look particularly at the problems surrounding religion, support both within the organisation and outside, the role of the State in child protection and the administration of the NSPCC on a branch and local level. It will discuss the evolution of concepts of child neglect and child cruelty, the links between the British and Irish societies, and the role of the NSPCC in provoking legislative reform. It will question the evolution of the Society in Ireland from 1889 to 1921, its relative standing by 1921 and who was in control at this time. An overarching theme is the NSPCC's attitudes to parents, families and keeping families together. The examination will extend to an analysis of child neglect cases, the sentencing of mothers to inebriate reformatories and the transferral of children to industrial schools. Throughout, the importance of class and gender in cases will be tackled, as will the impact of the Society on the children it was protecting.

The Society's beginnings in Ireland

The Dublin Aid Committee, the first branch of the NSPCC in Ireland, was elected on 12 June 1889 at a meeting in the lecture theatre of the Royal Dublin Society.[2] In September, it began its work in Dublin and in 1890 became known formally as the NSPCC. Therefore, while the Dublin committee did not hold the title NSPCC until 1890, it was the same organisation renamed. Following the opening of branches in Cork and Belfast in 1891,[3] Waterford in 1893, Derry in 1896, Kilkenny and Carlow in 1897, Clonmel in 1899 and Athlone and Wexford in 1901, the branches reached fourteen in number by 1904. Yet, interestingly, it was not until 1956 that the Irish Society for the Prevention of Cruelty to Children (ISPCC) gained autonomy from the NSPCC and took control of the assets and responsibilities of the Society in the Republic. It is this author's contention that the transfer was a result of changes within the British NSPCC as opposed to pressure from the Irish branches. In 1953, the Liverpool SPCC became the last branch to integrate itself into the national group, and it appears in this period that the NSPCC was reorganising and reinventing itself, hence the need to give autonomy to the ISPCC. Yet what is certain is that the connections between the Irish and British branches are critical throughout the nineteenth and twentieth centuries, but particularly in the earlier period.

Principal child protection agency in Ireland

From its foundation, the Society was the principal child protection agency operating in Ireland. Child protection moved past previous attempts at reform and relief – i.e. the operation of orphanages and 'ragged schools' – towards active lobbying for legislative change. In short, the NSPCC utilised legislation to effect change within the home. It becomes clear that throughout the nineteenth century, and especially from the 1880s, there was a shift in child welfare reform from a concern over the rescue and reclamation of children through philanthropy to the active involvement of philanthropists and the State in moulding children and families through education, social and health work. As part of an international 'child-saving movement', the Society's role is crucial to understanding the changing treatment of children and families by the State and its agencies. Harry Ferguson argues that it was between 1880 and 1914 that 'the modern concept of "child abuse" was constructed',[4] and the NSPCC was at the forefront of this construction. Although the Poor Law had restricted and questioned parental power (particularly that of fathers) from the 1830s, the NSPCC deliberately advanced legislative reforms that increasingly involved the State in the private lives of families. As the quotation opening this chapter elucidates, unlike 'other societies', the Society was focused on reforming parents through the threat of prosecution, and as charity work took on a greater class consciousness and class fear in the nineteenth century, the children of the poor became a primary focus.

An analysis of those involved in the early years is important in establishing how and why the Society expanded so swiftly in Ireland. It is also integral to the issue of the connection between the British and Irish branches, although at times this relationship was ambiguous, and it is impossible to ascertain why particular measures were adopted and others were rejected.

Emerging from the Dublin Aid Committee, the Society was made up mostly of members of the Dublin elite. Its first president was the Duke of Abercorn, and over the coming years the prominence of members of the Anglo-Irish Ascendancy would be the norm in most branches, at least as figureheads. The extent to which they were involved on a regular basis in activities other than fundraising cannot be ascertained here. The chairman of the Dublin Aid Committee was T. W. Grimshaw,[5] who would remain chairman of the Dublin branch until his death in 1915. Other members included the incumbent president of the Royal College of Surgeons (a position that changed annually). All were influential figures in Dublin at the time, and it appears from the subscription and membership lists that support for the Society was in vogue in Ascendancy circles over the next twenty years. In the first report of the Dublin Aid Committee, the following statement was included:

> Be it known that by the recent Act of Parliament for the Prevention of Cruelty to Children, every person –
> Who illtreats, neglects, abandons or exposes a child
> Who sends a child out to beg, though professedly to sell or perform
> Who sends one out under ten years old to hawk anything
> Who sends one out to hawk after ten o'clock at night
> Who employs a child under ten to publicly perform
> IS LIABLE to three months' imprisonment with hard labour and £25 fine.
> After this notice proceedings will be taken against all such persons by the NATIONAL SOCIETY FOR THE PREVENTION OF CRUELTY TO CHILDREN.

All information was to be sent to the secretary, Mr Hamilton Leslie, 62 Dawson Street, Dublin. At the end, it recorded: 'The informant's name will be kept strictly private'. The inclusion of this section of the 1889 Prevention of Cruelty to Children Act was significant, as were later references to people's ignorance of the act. It was a landmark piece of legislation, one driven by the Society in Britain, and its significance in the history of child protection is such that it was known by the NSPCC and other bodies as the 'Children's Charter'. The report also stated that 'one example made of those who commit a gross offence against a child reforms a neighbourhood'.[6] In clarifying the role of the Society, the authors stated: 'It differs from the work of the Police ... It differs from the aims of the Public Prosecutor ... It does not seek the removal of children from their parents' into ideal circumstances ... It does not seek merely to punish'.[7] For many families over the coming years these differences would not be as clear-cut.

While the motives of individual members cannot be fully ascertained, qualifications for membership of the Society were purely financial: for patrons, a once-off payment of not less than £500; for a 'life councillor' a once-off payment of at least £100; for a 'life member', a once-off payment of not less than £10; for an annual member, a yearly subscription of at least £1; and for an associate member, a yearly subscription of not less than five shillings. As was the norm for charitable and voluntary organisations, the names of members and the amounts of donations and subscriptions were printed in the annual reports. By March 1890, the committee had received £223 19s 6d in subscriptions and donations. £35 4s 3d of this was spent on advertising, indicating the importance of the press to the Society in the early days, and an inspector's salary is recorded as £55 5s 9d.[8] By the 1930s and 1940s, this sum would range between £250 and £350 per annum, depending on the branch.[9] Not only did the Society thank the press at the end of most reports, in 1897 the Cork branch report contained a supplement with extracts from the *Cork Examiner*, *Evening Herald*, *Cork Herald*, *Cork Constitution* and *Skibbereen Eagle*, all praising the Society's work. By 1911, the Society had 146 local 'organisations'. These were not all functioning branches but fundraising groups and branches of the Children's League of Pity, which was principally a means of getting middle-class children involved in fundraising. The 'Lady Collectors' were also critical to raising funds up to the 1940s, but while flower days and other fundraising activities increased awareness of the Society's work, the bulk of the money in the early years came from subscriptions and bequests. In 1903, for example, contributions to the Dublin branch totalled £2,458, with £1,000 coming from a bequest left by the late Richard Hawkins Beauchamp.[10] Bequests were encouraged in the annual reports, but could not exceed £5,000 in cases of private property.

The expansion of the Society from 1889 to 1914 was notable, as measured in the number of new branches opened, the number of inspectors hired, the amount of money raised and the number of families investigated. In 1899, for example, the Dublin branch dealt with 2,067 children. In the following year the figure rose to 4,027, and by 1909 the branch had dealt with 18,450 cases, resulting in 1,435 prosecutions, 15,951 warnings and 736 otherwise dealt with. The remaining 328 were dropped. At this time, there is no question that many families were living in poverty and children were suffering neglect as a result. However, the question must be posed – to what extent did the Society merely punish parents for that poverty?

The earliest file in the NSPCC archive in Ireland dates from 1919. In the context of this discussion, it is necessary to look at the details it recorded. The investigation form which came to be used as standard practice in inspectors' case-work contained the following information: the child(ren)'s name(s), age(s), address, religious persuasion, and relationship to the accused. Also included were questions on whether or not the child(ren) was illegitimate, whether or not the child(ren) was insured and for how much, whether the parents were living, and the whereabouts of the child(ren). Under the allegation section, the nature of the offence, the time of the offence and the locality were recorded. Following this, details of the accused and witnesses were recorded. Finally, the action taken, the result and how the child(ren) was dealt with were addressed. This first recorded case in one of the inspector's notebooks (as opposed to the generic file used) involved an allegation of 'neglect to provide'. The father of two children was accused of deserting his family. The inspector recorded: 'it is alleged that he parted from his wife on good terms and promised to write and send money weekly for their support, but since then it is alleged that he has not written or sent any money.'[11] The file included a statement from his wife: 'his people were not satisfied to keep me and our children without payment and I came back to [location withheld] to live and reported my case to the inspector of the NSPCC Society who has since been endeavouring to trace my husband ... I hope you can get my husband arrested and dealt with for his cruel neglect.' The language of the woman is quite formal, almost as if she had been instructed on what terms to use. It appears to be in her own handwriting, as it is different from the inspector's entry, but she may have been told what to write and sign off on. The files in the 1920s and 1930s contain many desertion cases, as emigration resulted in many husbands not returning home. The Society would become a place for these women to use the British connections to track their husbands for maintenance.

Apart from the case files, the inspectors' books (small notebooks kept to record case details) contain entries from 1920–21, which deal primarily with different 'types' of neglect, the placement of children in industrial schools, separation wives (wives of soldiers, often referred to as 'on the strength' because of their eligibility for state payments) and illegitimacy. In May 1920, a small card was sent by the mother superior in St Aidan's industrial school to the Wexford NSPCC Inspector:

> Dear Mr Sullivan,
>
> Many thanks for [your] kind letter. I am happy to say the two children arrived today. The Police were busy. Thanking you most sincerely for your kindness to us. If you have any more children you won't forget St Aidan's.

I would argue that this quotation relates to the acquisition both of money and of a soul. The continuation of the capitation grant for industrial schools encouraged institutions to remain full.

How did the inspectors view their role? The *Inspectors' Quarterly* was a newsletter for officers of the NSPCC set up in 1913, which contained details on British and Irish branches. In its first edition, it advertised a meeting for officers in Ireland to be held in Cork. The newsletter included 'Hints' for officers – for example, the keeping and forwarding of all news cuttings from local papers on matters concerning children to the Central Office. In the second edition it stated that 'care should be exercised in calling a doctor to a case ... no child should be allowed to suffer, but an Inspector must exercise wide discretion and consult his Honorary Secretary in times of doubt, before incurring expense'. It also discussed a case in which 'inattention to instructions' led to a situation in which an inspector entered a child's religion as Protestant. The child was removed to an institution, but soon afterwards fell ill and was removed to a hospital where it was discovered that the child was a Catholic. It stated that the child had therefore been 'improperly placed in the wrong Home', demonstrating the importance of religious affiliation and fears of proselytism. The same volume recorded the retirement of Inspector Maher of Kilkenny, who had worked for sixteen years as an inspector. It stated: 'his best work has been done in warning neglectful parents, and he had only lost one case in court during the whole period he has been an inspector.'

The role of women in the NSPCC, and the gender bias of inspectors and those being investigated, is worthy of further discussion here. Women did not act as inspectors in Britain until the First World War, and in Ireland until the 1920s. This was perhaps due to the perception that inspectors needed to be viewed as strong, powerful and authoritarian – qualities not attributed to women generally in this period. These qualities were listed in the *Inspector's Directory*, as has been noted by Maria Luddy in her article on the Society's beginnings in Ireland. What it demonstrates is that the inspectors were not benign figures, or even the equivalents of today's social workers; families were wary of the inspector, particularly in working-class areas.

Societies for the prevention of cruelty to children and the debate on child abuse

It is necessary to place the child welfare movement in Ireland in its international context. By 1890, the year in which the first Irish branch of the NSPCC was founded; there were thirty-four SPCCs in the United States and fifteen elsewhere. The movement had emerged in New York in 1874 after a landmark case in which a lawyer successfully used the cruelty to animal acts in a case of ill-treatment of a young girl. Linda Gordon and other scholars have demonstrated the ferocity of the campaigns that ensued, emerging as they did from existing philanthropic endeavours. After a visit to New York in 1881, British businessman Samuel Smith began lobbying for a British SPCC. In 1883, the Liverpool SPCC branch was opened. The ethos of the Liverpool Society can be demonstrated in a comment by Smith in 1883: 'no relief is to be found in any remedy which does not aim at producing individual virtue with independence; the proletariat may strangle us unless we teach it the same virtues which have elevated the other classes in society'.[12] Throughout the 1880s, Smith wrote frequently about the poor in Liverpool, arguing that while Britain had sent men overseas to reform 'savages', they had not set their domestic scene in order. His references to the 'impulse of humanity' and responsibility were also mixed with indignation that middle-class gains secured by business and trade were now threatened by economic depression and could be further eroded by the 'thriftlessness and moral incapacity of the poor'.[13] Smith was not alone in his sentiments, and for many in the middle and upper classes in the late nineteenth century the emergence of the SPCCs and the child-saving movement was seen as a long-awaited opportunity. While there were still a minority of reformers who became involved in the NSPCC and comparable organisations to improve the lives of children and families, most appeared to be primarily motivated by a need to organise and regulate the lives of the poor, encouraging class-biased legislation as a means of inculcating 'a sense of responsibility' into people of the working class. Linda Gordon argues that the 'child savers' (a general term she uses for the SPCCs) in the US were attempting to impose a new, middle-class urban style of mothering and fathering on working-class families. Mothers were to be gentle, moral and temperate, while fathers were to provide adequate economic support. As the family was 'reordered', a modern version of male supremacy replaced patriarchy. Fathers were to support their families economically, children were to attend school, and mothers were to provide comfortable homes with all the modern ideals of cleanliness and domesticity.[14]

The NSPCC in Britain would remain an important influence on the Irish branches. Over the period of examination, there were numerous publications by prominent members and presidents, particularly Benjamin Waugh and Robert Parr. Both would have an enormous influence on the Society's actions.[15] Aside from NSPCC publications, in its early years and at times of heightened campaigns and fundraising, the Society's *Child's Guardian*[16] often published alarming images of child abuse (which were very much the minority of investigated cases), as well as over-publicising the handful of cases involving middle- or upper-class families in order to appear non-class biased.[17] In the Irish branches, aside from the Cork branch report in 1893 which contained a shocking picture of a starving child sitting on an inspector's lap, and the Dublin reports in the early years which contained pictures of children in the shelter in Dublin, such images were not utilised to a great extent. There is no definitive answer to why this was, but it could be argued that potential Irish donors were not as susceptible to the images, and that in fact they would appear to show the poor Irish in a pitiful state. As most members of the Irish branches of the NSPCC were Anglo-Irish, this could cause tensions.

As Chapter 1 addressed, aside from workhouses and orphanages, 'ragged schools', industrial schools and reformatories were all set up to cater for dependent and orphaned children from the middle of the nineteenth century. Children were not the only group in society to be favoured by philanthropists, but they featured largely. Images of starving and neglected children sparked sympathy in potential donors. An idealised view of childhood has been identified as a motivation for philanthropists internationally, and Ireland was in keeping with this trend. What all these institutions had in common was a concentration on the rescue and reclamation of destitute children, and this philanthropic ideal was extended from the 1880s with the setting up of the NSPCC. While reformers were concerned with child rescue prior to the 1880s, from this decade on a more determined and extensive child-saving phase developed, one that shifted responsibility from philanthropy to the State.[18] The Society's role in Britain was twofold. As a lobbying group they pushed for legislative reform that shifted discussions in parliament from problems resulting from urbanisation (in particular poverty, overcrowded living conditions and unemployment) to an emphasis on the responsibility of parents to provide a defined standard of living to

The NSPCC in Ireland, 1889–1921

their children. By entering homes, inspectors criticised parents for their children's appearance and the environment they were living in. The problem with the standards of health care, hygiene and cleanliness was that it was based on a middle-class domestic ideal that working-class parents could not possibly meet. The definition and enforcement of this ideal will now be addressed, as will the environment in which it emerged.

How extensive was this philanthropic work and who were the philanthropists? In 1884, Dublin had over 120 educational institutions, orphanages and refuges, the majority of which were opened from the beginning of the nineteenth century.[19] This demonstrates the scale of the philanthropic endeavours that had developed. Men and women became involved in philanthropic activity not only to save children from the corruption of the streets and proselytisers, but also to keep them out of the workhouse and teach them middle-class ideals of home and school. The notion of moulding 'the children of the nation' emerged from discourse in Britain in the late nineteenth century. This coincided with changing ideas about the age at which children were still viewed as children and not as working men and women. Between 1880 and 1910 in Britain, as Harry Hendrick has demonstrated, the age of consent was raised, compulsory education up to the age of twelve was introduced, and child labour laws came to be enforced.

Another critical issue is the relationship of the Irish branches to the British Society. In 1912, the 'Society's duties' were outlined in the Wexford District branch's report:

> ... to prevent the public and private wrongs of children and the corruption of their morals. To take action for the enforcement of laws for their protection. To provide and maintain an organisation for the above objects. To do all other such lawful things as are incidental or conducive to the attainment of the above objects.[20]

In the same report 'The whole work of the Society' from 8 July 1884 to 30 June 1912 was recorded:

> The Society has enquired into 717,249 complainants of cruelty, of which 682,634 were found to be true, affecting the welfare of 1,981,140 children (of whom 11,518 children died), and involving 942,394 offenders. 574,830 cases were warned; 51,036 resulted in prosecution, 96 percent being convicted; and 56,718 were dealt with by transfer in other ways. 9986 years of imprisonment and £12,525 in fines were inflicted. Orders were made for 1209 years' detention in Inebriate Reformatories. 517,919 children were known to be insured for a total sum of £2,708,604.[21]

A few observations can be made which demonstrate the ethos of the Society as a whole in the early years: the death of almost 12,000 children; the success rate of convictions; the inclusion of the inebriate reformatory detentions; and the awareness of child insurance. The breakdown of all cases investigated was: 'Neglect and starvation – 584,111, ill-treatment and assault – 77,269, manslaughter – 172, abandonment – 6547, exposure –

11,610, exposure for begging purposes, &c. – 13,465, moral offences – 14,853, and other wrongs – 9,222.' The high number of 'moral offences' and 'other wrongs' is interesting, as is the number of neglect and starvation cases. Overall, the figures demonstrate the number of families the NSPCC in Britain and Ireland was now investigating, and the growth of the Society over such a short period of time.[22]

The sharing of statistical information was not the only connection between the Irish and the British Societies. Both financially and with regard to policy, the official reports demonstrate that the Irish branches of the NSPCC replicated many of the tactics and procedures of the British branches. Having examined British and Irish reports in the period, both the language and the offences being investigated are similar. A key difference was the greater focus on intemperance by the Irish Society, an issue that will be discussed later in the chapter. The presidents of the NSPCC in Britain spoke to the Dublin branch on a number of occasions. In 1902, speaking about the Dublin branch, the then president Robert Parr[23] stated: 'they have established some fair amount of public confidence. That confidence has been passed out of Ireland, and has reached England ... They ask the public to join them in carrying out, in Ireland, the principles of the Charter which the Society has received at the hands of Queen Victoria. They ask them to unite themselves with a Society which has at its head the King of the realm.'[24] As previously discussed, the involvement of prominent Ascendancy figures in the Society strengthened this Irish–British connection in the earlier years, particularly in Dublin. However, as with other philanthropic societies in the nineteenth century, much of the fundraising on the ground was done by the middle classes.

Did this involvement of Ascendancy figures lead to any conflict with those in the churches also involved in child welfare? Maria Luddy argues that the Society was unique in that it did not suffer from religious sectarianism.[25] In 1902, this issue was addressed by the chairman of the Dublin committee:

> The ghoul of proselytism has dogged the stages of our Society from the beginning. Its shadow has threatened but never touched us. I say that no matter in what guise it comes, and no matter from what quarter, that vile traffic has never found, and never shall find, a foothold among us. We have been in existence now thirteen years, exposed to eager, jealous watching, and during that time no definite charge of this description has ever been made against us. Some years ago there seemed to be a reflection of this kind thrown upon us in the columns of one of Dublin's newspapers in connection with a case dealt with by the Society.[26]

He goes on to state that following a letter from Robert Parr to the paper, a full retraction was printed and it was claimed there was 'no ghoul of proselytism'. Yet one of the most interesting differences between the Irish branches was that the Cork committee in the early years appears to have been strongly influenced by clergy from different churches working in tandem. The annual reports list donators and contain the minutes of meetings which involved both Protestant and Catholic clerics. It also appears that this amount of influence and cooperation was unique to Cork, and the comments of Cork clergymen are scattered throughout other branch reports. In 1910, the Wexford branch printed a supplement to its annual report entitled 'Some opinions regarding the Society's work in Ireland'. It cited a number of influential people, notably the Inspector of the Local Government Board and the Recorder of Dublin, F. Falkiner, who wrote:

> I wish to take this opportunity of saying what a blessing both the Inspector and the Society he so well presents have been to the city ... The good the Society is doing cannot be exaggerated, and God only knows what a hapless fate would be that of many innocent little ones but for its intervention. Thank God there is such a Society in the city.[27]

The majority of names, however, were clergymen from Cork. The Revd Robert Browne, the Roman Catholic Bishop of Cloyne wrote: 'The purpose of the Society has my fullest sympathy and encouragement. Cruelty to Children in any form is a hideous vice ... I enclose a subscription in token of my approval of your good work, and my heartiest good wishes for its success and extension wherever it is needed.'[28] Comments were also included from the Revd Meade (the Protestant Bishop of Cork, Cloyne and Ross), the Revd McSwiney, and Sir John H. Scott who stated: 'I have personal experience as a Magistrate of the great benefits which the Society has conferred upon the city'.[29]

Child abuse, cruelty to children and child neglect

What were the aims of the NSPCC? As previously mentioned, the term child abuse was not used in the nineteenth century, but many scholars have identified the offence of 'cruelty to children' as its equivalent. Yet what constituted cruelty was not always clear. Both Christine Anne Sherrington and Harry Hendrick discuss the ambiguity suffusing the debate on child abuse, particularly in the period 1880–1908.[30] One of the issues in the debate was the perceived link between child abuse, poverty and a person's moral character. Reformers argued that by altering the conditions in which children lived, there would be an indirect effect on working-class men and families, as can be seen by the fact that the child welfare movement emerged from an initial concern with the housing conditions of the poor working class.[31] Evidence at the Royal Commission on Housing of the Working Classes (1884–85), set up to examine the slums of London in particular, referred not only to the deplorable living conditions but also to the perceived connection between overcrowded living areas and incest in families. Debates on what constituted child abuse also centred on the SPCCs' shift internationally from an emphasis on cruelty to children to an emphasis on child neglect. Definitions of both are obviously problematic, but examples from the Irish reports can be given. Initially, the Society highlighted three types of cruelty: intentional (beating, starving, systematic persecution), which all came under the law; unintentional (allowing children to suffer by want of personal bodily attention, sour and improper food), which did not come under law; and accidental or careless (drunkenness, gossiping, falls, burns, scalds, run overs), which could be amenable to the law.[32] Yet from roughly 1900, neglect began to constitute the greatest offence addressed by the Society in both Ireland and Britain. Changing interpretations and treatment of neglect by the NSPCC will be referred to throughout, but three key questions must be asked: what was child neglect understood to be? How could an inspector decide what 'wilful neglect' was? How did they treat neglect resulting from poverty? As one inspector wrote in 1908,

> no word picture, however complete, can accurately portray a case of real 'Neglect' as our men discover by the thousand every month ... Each will accept the description in a comparative way, and each determine the depth of the evil by his or her own experience – just because we cannot put the things that count into words. The yearning of the child for mother – and father-love, the aching pangs of hunger, the bitterness of the cold wind upon the shivering form, the 'smell'.[33]

As this quote highlights, and as an examination of the *Inspector's Directory* demonstrates, what constituted child neglect tended to be very subjective. Yet it represented the majority of NSPCC cases. There were also other categories – for example, exposure, assault, immoral surroundings – but neglect was a principal focus. In the Irish branch reports, up to the 1920s, there were only two categories of neglect recorded – neglect, or neglect and starvation. From 1921 the categories expanded to include neglect to provide, moral neglect, neglect to provide proper guardianship, and medical neglect. Examples of these will be provided in Chapter 3, but the expansion of the category is worth noting here, as it represents a professionalisation of the Society's social work from the philanthropic actions of the early years.

Another element of the debate on child abuse was the bias of individual inspectors. While a genuine concern for the children involved in investigations can be seen in the inspectors' writings, this was not the case with regard to the parents. Throughout the files, descriptions of poor and working-class 'clients' as 'careless', 'useless', 'lazy', 'immoral', 'excitable', 'foolish', 'indifferent', 'fond of drink' and 'quarrelsome' depict images of degenerate, incapable and abnormal individuals. In contrast, the inspectors' personal writings project an aura of righteousness associated with their self-perception as saviours of the poor.[34] The following sample case from the Dublin branch in 1910 is typical of the cases cited in different branch reports in the period:

> Family of 5 children, aged from 10 to 5. The mother was addicted to drink. Their home life can be imagined from the Inspector's report – 'Mother hardly able to speak from effects of drink; children dirty and neglected. Children's clothes, boots and bedclothes pawned. Rooms in foul, dirty

state. Mother drunk in bed, children half naked, and dirty, one crying on the street.' Every chance was given to this woman to amend her ways, but it appeared impossible for her to abstain from drink. Finally she was convicted and ordered to be detained for one year in Inebriates' Home at Ennis.[35]

The removal to Ennis State Inebriate Reformatory will be discussed later in the chapter, but what is noteworthy is the detail recorded by the inspector. The physical condition of both the house and the children were the primary details documented in the early years, and both were seen as a mother's responsibility. This was an international trend in the SPCCs, as with the shift from cruelty to children to child neglect. However, in Ireland, 'intemperate' mothers were viewed as the most neglectful by the NSPCC. Although Sherrington has demonstrated that drunkenness and intemperance were issues addressed by the British Society in the early years, all the sample cases in the Irish reports examined have involved some reference to drunkenness.[36] Much of this has to do with inspectors' perceptions. Numerous scholars have demonstrated how, in the early years, child protection workers viewed the mistreatment of children through their own narrow cultural lenses, as demonstrated by the focus on drunkenness, cleanliness and children working or playing on the streets. The middle-class ideal of domesticity that was highlighted through the emphasis on neglect was impossible to achieve for many families. Neglect and poverty were not the same, but many cases of neglect arose as a result of poverty. This was particularly evident in Dublin city, where one-fifth of the population of Ireland resided and the slums were described as the worst in Europe. While previous child savers had focused on orphans and illegitimate children, the NSPCC was claiming the right to intervene in all families and all homes. George Behlmer argues that their 'interconnected roles as national pressure group and local watchdog of parental conduct gave the NSPCC a philanthropic cachet that fuelled spectacular growth'.[37] Even though this is a fair assessment of the Society's expansion, Hendrick rightly criticises Behlmer's later assertion of the Society as classless. Although Behlmer correctly maintains that reformers in the United States viewed cruelty to children as 'a vice of the inferior classes and cultures which needed correction and "raising up" to an "American" standard', his contention that 'no equivalent impulse coloured English child protection efforts'[38] is questionable. Luddy also emphasises the Society's classlessness, arguing that it 'made a virtue of its attempts to investigate all cases of abuse no matter what strata of society were involved'.[39] She later backs up this assertion, stating that 'as previously noted, the Society made it clear that cruelty to children was a classless crime, and the Irish branch of the Society echoed this belief'.[40] Although the NSPCC occasionally asserted its status as saver of all children, there is an obvious gulf between this rhetoric and the Society's actions. In the 247 files that have survived from the 1930s, no case involved a family outside the working class or the poor. Also, in its focus on the family rather than on institutions, prisons or schools, the Society was consciously deciding not to address corporal punishment, whipping of children for minor offences or abuse in industrial and reformatory schools. Again, in its shift in emphasis from cruelty to children to neglect, the Society was, it appears, making a decision to address only certain aspects of child welfare. As Hendrick points out, as the Society gained experience, its early character and emphases changed and cruelty remained an issue 'only within limited parameters'.[41] The existence of cruelty to children in society as a whole was a reality, but it raised more issues than reformers felt they could contend with, since it spread beyond the behaviour of the poor.[42] These and many other aspects of the NSPCC's policies make it difficult to view it as classless.

As mentioned in the literature review, in Britain the history of the NSPCC has been written and challenged,[43] but in Ireland the story of the 'cruelty man' or the role of what NSPCC inspector Robert Parr termed the 'children's man'[44] has yet to be fully told. The effect the Society had on the 'public awareness' of child cruelty in the early years has been considered by Maria Luddy in her article on the early years of the NSPCC in Ireland. In general, concern for child welfare was not new, and the emphasis on the unhappiness of children and the worthlessness of parents in this chapter's opening quote remained the philosophy and discourse of the Society up to the First World War, and to a lesser extent beyond. The rhetoric and class bias is in keeping with writings by reformers such as Samuel Smith (who was discussed previously), but the Society took this a step further by threatening to prosecute parents living in poverty for their inability to provide for their children a standard of living that they could not afford. In doing so, the Society was differentiating itself from other philanthropic societies, religious orders and the Poor Law guardians, who dealt only with 'dependent' children, orphan children and illegitimate children. Quite radically, the NSPCC was proposing to intervene in *all* homes deemed 'unsuitable', and to force parents, through the use of the threat of punishment, to meet their prescribed ideal of child-raising. What is most significant is that the agenda set out by the Society initially had no legislative basis on which to follow through with such threats. Yet, as will be demonstrated, in a surprisingly short period of time the 'cruelty man' had the power not only to enter any home but also to remove children from their parents without a police officer or any other state official being present. Before looking at how this situation came about, the expansion of branches in Ireland must be addressed.

Intemperance, poverty and 'being a habitual drunkard'

In the first twenty years of the NSPCC's existence in Ireland, intemperance was the chief explanation provided for child cruelty, and was discussed in every report. Drinking in Ireland was also frequently discussed in the British press. There is no doubt that drinking was an issue for families, particularly those in poverty.

It was not only the British press that focused on drunkenness; the Irish press also connected drinking to cruelty to children and child neglect, regularly reporting on cases in the courts. In 1907 the *Irish Independent* covered the visit of Viscountess Gormanston to a fund-raiser for the Dublin branch NSPCC. Gormanstown claimed:

> there was very little cruelty to children in Ireland compared to other countries. But there was a good deal of drinking, and that was the cause of much suffering to the little ones. As the child was father to the man, they should strive to redeem the children from all suffering, and make them grow up to be useful men and women.[45]

The sharing of statistical information was not the only connection between the Irish and British Societies. Both financially and with regard to policy, the official reports demonstrate that the British ethos and model was influential in most Irish branches, especially the Dublin branch. Having examined British and Irish reports in the period, both the language and the offences being investigated are similar. A key difference was the greater focus on intemperance by the Irish Society. In the early years, discussions by the Society and most prosecutions were centred on 'drunkenness' or situations emerging from poverty. At a Dublin branch meeting in 1902 the chairman specifically addressed the connections between poverty and drink, arguing that 'poverty frequently engenders drink, and drink aggravates poverty'. In the first fifteen years of the Society, almost all sample cases cited in the surviving branch reports involved one or two parents who were 'addicted to drink'. Poverty in Dublin was also frequently discussed, with the Dublin branch in 1904 'driven to the conclusion that at least 100,000 of the people of Dublin are living in abject poverty, insufficiently supplied with even the barest necessities of life'.[46] Yet intemperance was used to differentiate the deserving from the undeserving poor. Intemperate mothers were seen as the most unnatural of mothers, pawning their children's clothes for drink, neglecting to maintain their homes and not caring adequately for their husbands. In 1903, two equally revealing and disapproving captions were contained in the Dublin report: 'INTEMPERANCE THE CHIEF CAUSE OF SUFFERING ... OFFENDING MOSTLY WAGE-EARNERS', while the 1904 report highlighted that 'the average wage of those offenders in work was 21/6'.[47] To spend money on drink when earning a wage was the most frowned-upon form of child neglect, and it was child neglect that became the focus of the Society from this period on.

In response to the issue of drunkenness, and the drinking habits of working-class parents in particular, temperance campaigners and the NSPCC in Britain succeeded in forcing legislation to deal with the 'habitual drunkard'. The result was the passing of the 1898 Inebriates Act and the opening of inebriate reformatories throughout Britain and to a much smaller extent Ireland. With regard to the inebriate reformatories, it is perhaps best to situate them in the discussion of other institutions at the time – from prisons, to reformatories and industrial schools, as institutionalisation was used as a way to take care of any perceived social problem. The idea that the 'drunkard' could be rehabilitated and brought back to the middle-class ideal of a temperate, pious mother or father by being incarcerated for three years is interesting. Three years was a standard sentence in many of the cases investigated, and must have been seen as an appropriate sentence for reformation. That women constituted the greatest numbers sent to the reformatories is also worthy of further investigation. The use of the reformatories tied into the NSPCC's agenda, and its role in the placement of mothers in particular was significant as their absence would affect the entire family dramatically. Although in comparison to Scotland[48] and England removals in Ireland was on a much smaller scale, an examination of the reformatories is critical to this study as many of the women and some of the men placed there had been convicted of cruelty to or neglect of their children as well as for being a habitual drunkard. George Bretherton alludes to this connection and in particular a report from the governor at Ennis State Reformatory in 1914 which highlighted that in all these cases, such child neglect 'was a material factor leading to their trial and incarceration'.[49] While it is not possible to discuss the reformatories in detail here, the connection between them and the NSPCC is noteworthy, as in Ireland, the inspector's urging of a mother's placement often swayed the judge.

In Britain, support for the 1898 Act came from various groups including temperance advocates, local governing bodies (in particular Poor Law guardians) and members of the clerical and medical professions. Yet the temperance movement and support for the reformatories in Ireland never received the level of support the British movement did. Why? Was it that, as with other philanthropic campaigns in the period, religious sectarianism and the Catholic Church's fears of proselytism suppressed support? In Britain, many of the reformatories were set up and run by religious orders. In Ireland, aside from the St John of God order in Waterford, religious orders from both the Protestant and Catholic denominations did not support the initiative. From 1899 to 1920 four institutions opened in Ireland – a Retreat in Belfast called 'The Lodge', the State Inebriate Reformatory, St Patrick's Reformatory in Wexford, and St Brigid's Reformatory in Waterford. 'The Lodge' was opened by the Irish Women's Temperance Union in 1902 and accepted 'only Protestant women of the better working-classes'; the State Reformatory was opened in Ennis in 1899; St Patrick's opened in 1906 and admitted only men; and St Brigid's opened in 1908 and admitted only women. Ironically, as Bretherton points out, the State Inebriate Reformatory in Ennis was the least restrictive and prison-like. On average, in the sample of cases of those sent for being a habitual drunkard as well as offences of cruelty to children, the sentence was two years. Three years appears to have been the maximum and was opted for in more severe cases.

In 1904, a woman was convicted of the wilful neglect of her two children by the Recorder of Dublin. She was also convicted of being a habitual drunkard and received a sentence of eighteen calendar months in Ennis State Inebriate Reformatory. In her memorial, her character is described as 'indifferent'. The file contains a deposition from Inspector Thomas O'Reilly of the NSPCC and her husband. The inspector's deposition states:

> Since 15th Dec 1903 I have had this lease under observation. Deft wasn't at home. I went to George's Quay to look for her and next morning she called to the offices and I arranged to meet her in her husband's place on the 17th Dec. I told her her husband's complaint against her and she said she wasn't as bad as he said. She was under Notice to Riot on account of her drunken misconduct. On 4th January 1904 I visited her at Cross Kevin St and found her under the influence of drink. The younger child was lying on the bed. On the 21st January 1904 I visited at 7pm and found the child in bed. Deft was absent and didn't know where his wife was. Later on in the month 22nd January 1904, I found her again under the influence of drink. I spoke to her several times tasked her to take the pledge. She said she would but didn't do so. The little boy is in a very helpless state and requires constant attendance which of course he doesn't get, he is now in hospital.[50]

Similarly, her husband gave evidence supporting the inspector's observations:

> Deft is my wife. She has two children living to me under 16 year's age. I have been 20 years in Guinness's and earn £1-6-0 per week out of which I give her £1-3-0. My wife is of very drunken habits and has been so for the past six or seven years. She took the pledge once and kept it for a day. Latterly she is drunk almost every day in the week. I have had to wash my own clothes many a time. She had taken away the Children's Clothes and the furniture and bedding and pawned them for drink. I have often had to cook dinner both for myself and the children. On the 9th Dec 1903 I found my little boy with her in George's Quay and I had to take him to the hospital. On the 21st January I came home at 6 pm and found her drunk. She had been drunk all the previous week. She has neglected the children badly. I have washed the little fellow who is unable to walk. The children often told me they were hungry when I came home in the evening. My wife is unfit from her drunken habits to look after my house and my children.[51]

In the reports from the reformatory in Ennis, it was argued that it would be better to leave her for longer than the eighteen months, as 'she is not reformed enough and does not have the willpower to not drink'.[52] The fact that the courts and the system in general actually believed there was a time period for 'reformation' was probably based on observations of other institutions. .

In June 1909, a forty-seven-year-old woman from Belfast was released a year early on licence to her husband. In 1907 she had received a conviction of three years in the reformatory from the Belfast Recorder for neglect of her three children and for being a habitual drunkard. The licence was granted due mostly to a letter from the NSPCC inspector involved in the case:

> I would say that upon your strong recommendation of the conduct of this woman and having satisfied myself she is likely to receive real encouragement in her home, then I think this a case which may be dealt with by licensing without placing this woman's future in unnecessary jeopardy... I presume, of course, provision is made for her immediate return to the Reformatory should she in the slightest degree begin to take intoxicating liquor.[53]

What this demonstrates is that the inspector could influence both the committal and release of prisoners. In a similar case in Dublin in 1906, a woman was convicted of neglecting her three children and being a habitual drunkard and was sentenced to eighteen months in Ennis. Her character was described as 'indifferent'. The file states she had been 'addicted to drink since her marriage and for the year before her committal ... She took the clothes of the children and pawned them for drink'.[54] The report goes on to state that 'chiefly owing to her drunken habits her family are in poor circumstances. She has served but nine months of her sentence which is too short a time to eradicate the drink craving.'[55] As these cases demonstrate, sociological or psychological explanations were not considered.

In some cases, the reformatory was used as a last resort. In a case before the Recorder of Cork in 1914, the judge looked 'very unfavourably' on the defendant's previous convictions, of which she had forty-four for larceny, assault, drunkenness, malicious damage and obscene language. She was given two years in Ennis. The reformatory's report stated the woman was: 'bad ... married about 19 years ago, she commenced to drink 2 years later through bad companionship and gradually drifted until she became a confirmed drunkard. Thirteen years ago she commenced an immoral course and has since led a deplorable life...she is a mischief maker.'[56] All memorials were unsuccessful and the file does not state what happened to the woman after her release.

Aside from the NSPCC, the focus on women and drunkenness was also a concern of the Poor Law guardians. In Cork city during the First World War, numerous articles were published in the local press regarding the drunken habits of separation women,[57] and a brief look at the Circuit Court indexes for Cork from 1914 to 1920 does demonstrate an unusually large number of cases of neglect and cruelty to children. In 1914, Margaret Healy was sentenced to two years in Ennis Reformatory for the neglect of her four children and being an habitual drunkard; in 1915, Anne Creedon was also committed to Ennis for one year for neglect of one child; in 1916 there were numerous cases of neglect in the Cork borough, many resulting in transfers to Ennis and, finally, in a case in 1917, Hannah Walsh received eighteen months with hard labour for the neglect of her eight children. Yet in 1914 the RIC issued a report after an investigation into the 'Misuse of Separation Allowance to Wives of Soldiers', stating that 'there are no grounds for thinking that any marked increase has recently taken place in the drinking habits of wives of soldiers'.[58] For Cork East the report states: 'No increase in drinking habits. On the contrary the women and children are better clothed and fed and many are saving money'. Similarly, in relation to Cork West the report states: 'Generally the money is spent wisely. One case of drunkenness was adjourned by Magistrates and the woman is now saving money'.[59] Throughout the period, Belfast also had a very high number of committals to Ennis. In 1901, a woman pleaded guilty to ill-treatment and being a habitual drunkard and was sentenced to twelve months by the Recorder. The file states that she had three previous convictions for 'threatening her husband', 'drunken habits' and 'cruelty to children'. She is described as the wife of an ex-RIC constable with a pension of £42 a year. The file also contains a note stating that one of her brothers 'had for some years past been a religious maniac in Mullingar Asylum', while another was a clergyman of the Protestant Episcopal Church in Australia. The charge was initially brought after the NSPCC inspector called to the house and found her drunk. Interestingly, the file contains a letter from her husband asking for her release 'on the ground that if he did not do so, she would make matters unpleasant for him on expiration of her sentence.'[60]

What were individual inspector's opinions on the reformatories? In a chapter entitled 'A Habitual Drunkard' in *The Cruelty Man*, Robert Parr tells the story of a mother 'who sold and pawned everything the family had'. She was sent to an inebriate reformatory for three years after a conviction of child neglect and for being a habitual drunkard. He describes the circumstances for the family as he saw them, and perhaps gives an insight into why the Society felt it preferable to send mothers to the reformatories, as they would usually not be the principal wage earners in the home:

> It is not within my knowledge how the experiment of reforming the inebriate acted in this particular case, but I am concerned to point out that the removal of this, for the time being, useless and dangerous element from the Roy family group brought about an immediate change for the better. The money the woman had hitherto wasted could now be spent on food and clothing; the home, under kind and helpful supervision, became a place of moderate comfort; and the children, the chief concern of the Society, although bereft of 'parent' were, for the three years at least, allowed to live a tolerable existence.[61]

However, this mentality did not last long and the process of coercive 'reformation and rehabilitation' in the reformatories was set aside during the First World War in Britain, probably due to the fact that women were needed in the home and at work. In Ireland, the last reformatory closed in 1920. This is a significant marker in the context of the NSPCC in Ireland, as from this period onwards the Society attempted to adjust its role in post-independence Ireland and the issue of intemperance was replaced with other concerns.

Children's shelters and the industrial school question

One of the few pictures published in the annual reports of the Irish branches in the early years was a photograph of a group of children in the Society's shelter in Dublin in 1894. This photograph was taken by a M. Glover, who appears to have taken all of the Irish Society's photographs in the early period. The shelter, at 20 Molesworth Street, was utilised by the Society in the early years, and also contained the offices of the Dublin branch. Interestingly, 19 Molesworth Street contained the offices of the Inspector of Industrial and Reformatory Schools, Dublin Castle. The shelter appears to have taken in, on average, forty children per year. In 1896, for example, forty-four children passed through the shelter and twenty-nine were recorded as being sent to industrial schools.[62] Although much more research is needed, in Britain it appears that shelters opened across the country's major cities, yet this was not the case in Ireland. Why? From the documentation it is not possible to provide a definitive answer, but a few observations and speculations can be made.

Initially the Society did attempt to develop the Dublin shelter and open shelters in other cities. The following appeal was included in the first report of the Dublin Aid Committee:

> The great drawback to the working of this Society in Dublin is the want of a Shelter. Shelters are not Homes, but places of safety. They provide temporary relief for the children of parents who are charged, pending trial, under the clauses of the Prevention of Cruelty to Children Act, 1889. They are to meet the requirements of the magistrates under this New Law, which provides for the keeping of injured and neglected children, until such time as their cases are determined, out of the custody of those who injured, ill-treated, or neglected them; and to shelter children, when one or both parents are sent for short periods to prison for offences committed against them ... At the Inaugural Meeting of this Society in Dublin, the necessity for such a Shelter was recognised. The Committee now appeal for such funds... The cost of the house, fittings, etc., would be about £800, towards which your valuable assistance is desired.

In the first subscription list, £47 3s 2d was collected. However, although collections continued over the coming years, the shelter was never opened. It is probable that the system would have been in conflict with industrial and reformatory schools, orphanages and mother-and-baby homes, all now run principally by the Catholic Church. This issue appears to be the first of many compromises and concessions made by the Society when it came to potential conflict with the religious orders, as can be seen more prominently after 1922. Although the relationship between the industrial schools and the NSPCC cannot be fully addressed here, it is worth noting that in its early years the Society was completely opposed to their operation. However, it was forced to roll back on this once it became apparent that the shelters would not be supported, and if it was going to prosecute parents who could then be imprisoned, children would need to be placed. Aside from the conflict with other institutions, shelters would need to have been staffed and maintained around the clock, and perhaps in areas outside of Dublin the resources, both financial and voluntary, were not available. Either way, the fact that they did not develop is significant, as to have had a temporary facility for children that was not the workhouse or an industrial school would have been a considerable achievement. Internationally, criticisms of institutions had mounted in the second half of the nineteenth century, with the result that specialist homes and fostering were increasingly chosen. In 1886, W.P. Letchworth in the United States referred to children becoming 'institutionalized',[63] yet in Ireland this option would be repeatedly chosen. The NSPCC's inability to set up the shelters, therefore, represented a missed opportunity.

Conclusion

The NSPCC undoubtedly holds a prominent place in the history of child protection in Ireland. In contrast to religiously-motivated philanthropic and charitable organisations, the NSPCC, as the first established, secular, child-protection agency, suffered less from the effects of sectarianism and fears of proselytising forces than other groups. In this sense it thrived in a period of instability for other philanthropic societies. With connections to a highly motivated, upper-middle-class British organisation, and broader connections with an international 'child-saving' movement, the Society in Ireland gained support from the Ascendancy and other influential members of Irish society. This can be seen in its rapid expansion, increasing financial returns and in the number of children and families investigated by inspectors. From its foundation, the Society's inspectors entered the homes of thousands of working-class and poor families, identifying intemperate mothers, fathers failing to provide for their families, children on the streets and not in schools, and others who fell short of meeting the ideals of the middle-class home. The Society was part of a distinctive social movement, one in which children were the focal point, and the family the means to nurture the future citizens of Britain, Ireland, the United States and many other western societies. Its objective was the prevention of cruelty to children and the creation of safer environments in which childhood could be nurtured. However, its methods often had a detrimental effect. Where parents are being threatened with prosecutions, fines, imprisonment or institutionalisation, the environment for children rarely improves.

Notes

1 Annual Report of the Dublin Aid Committee (hereafter AR Dublin Aid Committee), 1889–90 (NSPCC, 1890), p. 9.
2 For a discussion of the NSPCC in Ireland from 1889 to 1921, see Sarah-Anne

Buckley, '"Saver of the children": The National Society for the Prevention of Cruelty to Children in Ireland, 1889–1900', *Conference Proceedings from the 2010 Nineteenth-Century Ireland Conference on Philanthropy* (forthcoming 2013).
3 The fourteen branches are as follows: Clonmel and District; Cork District; Dublin County; Dublin District; Galway District; Kerry; Kilkenny/Carlow/Queen's County; Limerick/Clare District; Mayo County; Meath District; North Louth/Monaghan/Cavan; Waterford and District; Westmeath/Kings County/Offaly/Midland Counties District; Wexford up to 1950. There were changes in the period to some branches which had to be amalgamated due to financial concerns.
4 Harry Ferguson, 'Cleveland in history: The abused child and child protection, 1880–1914', in R. Cooter (ed.), *In the Name of the Child: Health and Welfare, 1880–1940* (Routledge, 1992), pp. 148–49.
5 Cecil Thomas Wrigley Grimshaw remained as chairman of the Dublin branch until his death. He was born in Ireland, was a medical doctor and served in the Royal Dublin Fusiliers during the Boer War, during which time he kept a diary. The diary recounts his experiences as a prisoner of war in Pretoria at the same time as Winston Churchill. Later, he fought in the First World War, again with the Royal Dublin Fusiliers in the Gallipoli campaign. He was killed in action there on 26 April 1915. He had previously served as Registrar General for Ireland.
6 AR Dublin Aid Committee 1889–90, p. 9.
7 Ibid., pp. 6–7.
8 Mr Francis Murphy was the first NSPCC inspector in Dublin, AR Dublin Branch NSPCC (ISPCC, Limerick).
9 In 2011, £300 in 1930 was calculated as £98,010.00 (www.measuringworth.com).
10 AR Dublin Branch NSPCC, 1903, p. 7. In 1903, £1,000 was worth the equivalent of £801,600.00 in 2011 according to the average earnings calculator on www.measuringworth.com. Richard Hawkins Beauchamp was the nephew of William Hawkins Ball and Julia Ball. William Hawkins Ball was the eldest son of Benjamin Ball of Dublin and his wife Elizabeth, daughter of the Reverend James Hawkins, Bishop of Raphoe. He was born in 1797 and in 1845 married Juliana Salana, fifth daughter of Standish O'Grady, 1st Viscount Guillamore. He died at Ranelagh, Dublin, in 1864. Most of the Ball estate was in the parish of Kilchreest, barony of Clonderalaw, county Clare, but they also held a townland in the parish of Kilmihil. Upon their death, as they had no children, they left the estate to Richard, who bequeathed this sum to the NSPCC.
11 Ibid.
12 Cited in Sherrington, 'The NSPCC in transition', p. 61.
13 Ibid.
14 Linda Gordon, 'Family violence, feminism and social control', *Feminist Studies*, 12:3 (Autumn 1986), 453–78. In keeping with this argument, Deborah Gorham, looking at the motives of feminists and others in taking up the question of child protection in late-Victorian Britain, demonstrates how the professed solidarity of feminists with the working-class women was diluted by their commitment to 'hierarchical notions of authority that divided women along class and generational lines'.

15 The following is a selection of NSPCC publications: Benjamin Waugh, *Some Conditions of Child Life in England* (1889); NSPCC, *Acts Bearing upon the Welfare of Children* (1891); Robert Parr, *The Baby Farmer* (1908); Robert Parr, *Children Act, Abstracts of New Provision under the Act* (1909); Robert Parr, *The Seed of Hope: How the NSPCC Helps the State* (1910); Robert Parr, *Wilful Waste: The Nation's Responsibility for its Children* (1910); NSPCC, *The Society: What It Is, What It Does, Its Work in Ireland* (1911); NSPCC, *The Care of the Child* (1911–1913); NSPCC, *The War, the Child and the NSPCC* (1914–1918); NSPCC, *Infant Life Protection* (1916); NSPCC, *Illegitimate Children* (1918); NSPCC, *Assaults on Girls* (1919); NSPCC, *Child Adoption* (1919), *Child Adoption and Children Act – Part 1* (1926).
16 *The Child's Guardian* (Santry Library, Trinity College Dublin); *The Inspectors' Quarterly*, a pamphlet for officers of the NSPCC is also an interesting source (British Library, London).
17 See Sherrington, 'The NSPCC in transition', p. 86. In the Irish branches, aside from the Cork branch report in 1893 which contained a shocking picture of a starving child sitting on the inspector's lap, and the Dublin reports in the early years which contained pictures of children in the shelter in Dublin, images were not utilised to a great extent.
18 In France under the Napoleonic Civil Code a father whose child gave 'compelling grounds for dissatisfaction' could be imprisoned for a minimum of one month and up to six months. By the end of the nineteenth century, parental authority under the Napoleonic Civil Code began to be challenged, and from the 1880s the concept of the child who was *'moralement abandonné'* emerged, meaning that the child who was a threat as well as a victim needed to be rescued. Social workers began to question whether the issue was the parent rather than the child.
19 Luddy, *Women and Philanthropy*.
20 AR Wexford District Branch, 1911–12 (ISPCC, Limerick), p. 14.
21 Ibid.
22 Ibid.
23 Robert J. Parr was the president of the NSPCC after Benjamin Waugh, and he wrote extensively on the society's activities and child welfare from 1900 to 1930.
24 AR Dublin Branch, 1902–3 (ISPCC, Limerick), p. 30.
25 Luddy discusses how Benjamin Waugh wrote a letter to Archbishop Walsh of the Dublin diocese inviting him to attend the first meeting of the Society. It appears he did not respond; however, there are letters on the Society's work in various Archbishop archives in the Dublin Diocesan Archive. Luddy, 'Early years of the NSPCC', p. 72.
26 AR Dublin Branch NSPCC, 1902 (ISPCC, Limerick), p. 27.
27 AR Wexford Branch NSPCC, 1909–10 (ISPCC, Limerick), p. 19.
28 Ibid., p. 19.
29 Ibid., p. 20.
30 Sherrington, 'The NSPCC in transition'; Hendrick, *Child Welfare: Historical Dimensions*.
31 The Royal Commission into the Conditions of the Working Classes was set up in 1883. This report referred not only to the deplorable conditions in the slums of London in particular but also to the perceived connection between

over-crowded living areas and incest in families.
32 Cited in Sherrington, 'NSPCC in transition', p. 64.
33 Robert Parr, *The Cruelty Man: Actual Experiences of an NSPCC Inspector* (London, 1912), p. 24.
34 For a discussion of the Scottish NSPCC inspectors, see Gary Clapton, '"Yesterday's men": The inspectors of the Royal Scottish Society for the Prevention of Cruelty to Children, 1888–1968', *British Journal of Social Work Online*, DOI 10.1093/bjsw/bcn031 (March 2008). Sherrington discusses how there was a belief amongst certain NSPCC inspectors that their promotion prospects depended in part on the size of their case-load and the number of cases prosecuted, 'NSPCC in transition', p. 30.
35 AR Dublin Branch NSPCC, 1909–10 (ISPCC, Limerick), p. 15.
36 Sherrington, 'NSPCC in transition', p. 31.
37 Behlmer, *Child Abuse and Moral Reform*, p. 104.
38 Ibid., p. 105.
39 Luddy, 'Early years of the NSPCC', p. 63.
40 Ibid., p.78.
41 Hendrick, *Child Welfare: Historical Dimensions*, p. 30.
42 Ibid.
43 Behlmer, *Child Abuse and Moral Reform*; Cockburn, 'Child abuse and protection'; Creighton, *Trends in Child Abuse*; Hendrick, *Child Welfare: Historical Dimensions*; Wise, *Child Abuse*; NSPCC, *The First Hundred Years*. In the Irish context, the setting up of the NSPCC Dublin Aid Committee is discussed by Maria Luddy in *Women and Philanthropy*, pp. 93–5 and 'The early years of the NSPCC in Ireland'.
44 In *The Cruelty Man* Parr describes himself as the 'Children's Man', p. 10.
45 *Irish Independent*, 7 July 1907.
46 AR Dublin Branch NSPCC, 1904 (ISPCC, Limerick), p. 14.
47 Ibid.
48 In his article on the Irish inebriate reformatories, George Bretherton cites a paper delivered by Patrick McLaughlin, 'Inebriate reformatories in Scotland, 1902–21: an institutional history', presented at the Social History of Alcohol conference, Berkley, California, 4 January 1984.
49 George Bretherton, 'Irish Inebriate reformatories, 1899–1920', in I. O'Donnell and F. McAuley (eds), *Criminal Justice History: Themes and Controversies from Pre-independence Ireland* (Four Courts Press, 2003).
50 The deposition of Thomas O'Reilly, NSPCC, 20 Molesworth Street, Dublin City, taken 22 January 1904 at Kevin Street, cited in CRF/1905/D8 (NAI, Dublin).
51 Ibid.
52 Ibid.
53 CRF/1909/M35 (NAI, Dublin).
54 CRF/1907/B3 (NAI, Dublin).
55 Ibid.
56 CRF/1916/H16 (NAI, Dublin).
57 See CSORP/1914/22394 on the 'Misuse of separation allowances to wives of soldiers' (NAI, Dublin).
58 'Misuse of separation allowances to wives of soldiers', 17 December 1914, CSORP/1914/22394 (NAI, Dublin).

59 Ibid.
60 CRF/1901/D66 (NAI, Dublin).
61 Parr, *The Cruelty Man*, p. 45.
62 In the same year, of the 368 serious cases, seventy-seven persons were convicted for offences against children, amounting to nineteen years' imprisonment cumulatively. As the report recorded, four months per case was the average sentence, as opposed to two months in the previous year.
63 Robert H. Bremner, *Children and Youth in America 1866–1932, vol. 2, parts 7–8* (Harvard University Press, 1971), p. 296.

3

The NSPCC 'in transition', 1922–56

It shall be the first duty of the Republic to make provision for the physical, mental and spiritual well-being of the children, to secure that no child shall suffer hunger or cold from lack of food, clothing or shelter, that all shall be provided with the means and facilities requisite for their proper education and training as citizens of a free and Gaelic nation.[1]

Introduction

As addressed in Chapter 1, a growing campaign for the rights of children emerged in the early twentieth century, arising from the gains of nineteenth-century philanthropy. In the aftermath of the First World War, organisations lobbied the newly founded League of Nations to implement a declaration of children's rights. In 1924 they were successful. Yet, although international organisations were important in setting the tone of debates on children's rights, it was at State level that laws were passed and reforms implemented. The turbulence in Ireland resulting from the War of Independence, the Civil War and the foundation of the Irish Free State in less than ideal conditions meant that the State was perhaps not as diligent as other countries in this respect. The Democratic Programme of the First Dáil has been cited by numerous scholars in discussions of family welfare in post-independence Ireland as a paradigm of what could have been. Social democratic in tone and intention, it was far from the programme chosen by successive governments after independence, which used 'the spectres of socialism and proselytism'[2] as arguments against State interference in family welfare and (non-Catholic) assistance for poor families. While post-war Western states moved away from the nineteenth-century philanthropic tradition, the Irish State, guided by the Catholic Church, continued its policies of institutionalisation of children, stigmatisation of single mothers, and charity as opposed to welfare. As addressed in Chapter 1, many of the issues regarding child welfare, voluntarism and State interference in the family had been established before independence, but these intensified as the Catholic Church became an influential force in Irish social policy.

In examining the NSPCC, religious orders and the State, the effects of draconian policies on families can be observed. The State did not ignore families (although it did ignore many aspects of family welfare) but in fact interfered repeatedly in the lives of poor families in particular, continuously encroaching on parental rights. With regard to the NSPCC, the Society's professionalisation will be assessed in this chapter, with an emphasis on the compromises and concessions made by it from 1922 onwards, as well as the positive aspects of the Society's work. Its newly defined role as an advisory agency is central to this, as is its role as a State lobbying agency. Throughout the period, attention on the 'male breadwinner' and the regulation of female sexuality can also be observed – from the actions of voluntary and charitable organisations, to the discriminatory legislation put in place with regard to women. Overall, the chapter will address a number of themes, from the recategorisation of child neglect, to the relationship between the Irish and British branches of the Society. After an initial examination of developments in social work and an overview of the Society from 1922 to 1956 (when it became the ISPCC), the discussion will centre on other social work agencies, women's groups and the relationship between the NSPCC and the State.

The NSPCC 'in transition', 1922–56

Throughout the period, NSPCC inspectors fulfilled many roles: children's police, social workers, probation officers and school attendance officers. They were involved in providing material aid to families, prosecuting parents for various offences, removing children from the home and placing them in institutions.

As the Irish State after independence continued to rely on voluntarism over State welfare for provision of social services, the Society's role continued to be significant. In the Free State, financial and religious concerns heavily influenced the approach to social policy. Although the Catholic Church had increasingly gained control over the provision of education and health from the 1850s, from 1922 it became an even greater driving force in policy and the provision of social services. Partition and the emigration of thousands of southern Protestants meant that by 1926 the population was 92.6 per cent Catholic. This had numerous implications for the NSPCC: much of its financial support in its early years came from the wealthy Anglo-Irish, while the increasing prominence of Catholic Action lay organisations provided a range of challenges. In examining the NSPCC and the State in its earlier years, Mary-Anne Webb's image of 'parallel bars' has been employed by scholars of the British society to describe the relationship between statutory and voluntary services. But during the early part of the twentieth century in Britain, an 'extension ladder' relationship between statutory and voluntary services became more prevalent.[3] As the State assumed increasing responsibility (albeit in an *ad hoc* manner) to provide a basic minimum standard of living, voluntary agencies began to play a more supplementary role. In Britain, this assumption of responsibility by the State continued between the wars, and the introduction of 'cradle-to-grave' welfare legislation after the Second World War was regarded by many as heralding the demise of voluntary welfare there.[4] Legislative changes relating to issues such as adoption, fostering and incest were implemented in inter-war Britain but not in independent Ireland.[5] In 1922, legislation to amend the 1908 Punishment of Incest Act was passed in Britain; in Ireland this would not occur until 1995. In Ireland adoption did not become legal until 1952, while legislation was passed in Britain in 1926. Writing on the illegal adoptions that occurred in Ireland in the 1950s in particular, Moira Maguire claims: 'The child-centred tone of the English debates contrasts sharply with the obsessive concern among Irish lawmakers with questions of religion and faith, at the expense of the rights and interest of children and their biological parents.'[6] While the NSPCC did not attempt to effect change in the areas discussed, in redefining their role as an advisory agent and continuing to investigate families for child neglect they secured their position. Not only that, due to the State's continued fear of debt, it treated the NSPCC as a semi-State body, allowing its inspectors to act as school attendance officers, social workers, police and general observers of working-class and poor families.

In general, from 1922 to 1956, it could be argued that the NSPCC's role was both positive and negative. As an advisory agency, it did succeed in obtaining some material aid for destitute families. In its annual reports also, the Society highlighted pertinent issues such as male desertion, the inadequacy of home assistance, the need for a children's court outside of Dublin and the issue of overcrowding in urban areas. It was also in this period that two significant changes occurred in the focus of the Society's investigations – the inclusion of the category 'advice sought' and the expansion of child neglect. 'Advice sought' was a new category of investigation from 1922. It involved families approaching the Society for advice regarding poor relief, desertion, domestic violence and other issues. Throughout the 1920s and 1930s, the number of advice-sought cases increased, which was highlighted by the Society as a reason for their continuing operation. Although the 1927 report into the poor relief had stated that private charities should not be allowed to administer State aid, the case files and sample cases show that the Society often obtained poor relief for families. The expansion and recategorisation of child neglect will now be addressed.

Expansion and recategorisation of child neglect

Linda Gordon, Harry Hendrick and other scholars have demonstrated that one of the most important changes in the history of child protection work was the 'discovery' of child neglect between 1900 and 1922. Not only did it redefine cruelty to children as a family problem, with child neglect as its most common form, but it also placed the emphasis increasingly on parental responsibility for all aspects of children's lives. By the 1920s, neglect encompassed most child protection work, expanding to include moral as well as physical neglect. That neglect was vaguely defined (as it still is today) and difficult to address, does not mean that its existence was not real. Neglect, as Gordon states, was not identical to poverty, but many poor parents were accused of neglect when in fact their only crime was an inability to meet the standards expected by child protection workers.[7] Similarly, many cases of neglect involved 'multi-problem families', in which poverty was exacerbated by non-economic issues such as separation, alcoholism, violence or women's responsibility as both breadwinner and child-carer. What was certain, however, was that the family was now the core focus of child protection work. The following cases demonstrate different 'types' of neglect investigated by the NSPCC in the 1920s and 1930s. There follows an analysis of each type:

- In the course of conversation I asked Mrs. C if she knew a soldier of the Indian Army who has been on leave in ____ , she replied 'do you mean young Barnaville?' I replied 'yes'. She said yes! I know him and openly met and spoke to him. I then said 'that's enough I don't want to know any more'. She then said 'my husband was jealous of Barnaville ... did my husband tell you about him?' I replied he did not. She then said 'were you told it in Faghmans?' I said 'No'. She then said 'someone in ____ told you.' I said 'No'. She then asked me who told me of him. I said I would not tell her and she answered, 'I'll make you tell. You'll have to tell it in the Court.'[8] (NSPCC Inspector Book, 1925)

- Found children alone – L and M in the house. J and A in outhouse in yard. Lawrence (3) is sickly and hasn't walked – also dirty and unwashed. Aidan dirty of flesh and unwashed. No boots. M dirt of flesh and unwashed. No boots. John fairly well clad but in rags and worn boots. None of the children had attended school. John (9 yrs.) is illiterate. Bedding dirty and filthy in condition.[9] (NSPCC Inspector Book, 1925)

- 'John' and 'Paula Murphy' live with their five children in one room. They all sleep in one double bed. The children are aged between 2 and 7 years. They are all described as 'poorly clad and nourished'. One of the twins, aged 5, is described as being very 'sickly'. They pay 5/ week rent. (NSPCC Case file, 1938)

- In 1928, the mother of an 'illegitimate' 15 year old boy was investigated by the NSPCC inspector for 'neglect and failure to exercise proper guardianship'. He was committed to Glencree Industrial School until 1942, and she was fined £1.[10] (NSPCC Case file, 1938)

- Neglect to provide medical aid. Parent's good character, 3 children ages 4, 2 and 2 mths. Father labourer, G suffering from very sore eye from which is discharging. Not medically treated. Children seem poorly clad but fairly well nourished.[11] (NSPCC Case file, 1939)

- Investigating a couple with a daughter aged 9 years. She is a Roman Catholic and he is a Protestant and this seems to be the reason they are being spoken to.[12] (NSPCC Case file, 1939)

In the first case, the inspector was notified by a neighbour after the woman being questioned was seen talking to 'Barnaville'. The case is revealing in both the inspector's disgust and suspicion of the woman, and the woman's awareness of the situation. Adultery, or more specifically female adultery, was regarded as a justified explanation for 'moral neglect' by the Society. Whether or not this woman was having a relationship with the man is irrelevant; what is significant is that the NSPCC's jurisdiction now extended to the relationship between a husband and wife. The Society had always labelled some parents as immoral, but from the 1920s moral neglect was considered the most dangerous form of neglect. As a category, it was focused solely on the parents, in an understanding that the 'bad habits of parents' would directly create immoral, criminal children. Immoral parents should not pass immoral habits to the 'children of the nation'.

While 'neglect and starvation' was the only neglect offence investigated by the Society up to 1921, from this time on five specific types of child neglect emerged – neglect to provide, neglect and starvation, moral neglect, medical neglect and neglect to provide proper guardianship.[13] It would not be until the mid-twentieth century that emotional neglect would be added, with the acceptance of psychological explanations for social problems and a focus on 'the mind' of the child. Central to the Society's recategorisation and focus on neglect was the Society's own survival. Not only did the issue of neglect expand the areas into which the Society could intervene, it also provided it with a place in the State's child welfare apparatus. The NSPCC would continue to identify neglectful parents, obtain home assistance for some, and facilitate institutionalisation for others. It continued to champion particular issues, such as maintenance for widows and single mothers (from fathers, not the State), changes to the Children's Court and the treatment of juvenile delinquents, and improved housing for families in poverty.

With regard to the changing definitions of neglect, in comparison to the first case listed, the second (investigated for neglect and starvation) is far more in keeping with the emphasis on the physical appearance of home and child in the late nineteenth century. In the third also, the issue of overcrowding continues to be addressed, as the Society became more vocal on living conditions and State intervention in slums from the 1920s. Yet, if the first example represented the policing of morality, the fifth example characterises a new area of NSPCC work – the regulation and identification of the 'juvenile delinquent'. Although juvenile delinquency had been debated and treated since the 1850s, it was now being directly connected to the inability of parents to raise and control their children. Juvenile delinquency and child neglect were being moulded together in the discourse on parental responsibility for children's behaviour. This involved the responsibility of parents to keep their children passive and law-abiding, together with, in this case, the added stigma of the boy being classed as 'illegitimate'. The crime in this case was that this fifteen-year-old boy had allegedly been staying out late at night – sufficient grounds for three years' detention in an industrial school. Integral to the analysis is attitudes to adolescence, the effects of compulsory schooling on the separation of childhood and adulthood, and fears surrounding modern influences like the cinema, dance halls and motor cars. In the final example, medical neglect was addressed by the inspector. Medical neglect represented another aspect of physical neglect, defined on the basis of class-specific expectations and standards of living. Many of the untreated health problems found by the NSPCC were infected sores, lice, tuberculosis, colds and eye and ear infections. Parents often claimed ignorance, but it is probable that many could not afford treatment or hoped it would not be necessary. It could also be speculated that some did not completely trust modern medical practices, continuing to administer folk remedies for ailments. Although it will not be investigated in this examination, the controversy surrounding the 'Mother and Child Scheme' in Ireland in 1951 is key to understanding the relationship between the medical profession, the Catholic Church and the State on issues of child welfare and medical care for poorer children in particular.[14]

In 1933, the Dublin Branch NSPCC published a breakdown of the 'cause' of the cases of neglect that had come to its attention during the year. In all, the greatest number of situations are recorded as being the result of 'ignorance and idleness'; this was followed by 'bad housing, extreme poverty, jealously, immorality, interference by outsiders (usually mothers-in-law), living beyond means, drink, betting and gambling, other causes'.[15] That drink is listed near the bottom is interesting. As was demonstrated in Chapter 1, prior to 1922 drink and poverty were seen as the principal cause of all cases of cruelty to children and child neglect by the NSPCC. As Maria Luddy correctly asserts in her examination of the Society in the early years, the Society's effect on the public awareness of cruelty to children and child neglect was noteworthy. From 1921 child neglect featured regularly in the press and in the courts, and as early as July 1920, the *Irish Times* began to run a regular feature entitled 'NSPCC and child neglect', in which the offences for different branches were recorded.[16] While cases of neglect in the courts will be addressed in Chapter 6 in reference to gendered assumptions about culpability, the extent to which neglect had been integrated into the public discourse is noteworthy here. With regard to cruelty to children, only the most shocking cases made it to the press, often involving nurse children, but never those in industrial schools or reformatories. As with the issue of corporal punishment, the press and the courts were discriminatory with regard to which cases would be publicised and dealt with.

Offences investigated and 'advice sought'

In the period 1933–55, there were roughly 45,000 cases dealt with by inspectors involving approximately 100,000 children.[17] The Dublin branch alone dealt with 20,000 from 1930 to 1950. The Dublin branch is unique, however, as only fifty per cent of cases relate to 'neglect', with the other major categories being 'ill-treatment/assault', 'immoral surroundings/moral danger', 'other wrongs' and 'advice sought'. In the other thirteen branches, 'neglect' constituted the majority of cases investigated. With regard to cases of 'advice sought', in 1931 the Dublin branch stated: 'it is gratifying to see that these have again increased this year.'[18] The statistics are not the only difference between the Dublin branch and the other regional branches; there are also marked differences in the tone and content. While each year similar issues were highlighted by all branches, the Dublin branch was more detailed in its requests for legislative and welfare changes, and in the examples given to illustrate specific issues. As it was the principal branch in the country, with five inspectors, this is not surprising. The urban/rural divide in Ireland during the period of examination is a significant consideration when looking at annual figures. Conditions in Dublin, and to a lesser extent Cork and Limerick, were very different from those in rural areas, in the west of Ireland particularly, with regard to such issues as accessibility to schools, medical aid and other services.

Table 3.1 demonstrates the focus of the Society's investigations in Ireland in the late 1930s. While drunkenness was still a factor in a number of cases, that the majority involve neglect and advice sought is interesting. The increase in advice sought was probably the most significant change in the Society in the 1930s, demonstrating that families had begun to realise the NSPCC could also be used to obtain material aid and assistance.

Table 3.1 Number of NSPCC cases in Ireland, 1934–39, by offence

	1934–35	1935–36	1936–37	1937–38	1938–39	Totals
Total cases	4,476	4,542	4,288	4,460	4,450	22,216
Neglect	3,310	3,326	2,986	3,129	3,106	15,857
Advice sought	710	771	837	847	854	4,019
Ill-treatment	280	232	227	203	198	1,140
Begging	10	11	9	5	10	45
Corrupt morals	32	31	25	43	36	167
Other wrongs	134	171	204	233	246	988
Drink	530	568	484	525	508	2,615
Medical	34	21	27	30	22	134

Figures taken from the Annual Report of the NSPCC, Dublin District branch, 1939.

Children's courts, poor relief, illegitimacy and desertion

In the 1930s and 1940s, the Society also frequently addressed the need for children's courts outside Dublin (as legislated for in the 1924 court's act), the inadequacy of poor relief, illegitimacy and situations of desertion. These were issues that needed to be highlighted, but why the NSPCC did so is of particular interest. The children's court would allow those children labelled 'juvenile delinquents' to be dealt with outside the adult system, and adolescents kept within the family structure. Increased poor relief would keep more families intact, as poverty was the chief cause for the transfer of children to industrial schools. Illegitimacy and desertion were both part of the Society's emphasis on single mothers – both would be taken care of through prosecuting 'putative fathers', and not through maintaining women and children at public expense; if the latter was necessary, the payments would not be dispensed easily. Home assistance was administered to the neediest in society, who were unable to work due to disability, age or illness. In 1932, for example, there were 126,035 people in receipt of this assistance.[19] The NSPCC often acquired relief for families, but was also vocal on the meagreness of the payments and the difference between rates in rural and urban areas. The issue was addressed in the 1937–38 Dublin branch report:

> The rates of assistance in Dublin are fairly good, the maximum allowed being 25 shillings per week to a large family, but in the counties of Wicklow and Kildare, cases have been found where the allowance has been most inadequate. The maximum in many of these districts is only 10 shillings per week whatever the size of the family. It is obvious that such a small amount is not adequate to ensure proper nourishment.[20]

In the cases examined in this study (Wexford and Waterford primarily), the most regular payment was six shillings per week, a payment completely inadequate to maintain even a small family. In the 1938–39 report poor relief was again addressed:

> The scale of relief granted to destitute families in rural areas is often absolutely inadequate. It is realised that public funds would not be sufficient to enable a large increase in relief, but a larger allowance for children would be economical in that it would undoubtedly mean better health, and so less expense for hospitals and treatment.[21]

What was the economic situation for families investigated by the NSPCC in the period? Table 3.2 demonstrates the variations in rent and income from 1921, with the figures taken from individual cases. Taking into account the fact that inspectors were earning roughly £170–£350 in the 1930s, depending on the branch, the figures show the income disparity between the working-class families and middle-class inspectors. The table also highlights the high cost of rent for those on home assistance or other relief. Most families in such situations would spend what little they had on rent, food and heat. The table also demonstrates that the British Army pension was

Table 3.2 Sample incomes and rents from NSPCC case files, taken from sample cases in the inspector books and the case files

Year	Income	Other income	Rent	Rates	Children
1921		20s weekly BAP			2
1921			1/9 weekly		2
1925			9d weekly	3d	4
1925		UA	9d weekly	15s yearly	4
1928		£4 11s 4d quarterly BAP	3d weekly		4
1928	£1–15		1s 6d weekly		2
1930		UA	4s 3d weekly		9
1930		4s Outdoor Relief			1
1935			3s weekly		5
1935		6s HA			3
1938		14s 6d UA			5
1939		3s HA			2
1939		10s WOP			1

BAP, British Army Pension; HA, Home Assistance; OAP, Old Age Pension; UA, Unemployment Assistance; WOP, Widows' and Orphans Pension. Data taken from inspector books and case files, 1920–40 (ISPCC, Limerick).

one of the most sufficient payments, and most families did not represent the 'typical' large Irish family, but those containing between two and four children.

In the 1938–39 Dublin report, 'Slums, incurable children, legislation, illegitimate children, the cinema and the child – Father Devane, the begging problem and poor law relief' were all addressed.[22] Overall, the principal legislative changes proposed were those regarding desertion and specifically amendments to the Married Women Maintenance in Cases of Desertion Act (1886) and the Illegitimate Children (Affiliation Orders) Act (1930). As the report pointed out, the civil bill procedure to enforce the act was ineffective as it was too expensive for poorer women. Chapter 6 will address the specifics of the act, but the Society was correct in its assertion of the act's inaccessibility to working-class and poor women. Legitimacy was one of the few issues focused on and legislated for by the State in the early 1930s, yet the measures introduced were more focused on protecting husbands and fathers than on supporting mothers and illegitimate children. This was also the case with regard to deserting husbands and maintenance.

The Society also campaigned for the prohibition of advertisements in the press offering children for adoption.[23] In reference to the 'illegitimate child', the 1930–31 Dublin report stated that 251 illegitimate children out of a thousand died before the age of one, roughly one in every four in comparison to fifty-four in every thousand, or one in nineteen of legitimate children. This was a result of the poverty of single mothers and their children. As tenement dweller May Hanaphy stated in Kevin Kearns's oral study:

> And girls did become pregnant. Oh, and you were never kept once you became pregnant. It created girls being put out of their homes. A woman often went on the streets if the fella didn't want you. Some of them went into prostitution. And some of them drowned themselves. Out of despair. And the Church had no sympathy in those days. Oh many a girl took her own life. Oh, the Church, she's a good mother, but she's a hard mother.[24]

This issue of the Catholic Church's role in the regulation of the State and families has been questioned by a number of scholars, particularly with regard to unmarried mothers and illegitimacy. Maria Luddy, Lindsey Earner-Byrne, Moira Maguire, Paul Garrett and Clíona Rattigan have addressed the stigmatisation, emigration, poverty and recourse to infanticide that so many experienced.[25] Yet, as can be seen from May Hanaphy's statement, it was often the working class and the poor that offered the greatest devotion to the Church, and perhaps experienced the greatest hardship as a result. Yet the following case study of the Wexford Branch NSPCC in 1939 will demonstrate that, in many instances, those outside 'the family cell' (such as single mothers) were most in need of the Society's assistance.

Compulsory education and parental responsibility

In examining compulsory schooling, both the motives of the State in introducing and extending limits, and the effects of legislation on families must be addressed. In Ireland as elsewhere, compulsory schooling enabled socialisation, particularly in the 1920s when schools would deliver Irish children educated in the language and history of Ireland. Its enforcement was also one of the few educational measures pursued by the first Irish governments. As Mary Daly highlights, although the first Dáil in 1920 embarked on a restructuring of local government and welfare services through the abolition of workhouses and county services, education remained largely unchanged. The authority of the school manager remained, and the primary concern of the Department of Education was curriculum reform and specifically the revival of the Irish language. Even though the 1937 Constitution acknowledged the family as 'the primary and natural educator of the child', in the first fifty years of independence the Church and State did very little to uphold these rights. Church and State combined to exclude parents from educational matters, as any role for parents would have 'threatened the established equilibrium between church and state, or between church, state and the teaching profession'.[26]

Was the State aware of the effects of compulsory education up to fourteen years of age? In debates in the Oireachtas on the 1926 School Attendance Bill, there were varying concerns addressed by deputies. Some were focused on the cost of implementing the act, others discussed the need to have children in school until sixteen years of age, and one or two were aware of the financial ramifications for families. In 1925 Michael Heffernan of the Farmers' Party pinpointed the effects for farmers and households dependent on the wage of those under sixteen years:

> I am sorry to say that, although I do not differ from my colleague, Deputy Wilson, in the ideals to be aimed at, I differ from him with regard to the practicability of enforcing such a law if it were passed. I think it is one thing to be idealistic and it is another thing to take cognisance of the actual financial conditions of the country. My view is, that we should start off with the minimum of compulsion in every direction, and as we gain experience in time in the working of the Act, and see the advantages we are to gain by the Act, then there is nothing to prevent our expanding if the necessities of the case require it. As I read this amendment it means that in effect all children, unless they have been granted a certificate of proficiency and have also been apprenticed to some trade, are forced to attend school. This means in effect that the children of the farmers, who would not be apprenticed in the ordinary course of events, who would be employed at home on the farm, or if they happened to be workers' children they might be employed as paid workers on the farm, would not come within this category and would be obliged to attend school. I maintain that is not an economic proposition. Parents in this country would be unable, in most cases, to keep their children at school beyond the age of fourteen.

For those advocating the extension to sixteen years of age, compulsory education was seen to take care of the problem of child unemployment, as the following speech made by John Good of the Businessmen's Party regarding the Third Stage of the School Attendance Bill shows:

> I do not blame our Government for the backward state of education to-day. What is the position to-day in our city, having this amendment in view? Over 6,000 boys and girls leave our primary schools every year about the age of fourteen. Of those, some 6,000 register for employment at the labour exchanges. The labour exchanges are only able to find employment for something less than 1,000. Let us assume that another 2,000 find employment by other means. It is a fairly optimistic estimate to take, when the labour exchanges can only find employment for 1,000. Taking that optimistic estimate, what does it mean? That 3,000 boys and girls are set free in our city every year for whom there is no employment, with the result that we hear complaint after complaint from parents about these boys and girls getting into bad company and acquiring bad habits with disastrous results. What will this amendment do for those boys and girls? For those in employment, it will mean that the Minister will decide upon what classes or what further course it is desirable that they should follow up to the age of 16. For those who are not in employment, the Minister will also settle what hours of attendance they shall follow up to the age of 16. I have only given the figures for Dublin. Deputies can get the figures for their own areas and apply exactly the same argument. With regard to Dublin I would ask: is it a desirable thing that those boys and girls, upon whom

the future of the country depends, should have their education continued during those important years between the ages of fourteen and sixteen, or should they be set free to go to picture houses, to get into bad company, to give trouble to their parents, and to make wretched citizens? To my mind, this is one of the most important matters in connection with education.[27]

One of the principal concerns of politicians with regard to the extension of compulsory education up to fourteen years was the cost of enforcing it. The following estimate was made by the Minister for Education, John Marcus O'Sullivan:

> Then there is the financial case. I am not stressing it now. Our estimate is that it would cost to enforce the Act up to the age of 14, at the beginning, and initially, in or about £120,000 a year, and afterwards we may put it at about £200,000 a year. These figures, if they err at all, probably err on the low side. They were figures not intended [527] for this House, but figures intended to be put up to the Department of Finance. We do not generally exaggerate the cost when putting things up to the Department of Finance. They are generally the lowest figures, but, of course, I do not say that they are not the correct figures, but we certainly do not exaggerate. Then we calculate that if we were to extend the limit from 14 to 16 years of age, the cost initially would mean an additional £110,000 or £120,000, and might go up to £150,000.[28]

It is probable that the department's concerns about the cost of school attendance officers and the courts represented one of the principal reasons why the NSPCC became involved in the regulation of school attendance. This represented an area they could monitor, but also one that the government was unable or unwilling to provide in certain areas at particular times. In the NSPCC the government had a regulation force that was already monitoring families and one that already had a semi-official status. The 1929 Children Act, with its extension of court-ordered committals to industrial schools for school non-attendance, would increase the NSPCC's role as a regulatory body.

Aside from its role in monitoring school non-attendance, were there any cases in which corporal punishment was brought to the attention of the NSPCC? Occasionally, parents did complain to the Society about the punishment their children were receiving in school. In 1930, a woman went to the NSPCC inspector in Wexford with her son to complain about a 'punishment' he had received from his master that day. The boy stated: 'The master McGould lashed me across the thighs with a cane for mistakes in my copy which I had not corrected, I did not correct them as I was not told to.' The severity of the punishment can be observed from the inspector's remarks: 'Boy had two red welts on right thigh 1 six inches in length, the other 4 inches ... Boy broke glasses and suffers from defective vision right eye – receiving treatment at Co Hospital.'[29] The file does not state whether any action was taken by the inspector, although it is unlikely the matter was taken further than a warning. As Mary Daly demonstrates, the Church, the State and the teaching profession had monopoly control over what occurred in classrooms; parents had little say.

Case study: County Wexford and District branch, 1939

[P]arents have learned that even children have their rights.[30]

The County Wexford and District branch of the NSPCC covered Wexford, Arklow, Enniscorthy, Gorey and New Ross. It was chosen for this case study as it holds the most complete set of files up to 1940. From 1933 to 1955, the president and vice-presidents were all priests.[31] Before looking at the cases in 1939, extracts from the reports will briefly be referred to in order to understand the problems the Society was highlighting. In 1933 the sample cases cited involved a nurse child, a 'deformed girl' and a deserting father. Of the 136 cases, 104 were investigated for neglect and seventeen were 'advice sought'. In 1934 the three sample cases involved an illegitimate child and two concerned deserting husbands. In 1936, the headings in the report were 'forsaken', 'deformed' and 'living apart'. Under the heading 'living apart', the report states that 'disputes between husband and wife are not infrequent, and generally react to the disadvantage of the children, sometimes "causing unnecessary suffering".'[32] The occurrence and acknowledgement of domestic violence can be seen throughout the reports and case files, as will be addressed in Chapter 6, but the situation for women in violent situations was not addressed in any substantial manner.

In 1937 the Society continued to highlight the shift from cruelty encapsulated much of the work in the early years: 'since then the scope of the work has widened ... the name [NSPCC] inadequately describes the varied nature of the work undertaken by the Inspectors.'[33] The 1939 report asserted: 'it is seen that cruelty is little known in Ireland. Cases of brutality have never been numerous, but it is noticeable that in the early years more of such cases were found. There is no doubt that the existence of the Society has been a preventive and a deterrent.'[34] While this was most likely driven by the Society's need to redefine its role and to continue to receive financial support as it competed with Catholic charities like the St Vincent de Paul (SVDP), to what extent was this situation reflected in the courts? Interestingly, from 1936 to 1941 the number of persons bring prosecuted for both the indictable and non-indictable offence of 'cruelty to or neglect of children' decreased significantly. However, the number of persons prosecuted for offences against the Education and School Attendance Acts rose substantially. As these cases often resulted in the removal of children to industrial schools, was the Society altering its role to ensure its survival in 1930s Ireland?

In the sample from 1939, there were 205 cases recorded in the annual report involving 286 boys and 253 girls, in connection with which 1,617 supervision visits were made. Seventy per cent of these cases were inves-

Table 3.3 Breakdown of cases in sample of NSPCC files for Wexford District Branch in 1939, by 'nature of allegation' box on inspection forms

Allegation	Number of cases	%	Number of children	%
Neglect	60	66	145	66
Neglect only	27	29	85	40
Neglect to provide	9	10	12	6
Neglect and starvation	21	23	55	26
Neglect and failure to exercise proper guardianship	2	2	4	16
Neglect/medical	1	1	1	>1
Advice sought	21	23	49	23
Ill-treatment/assault	5	5	12	6
Exposure	3	3	3	3
Begging	1	1	1	>1
Indecent assault	1	1	1	>1
Other wrongs	1	1	4	2
Total	92	100	215	100

Sample of ninety-two case files for the year 1939 (ISPCC, Limerick).

tigated for child neglect, twenty-two per cent were 'advice sought' investigations, and the remaining eight per cent were related to abandonment, ill-treatment, exposure and assault. One-hundred-and-fifty-four cases resulted in warnings, thirty-eight cases were advised, six were prosecuted, six were otherwise dealt with, and one was dropped after investigation. The following analysis will be based on the ninety-two surviving case files. At almost half the case files investigated, this is a substantial sample. Table 3.3 outlines the offences investigated and the number of children involved.

Of the ninety-two cases, only thirty-two involved two-parent families. The remainder involved illegitimate children, widows and widowers, as well as eight cases involving nurse children. Thirty-eight cases, or 41 per cent of the sample, involved illegitimate children – a huge proportion when you consider that the percentage of registered illegitimate children born in the 1930s and 1940s in comparison to those born overall was between two and five per cent. The average number of children involved in each case was two, again a very different figure from the larger families associated with the rural Irish family. In the descriptions of clients, both class and gender bias must be considered, as inspectors often projected their own middle-class views in making judgements of families. Mothers deemed to be 'bad' were described in such terms as 'lazy', 'careless', 'useless', 'mental', 'morals doubtful', 'dirty', 'thriftless' and 'untidy' – all references which questioned their domestic virtue or moral nature. In contrast, fathers who were deemed to be of a bad character were described in stereotypically 'masculine' terms:

'violent', 'quarrelsome', 'fond of drink', or merely 'bad'. If they were seen to be unable or unwilling to support their family, they would not be described as 'giddy and irresponsible', as one single mother who had moved to England for work was, but as 'useless' or 'deserting'. The cases involving 'illegitimate' children and single mothers will now be discussed as the Society regularly addressed the issue of illegitimacy, and it was also an issue that was being highlighted by the State after independence.

The NSPCC and nurse children

As addressed in Chapter 1, with regard to the situation of nurse children, the NSPCC was very influential in the passing of the 1908 Children's Act, which consolidated a number of legislative reforms surrounding child welfare.[35] While the Infant Life Protection Act of 1872 had legislated for nurse children for the first time, the 1908 Act contained a provision that allowed the NSPCC inspector to monitor homes in place of a child protection officer.[36] After independence, the Society was also increasingly vocal in its annual reports and in the press on the neglect and ill-treatment of nurse children, as well as on the situation of the 'illegitimate child' generally.

The number of cases of 'failure to notify of a nurse child' was a small percentage but a consistent feature of the NSPCC's case-load. In 1905, the Dublin District branch of the NSPCC investigated thirty-four cases involving nurse children.[37] As there were fourteen branches in the country, this demonstrates that they were actively involved in the situation of nurse children. In 1914, the NSPCC investigated twenty such cases, and this steadily decreased in the 1920s. In the period 1933–50 for example, the Cork District branch dealt with seventy-six cases involving nurse children.[38] This appears to be similar to the other thirteen branches in the country. In one particular case in Wexford in 1934, a seventy-year-old woman, almost completely blind, was investigated on suspicion of ill-treating a nine-month-old baby. The child was allegedly starving, and the woman was almost incapable of looking after her own needs, let alone the child's.[39] In this instance, the child had not been registered, but the inspector involved in the case decided not to prosecute the woman. Generally, cases involving nurse children demonstrate the desperation of unmarried mothers who were unable to place babies in institutions because of their age or lack of resources. The State's responsibility in the treatment of unmarried mothers, and its inability to alleviate poverty in families, resulted in the greater suffering of those children most in need of State care. This can be seen particularly in the 1930s, when cases involving nurse children became more common in the courts. Yet unlike in Britain, where adoption was seen as a suitable solution, opposition from the Catholic Church and inaction from the State left placing children at nurse as one of the only options aside from institutionalisation.

In 1932, at the NSPCC's annual meeting, General Eoin O'Duffy spoke to the Society about the 'terrible figures' relating to deaths of illegitimate children, and the need to implement controls to deal with nurse children. He argued that the inspection of premises of nurses alone would not sufficiently address the problem and that the recommendations of the investigation into the Criminal Law Amendment Acts by the Carrigan Committee also deserved attention. In 1928, amendments to the 1908 Children's Act had been the primary concern at the NSPCC's annual meeting, particularly as changes had occurred in Britain in 1923. It was agreed that a number of changes be made, principally the obtaining of a licence twenty-four hours *before* a child was received, inspection of the premises by the Infant Protection Visitor, the keeping of a register of all persons holding licences and that institutions make sure to notify local authorities *before* a child was transferred to a nurse. The Society stated that in the area covered by the Dublin Union Commissioners, 1,100 children were visited by three Children's Act Inspectors, assisted in the city by the Child Welfare Officer in each district. However, it was acknowledged that rural districts were nowhere near as 'well policed'. Yet, the fact that 1,100 children were the responsibility of only three inspectors does not appear to have been 'well policed' in Dublin.

Aside from the issue of inspections, understanding the bind for parents of illegitimate children and the treatment of illegitimacy by societies such as the NSPCC and the State is crucial to understanding the motivations for placing children at nurse. Most families visited by the NSPCC inspector were not the 'ideal' two-parent family structure, and most cases were related not to child cruelty but to various forms of child neglect. This neglect often stemmed from severe poverty. Of the ninety-two cases mentioned in Table 3.3, only thirty-two involved two-parent families. The remainder involved illegitimate children, widows and widowers, as well as eight cases involving nurse children. Thirty-eight cases (forty-one per cent of the sample) involved illegitimate children – a huge proportion when one considers that registered illegitimacy rates in the 1930s and 1940s were between two and five per cent. The illegitimate child featured in numerous cases, both in this sample and in earlier files contained in the NSPCC archive. There was no stereotypical case, although a number of situations involved girls working as domestic servants in England and Ireland. In one such case a labourer and his wife were investigated for neglect and starvation. They were looking after their nine-month-old grandson whose mother was working as a 'domestic' in London. The child was illegitimate and they were receiving 7s weekly from a maintenance order. Both were in their forties and their income was 37s per week. On the first and only visit, the inspector described the child's condition: 'Found the child ill and wasted. Weighed child in clothes, weighed 12 lbs. Child appears to have been neglected for a long time.'[40] The boy was removed to the local hospital but died five days later. The inspector described the couple's character as 'fair' and no prosecution was brought.[41] In another case involving an illegitimate child, a 22-year-old woman approached the Society to request advice. The father of the child had been paying 5s weekly, up to a month previously. She wanted to give the child to the father's mother, who 'offered to take the child – although she denies that her son is the father'. The inspector 'advised the mother to retain custody and that she could not get rid of her responsibilities by adopting such a course'.[42] This reaction by the inspector was a more unusual one and probably demonstrates his own bias with regard to the young mother. If he had viewed her with greater empathy, as opposed to seeing her as someone negating her responsibilities, his response may have differed.

With regard to the ill-treatment of nurse children, the following two cases are representative of those investigated by the NSPCC. Both involve illegitimate children, which is significant as they were taken from the sample cases contained in the annual NSPCC reports. These cases, handpicked by the NSPCC, were often used to warn parents or demonstrate to the State or potential benefactors the NSPCC's focus. The fact that they were included in the sample cases of the reports sent to benefactors and potential benefactors demonstrates that the issue of nurse children was one that received support. In the first case, taken from the 1933–34 Dublin District branch report, the situation of a fourteen-month-old baby residing with a foster mother was investigated. The baby was found in a severely neglected state in the care of a woman who had two adopted children, two foster children and two other nurse children – for all of whom she had received payment. The report records that 'through the intervention of the Society the three nurse children had been removed – the baby to the County Home and the other two to more suitable homes'. The two adopted children were left and the mother was kept under supervision for a number of months.[43]

A sample case entitled 'A child we had to protect from her own mother' is included in the 1934–35 report:

> A young woman was found recently by a Guard lying in a gutter. She was under the influence of drink and beside her lay her thirteen months' old baby girl, who was 'sopping' wet and crying with hunger. The inspector learned on inquiry that this young woman would not stay in any of the mother and baby homes provided for unmarried mothers and babies. She gave trouble, neglected her baby, and set a bad example for the other inmates. She was also suffering from disease. The child had to be protected from her unnatural mother, who was prosecuted and sent to prison for three months. The child was removed from her custody and placed in a convent home.[44]

Why did the Society choose these two cases to illustrate ill-treatment? In keeping with the State's focus on unmarried mothers and illegitimacy, both cases involve illegitimate children and two different paths taken by unmarried mothers. In both, the mother was shown to be negligent or 'unnatural', and the removal of the second child to a convent home was presented as the most appropriate option. As with the NSPCC's sample cases of intemperate mothers in the late nineteenth century, the unmarried mother was now a principal focus of the Society. Yet even with this focus, the situation for nurse children was not improved. If placed at nurse, children were often ill-treated when payment ceased, and inspections were rarely carried out by the local boards. If boarded-out, a similar fate could occur. Yet never did the State or the NSPCC decide to support unmarried mothers in keeping their children, or legislate for legal adoption. In this way, unmarried mothers and nurse children were an intertwined 'problem', yet unlike infanticide cases, the abuse suffered by nurse children was reported regularly in the press. By framing the issue as one of parental neglect, cruelty and ignorance, the press demonised nurses and victimised the children involved without ever questioning why the situation occurred. Most cases in the courts also demonstrated the poverty in other families too, as most nurses took children purely for financial reasons. The results were often very detrimental.

As previously mentioned, it is clear that in some cases women became very attached to the children they were nursing, as revealed by a case that came to the attention of the authorities in 1928. In this instance, a seven-year-old boy who had been at nurse was sent to the Union infirmary in Dublin for treatment. Upon discharge, he was found to be receiving alms by an NSPCC inspector, and the Dublin Union Commissioners sent him to an industrial school. The woman who had being acting as the boy's nurse had applied to overturn the decision and was surprisingly successful. Judge G. P. Cussen, who would later chair the investigation into industrial schools and reformatories in 1934, stated:

> ... because a little boy or girl begs a penny or a few pence from a charitable person to buy sweets or cakes that therefore a case has been made for sending the youngster to an industrial school. The real test is – is the child in need of the necessities of life ... there is no evidence that this boy is in want of food or clothing [and] that is the end of this matter.

In this instance, the nurse wished to retain the child, be it for financial or emotional reasons, and the judge's verdict acknowledged her rights as a guardian. Yet the case also demonstrates the use of institutionalisation by the NSPCC and guardians, who appear to have ignored other alternatives in many instances.

It could be argued that this situation was not unique to Ireland. Yet when one examines the alternative measures that could have alleviated the situation for nurse children, principally the legalisation of adoption (which did not occur until 1952) and the introduction of mother's payments, the reluctance of the State to interfere could be viewed as negligent. In Ireland, the continued stigmatisation of unmarried mothers, both socially and economically, created an environment where women took desperate measures to care for and maintain their children. With regard to the women who took the children, they too were often in dire economic situations. Unfortunately, in many instances it was the child that suffered most.

Unmarried mothers after 1921

> Motherhood and childhood are entitled to special care and assistance. All children whether born in or out of wedlock, shall enjoy the same social protection. (Article 25, UN Declaration of Human Rights)

As numerous scholars have demonstrated, unmarried mothers in Ireland were stigmatised throughout the nineteenth century. However, in the post-First World War period, this stigma and fear of rising illegitimacy rates became engrained in the discourse of social workers, the clergy and the State. For the NSPCC and social reformers, individualism, the erosion of domesticity, and inadequate parental supervision became part of a discourse with the protection of the 'traditional family' as its core. In reality, the 'traditional family' being espoused was far from traditional in Ireland, representing instead a modern version of the family associated with urban, industrial society. As noted previously, by broadening the definition of cruelty to children to encompass that of neglect, the NSPCC had both increased its scope of intervention and narrowed its target to the family. Corporal punishment, child labour, child prostitution and other 'non-familial' issues were now ignored. Child protection was being used to punish parents who did not abide by the standards set out, but also to promote a particular type of family structure. The tension between what did and did not constitute appropriate family structures was greatest for single mother families.

In the 1920s and 1930s single mothers were consistently over-represented in the NSPCC's case files. In general, aside from deserted wives, single mothers were portrayed as neglectful, and an examination of why they appeared so often negligent illuminates both the historical construction of modern single motherhood and the modern concept of child neglect.[45] Yet despite their intentions, child savers had created agencies to which single mothers could come and plead for some material aid.[46] It is necessary here to point out the differences between single mothers in rural and urban areas. In agrarian economies there were fewer single mothers due to lower illegitimacy and desertion rates. Similarly, greater household flexibility, community responsibility and variable labour requirements meant that the children of single mothers could be integrated into extended or augmented families. In an urban setting, jobs were scarce, wages were low and there were fewer child-minding options. There were genuine cases of neglect, if neglect is defined by whether children should be supervised a certain number of hours, whether or not they should contribute to the family economy, and whether they could be sent to school every day clean and adequately dressed. Also, the work undertaken by many single mothers would not have been approved of by social workers or religious agencies. Taking in boarders could lead to charges of 'immorality', and other women were forced through economic necessity to earn their living through prostitution. The anxiety about single mothers within the social work and child-saving establishments can be seen in four related discourses relating to desertion, illegitimacy, women's employment and mothers' pensions. The apparent discrimination against single mothers resulted from observation of actual conditions where it was difficult to combine breadwinning and child-raising, from ideological anxieties about pauperisation, and also from fear of destabilising male and female roles.[47]

As Lindsey Earner-Byrne has highlighted with regard to unmarried mothers after independence, 'in the Irish "social order", the concept of illegitimacy extended in practice, if not in name, to the unmarried mother: she was an illegitimate mother'.[48] While widows would receive some financial support from the State, and deserted wives could approach the NSPCC for material aid and assistance to a limited extent, unmarried mothers were simultaneously ignored and increasingly focused upon. As the State refused to provide aid, religious orders, through fears of proselytising forces, developed institutions and informal structures both at home and abroad to cater for unmarried mothers. For those that did not wish to enter these institutions, or in the case of fee-paying homes, could not afford to, the following cases illustrate the desperate situation they faced.

In 1939, a twenty-two-year old woman requested advice regarding her two-year-old baby from the local NSPCC inspector. The mother and child were being kept by her parents when the request was made. The inspector recorded:

> Putative father paid 5s weekly for the maintenance of the child from birth up to about a month ago when he went to England and has not since been heard of or sent money. The man's mother now offers to take the child – although she denies that her son is the father of the child. Mother seeks advice re handing over the child. Advised mother to retain custody and that she could not get rid of her responsibilities by adopting such a course.

The inspector goes on to record that after five visits there was still no trace of the putative father, but 'child left with mother, case now satisfactory'.[49] That the inspector chose to highlight the mother's responsibilities in this case is interesting, as in the treatment of deserted wives the man's putative role would usually have been the focus. Not only would it have been the focus, but deserting husbands were tracked by inspectors of the NSPCC throughout Britain, Ireland and, in one instance, the United States, with great effort. It is probable that as this girl was an unmarried mother, the inspector did not feel her case worthy of such efforts.

In most cases, girls who became pregnant outside marriage would not be given a choice as to how they would rear their child. In 1939, the following letter was sent to the Wexford inspector:

> Dear Mr O'Connor,
>
> It has occurred to me that you might be able to help us with a little trouble. You will remember from the transactions we had in your Gorey Office and it is on that acquaintance that I presume. One of my girls to my surprise

and annoyance got herself into trouble with a neighbouring boy and a baby boy was born in Enniscorthy Co. Home last Sunday. I had to send her there to keep the peace as her father and the brothers were furious. After considerable persuasion they are willing to take her back, but will not allow the baby to come. She is a little mentally deficient and I cannot afford to pay for the baby anywhere else. You might be able to help me by using your influence to get it into a Catholic Orphanage or Home in Dublin. I would be very grateful to you because I am very tormented and I do not know what to do and I dare not bring the child here neither can I pay a fee for adoption as Mick is not fit to work now and I have three small children and the Mother will naturally have to earn her own living[;] if you can help me in my trouble I will try to express my gratitude later on.[50]

There is no suggestion that the girl would be allowed to keep the child, but the letter is interesting in the options it lists for the placement of children. As a fee was needed for adoption (although illegal), and often also for an orphanage or industrial school (again informal), many women chose to place their children with nurses. Chapter 1 briefly addressed the issue of nurse children and cruelty to children, but from the beginning of the twentieth century, the situation began to receive much attention in the press and in NSPCC official reports. The press in particular highlighted sensational cases of shocking cruelty. In 1915 the *Irish Independent* reported the following:

> Gross Neglect of a Child – Stating that the defendant was less guilty than a murderess, and that it was God's Providence she was not in the dock for murder, Mr. Mahony sent to jail for 6 weeks Mrs. Annie Hunter, Buckingham Buildings, the wife of a carpenter who was charged with neglecting Patrick Ryan in a manner likely to cause unnecessary suffering. Inspector Nelly said the woman told him the child's mother arranged to pay her 16s a month for its support, but she had not got any money ... While the defendant's own three children were fairly well looked after, the nurse-child was in a sad state.[51]

In 1931, the *Irish Independent* reported another case in which a woman received six months' imprisonment with hard labour for the neglect of a nurse child in her care. The NSPCC inspector investigating the case described it as follows: 'the worst case ... I have had extensive experience of nurse children and their conditions but I never came across a case as bad as the present one.'[52] Although the press did tend to cover the most sensational cases, there was an issue with nurse children in Ireland. As the State, in keeping with the previous policies of the Poor Law guardians, was extremely reluctant to board children out, mothers who did not want to commit their children to industrial schools for up to fourteen years were forced to trust that the woman they left to nurse their child would care for it. Unfortunately, it appears that once money stopped being sent by mothers, many nurses chose to leave children, usually babies, to waste away. The bind for unmarried mothers was not merely the choice between industrial schools or not; most industrial schools refused to take children under the age of six, and it became very difficult to get babies into Catholic orphanages or mother-and-baby homes. So this form of neglect, although not directly related to single mothers, represented another way in which their ability to raise their children was restricted.

Widows and widowers

> It turned out that the father only received fifteen shillings a week. He seemed to have done his best for a little while after his wife's desertion, then, demoralised by the weight of his many difficulties – and after trying one loose woman and another as a housekeeper – he had given way and sought solace, as thousands do, in drink. So the little wage was made less, and the children's chances of a tolerable existence became less also.[53]

Throughout the 1930s and 1940s there was a clear distinction between widows and widowers with respect to how the Society viewed and treated them. The former would constitute one of the first groups to be supported financially by the State through the Widows' and Orphans' Pension Act (1935), while the latter would be viewed with suspicion. The treatment of each category reflected dominant gender assumptions in the period and although both were viewed by the Society with suspicion, this was often for very different reasons. When looking at the cases involving widowers in the files, two issues become apparent: a mistrust of fathers being left with daughters, and the related problematisation of the absence of a woman in the home. Similarly, the inspector's own cultural and moral biases can be seen in numerous cases. In examining the treatment of widows, suspicion was normally focused on their position as single mothers, specifically with regard to any relationships they may have had or were believed to be having with men. In the only case in the sample investigated for 'Other Wrongs', the Society investigated a forty-year-old widow and mother of four children aged between seven and fifteen years. The family was living on a 10s weekly widow's and orphan's pension, and the four-roomed house they were renting cost 7s 6d per week. The inspector describes the woman as 'careless and indifferent'. However, aside from the eldest girl who had 'sores on her face', the family were 'fairly clean' and 'well nourished'. The following extract explains how and why the family were under investigation:

> Mrs. 'Murphy' is a widow for some years past. A widower named ⸺ whose two children are at nurse often frequents the place and gets his meals there. The presence of this man was resented by Mrs. 'Murphy's' eldest son who left and joined the British army. A second son has been committed to an industrial school … The mother seems infatuated with the man and is neglecting her children.[54]

How the case came to the inspector's attention is not recorded, but from the nature of the 'crime', assumptions can be made. Most likely, a neighbour or 'concerned citizen' informed the inspector. (The involvement of the 'general public' in reporting cases was briefly addressed in Chapter 2 with reference to the Society's early years.) The following letter, from 1939, is an example of one such notification to the inspector.

> Dear Sir,
>
> Thanks for sending the N.S.P.C.C. reports, which I have read with interest – I wonder very much what will be done with the Rowe case – as I think this is the nite [sic] he comes out official. I heard that he had become mentally affected but do not know if it is true – I shall be very interested to hear further as you can imagine ... I see you have 3 cases of exposure for begging which reminds me of that Mrs Purcell and her children who hang about New Ross. Can anything be done about them?
>
> Yours Truly,
>
> C.C. Tyndall.[55]

This last sentence – 'can anything be done about them' – sums up many of the letters to the NSPCC. It is not so much genuine concern that characterises the tone of the letters as anxiety over dealing with unsavoury elements of society – particularly those cases on public display, such as children begging. In another case in the sample, a letter was sent from the Garda at Oylegate to Inspector Leacy regarding a ten-month-old girl:

> I wish to bring to your notice an instance of alleged neglect and abuse of an illegitimate infant in this area. A girl named ____ , who resides with her parents ____ and ____ ... gave birth to an illegitimate child some time ago. She had been away at domestic service, and returned home, where she gave birth to the child. It is alleged that after she gave birth to the infant, she was put out of the home by her father, and was obliged to sleep in an outhouse on a few occasions, and as a consequence the infant was neglected. It is alleged that the infant is very seldom fed, and lies from one end of the day to the other in a cot. I cannot say to what extent the allegation is true, if at all, but if you could see your way to look into the matter, it would be a good thing for all concerned, as in nearly all such cases there is generally always some neglect.[56]

Though there may well have been neglect in this case, again the lack of concern for the girl and even the child are very apparent. With regard to widowers, the mistrust of fathers with girls can be seen through the number of girls as opposed to boys removed to industrial schools after the death of a mother. In one such case involving a family of ten, five girls and five boys between the ages of three months and eleven years, the four younger girls were sent to schools, 'the eldest girl being kept to look after the boys'.[57] Or perhaps it was not so much the mistrust of fathers as the usefulness of boys as opposed to girls in the period? Either way, one of the offshoots of such a policy would be the consistently higher number of girls than boys in industrial schools throughout the twentieth century.

Childcare was an obvious problem for single-mother families, one which the NSPCC addressed but did not actively campaign to reform. As clearly defined standards of childcare had begun to emerge with the introduction of compulsory schooling to the age of fourteen years, single mothers were under increasing pressure to find adequate childcare. Family, if they lived close by, were the most logical and cheapest option usually. Yet this was often criticised by the NSPCC inspector if the person chosen to mind the children was not deemed suitable:

> Case involving six children, aged between one and fourteen years, single mother: 'The children are generally handed out to the care of an unmarried aunt who is mentally incapable and of reported immoral character.'[58]

In this situation, it was often rural women who had the most support, particularly if a child could be integrated into the larger extended family. Often, widows perceived to be out of control of their children or perhaps lacking adequate childcare were scrutinised. In 1939 a 55-year-old widow was investigated by the inspector for the neglect of her fourteen-year-old son. The inspector described the woman as 'careless and indifferent' and warned the woman that she would be prosecuted and her son sent to a reformatory or borstal institution if she did not reform her habits. The complaint had been made by a neighbour who stated that the boy 'was out of control'.[59] The boy had apparently been staying out late and it was felt that his mother did not have the ability to control him. In this case the gender bias was multifaceted. As a single mother, the woman had the added pressure of being the breadwinner and sole carer, yet the inspectors were often sceptical of a single woman's ability to control a teenage boy. This scepticism also applied to widowers rearing young girls. Widows had always tended to outnumber widowers, and to some extent the focus on widows developed in the post-First World War period, due in many cases to the emphasis on separation wives. In another investigation in 1921, the case of a mother, the widow of a soldier, was recorded by the Wexford inspector as follows: 'Widow. Believed drinking and neglect – children, under age Boy age 15 years Girl 13yrs, Boy aged 10 years and Girl aged 9 years and not insured. 2 Room Home rent 1/9- mother out believed drinking and alleged shopping.'[60] The following section will address poverty in an urban setting – another issue highlighted by the Society after independence as well as before.

Dublin: a case study in overcrowding

> We talk a great deal about the condition of the poor, but do we ever try to realise the conditions under which they live, or try to understand them? No, we don't or find out anything disagreeable, but the time had come for us to face facts. What are the ordinary tenement houses like in Dublin? In the first place most of these houses are owned by some man or woman who

tries to make a living out of the profits. They have themselves never learned or thought anything about ordinary modern ideas of health or sanitation. All they generally think of is, 'will the rent be paid regularly?'[61]

That extract, taken from an article in the *Irish Citizen*, outlines the conditions of the Dublin slums in 1915. It highlights how they were never intended for one-room tenements, being the old houses of 'the rich people of Dublin', and how they were never designed to contain a number of families. Not only is the overcrowding outlined; the lack of water is described, which forced women to carry buckets up four or five flights of stairs. The author concludes by asking:

> Cannot we do something to help and give the poor a chance of leading decent, respectable lives? Help them to help themselves, and don't give indiscriminate charity; it does far more harm than good ... and see if we cannot help in some scheme for the better housing of our poor in Dublin.[62]

The issue of overcrowded living conditions was one the NSPCC in Dublin particularly highlighted. The 1926 census recorded 800,000 people living in overcrowded conditions, or a quarter of the population. Yet discussion of overcrowding in the Oireachtas and in the press was sparse. Overcrowding had been addressed by the NSPCC from its foundation, but from the 1920s onwards it became one of the Society's most pressing concerns. Table 3.4 demonstrates the numbers of families it had investigated living in overcrowded conditions in the 1930s. That this table was included in the Society's Golden Jubilee Report is significant.

While the figures show a decrease in the number of cases involving families in one-roomed housing, the numbers are still very high, particularly the number of children living in such conditions. The following case featured in the 1933–34 report of the Dublin branch.

Table 3.4 Number of families investigated by the NSPCC for living in overcrowded conditions, 1934–39

Year	One room			Two rooms		
	Cases	Adults	Children	Cases	Adults	Children
1934–35	1,126	2,059	2,767	887	1,770	2,889
1935–36	1,099	2,062	2,942	861	1,721	2,841
1936–37	897	1,666	2,322	780	1,569	2,626
1937–38	855	1,498	2,040	850	1,617	2,705
1938–39	804	1,419	2,074	871	1,646	2,977
Total	4,781	8,704	12,145	4,249	8,323	14,038

Figures taken from the Annual Report of the NSPCC, Dublin District branch, 1939.

> The inspector's attention was directed to a family living in one room in a tenement house. In this one room fourteen persons (seven adults and seven children) [of] mixed sexes, lived, slept and ate. The room was about 17ft. by 10 ft., and contained two beds only. Several members of the family had to sleep on the floor. The inspector was informed that several applications for better accommodation had been made to the Housing Authorities by the family, and they were told that there would be none available until next year. It was hoped that some of the elder children would be able to sleep at relatives' homes and thus enable the younger children to have more accommodation. A recent visit, however, shows that only one boy has left the home, and the family are still pressing for other quarters.[63]

In an earlier report by the same branch, the inspector detailed the case of a family comprising an unmarried mother with two children, her own mother, her three sisters and her brother. The one-room living area was described as a 'foul hovel'; the family lived on eight shillings per week home assistance. They were found 'without food, practically naked and bootless ... The conditions altogether were the embodiment of squalor, ignorance and immorality.'[64] The parents were warned, but they refused to enter the County Home. As a result, the children and their mother were committed to the County Home for one year by the courts, while the others remained.[65]

The case above demonstrates the lack of options for families in similar situations of destitution. In many discussions of families in overcrowded conditions, the NSPCC inspector would automatically suggest that the children be removed, or the family move to the County Home. Not only did the County Home have stigma attached to it for families who had been self-supporting, but it could also result in the separation of families, something most wished to avoid. As the workhouse renamed, the County Home continued to be associated with the stigma of the workhouse, and many families were reluctant to enter it. In the 1937–38 Dublin report the following case featured:

> Ten persons, the parents and eight children, were found to be living in one room when the inspector called to see about a boy requiring orthopaedic treatment, recommended by the School Medical Officer ... The living conditions were miserable. This ten-roomed, three storied house contained ten different families, one to each room, a total of 41 human beings altogether. There was only one lavatory and one water tap in the back yard, for the use of them all.[66]

That the conditions described above were still prevalent in 1938 is quite shocking. Yet other than acknowledge the conditions, the NSPCC did not suggest any reforms. The concerns of the NSPCC and the State were not principally for the families in tenements *per se*, but rather for the effects of the conditions on children and the risk of exposure to immorality and criminality. The 1935 Report of the Committee on the Criminal Law Amendment Acts (Carrigan Committee) referred to this situation:

> in this country the children of the poorer classes are less protected than in Great Britain. In Dublin, the necessity in the case of many families living in tenements, for the parents, both father and mother, to leave children to look after themselves in the daytime while they themselves went out to earn their livelihood, was a constant source of danger. In rural districts girls of fourteen years are sent out to service, which deprives them of the protection they had with their parents.[67]

What official reports demonstrate is a complete misunderstanding of the ways in which families could be helped. As Kevin Kearns's and Jacinta Prunty's examinations of life in urban Dublin have shown, families did not want to move from the city, and basic welfare reforms could have enabled many of them to survive and improve their conditions.[68] Yet the focus of the NSPCC and the State remained on parental responsibility to provide suitable living conditions, and if parents could not do so, children were removed for their 'protection'.

Competing to save the poor? The SVDP and proselytising

> The material relief is only a means to an end.[69]

Proselytising and fears of proselytising did not end in the nineteenth century in Ireland. The SVDP was one of the principal agencies working with poor people to promote Christian principles. Formed in 1833 by seven students at the University of Paris, the SVDP held its first conference in Dublin at the White Cross Rooms in Charles Street on 16 December 1844. By the end of 1923 there were 490 conferences in Ireland and over 4,000 members. The SVDP appears to have been better financed than the NSPCC in the 1920s and 1930s, and its agenda, while focused on helping the poor and the working class, was also centred on maintaining and expanding Christian principles. In the 1920s and 1930s the SVDP underwent rapid growth, endorsing its 'special works' in particular in its annual reports. These consisted of a number of institutions and committees, principally the Orphanage of St Vincent de Paul in Glasnevin,[70] the 'penny banks' throughout Ireland, a night shelter in Dublin, a labour yard in Dublin, the Seamen's Institutes in Belfast and Dublin, the Prisoners' Aid Societies in Dublin, Cork and Belfast, night schools for the 'backward boy' in Dublin and various committees that conducted hospital visitations. Honorary members of the Society paid an annual subscription and were expected to attend a quarterly mass and receive the sacrament of Holy Communion.

Unemployment was frequently discussed at conferences held throughout the country in the 1920s and 1930s, as were the ways in which the 'moral welfare of the poor', and children in particular, was being catered for under the guidance of Catholic schools. With regard to the families visited, the conference reports primarily feature cases involving situations of desertion or separation, and regularly those in which one parent or a group of relatives were Protestant. Reports often specified if parents were temperate, or 'never smoked'. If the 'deserving poor' were frequently discussed in the nineteenth century, in the 1920s and 1930s it appears that the deserving poor were Catholic (or willing to convert to Catholicism), temperate and unemployed 'due to no fault of their own'. Spiritual and moral improvement was constantly referred to, and families remained on the SVDP list for months and years 'in the hope that eventually permanent improvement [would] be effected'.[71] Schools were a key factor in the recruitment of new members, and the Christian Brothers are discussed as being central in encouraging young men who were not yet junior members to participate upon leaving school. Upon the death of Brother Francis P. Thunder, a previous president of the Conference of Our Lady Help of Christians in 1923, the 'zealous' work of the brother was espoused, from encouraging the Family Rosary to impressing on all the brothers that the spiritual aspect to cases was without question the most important.

The SVDP grew in membership and in funds in the 1920s and 1930s. In the 1927 report, a substantial increase in membership and an increase of £12,000 in receipts were noted. The SVDP's 'propaganda work' was highlighted, specifically with regard to juvenile membership. The report asserted with regard to proselytising and poverty: 'the eagerness with which the poor adopt the suggestion of having their families consecrated by the Sacred Heart is very edifying'.[72] Lindsey Earner-Byrne's study of motherhood and child welfare in Dublin from 1922 outlines how many Dublin mothers became proficient in using the religious and charitable organisations to feed their families; mothers knew there was only one thing more precious to the Catholic Church than their souls – the souls of their children.[73] In 1929, the SVDP visited 8,000 families, or 35,000 individuals, and raised £19,850 or £2.10s per family visited.[74] Obtaining employment for men in families remained one of the principal aims, as it ensured the 'self-supporting' nature of the families. In 1930 the SVDP again claimed an increase in membership and conferences, and added that with the re-establishment of Dublin Corporation many of the families needing assistance would be dealt with by that body. With regard to Cork, the report states: 'the year 1929 was a great year of prosperity, with the result that the families on the books of the Society were adopted cases only',[75] yet in 1930 the employment environment was completely changed with the closing down of one of the major industries. For this reason the number of families on the books had doubled. Penny banks were closed down in 1930, and the encouragement of juvenile conferences was again highlighted. There is a record of 6,165 active members, 241 aspirant members and 1,187 honorary members. 26,932 families were visited, or 104,000 individuals, and 293,194 visits were made. £96,470 was received, down on the previous year. In today's terms, this is the equivalent of over £5 million. Also in 1930, the president and honorary secretary highlighted the primary objective of the SVDP: 'to make ourselves and those whom we visit better Christians'.[76]

Aside from the interest in 'downtrodden' men, the SVDP focused its attention on vulnerable children. In 1855, the Glasnevin orphanage was opened under the direction of Cardinal Cullen, and in the 1930s was the oldest of the SVDP's 'special works'. The 1928 report states: 'Religion is the dominant influence which is relied upon to shape their characters ... Their weak human wills are strengthened by the frequent reception of the sacraments.'[77] From his appointment, Archbishop Byrne became the patron of the orphanage. There were no women on the committee or in positions of influence. In the 1932–33 report the committee states that 1,900 boys had entered the school since its establishment. It appears from the reports that the school was very much a 'civilising' influence on the boys, and perhaps a way to encourage the entrance of young educated men into the priesthood or the Christian Brothers. What is apparent in the reports is the need to keep any children in danger of proselytising forces out of harm's way. In 1930, the Revd P. Dunne wrote to Archbishop Byrne requesting £146 15s (initially) for the maintenance of three families. He requested £100 for one family in particular, in order to place four children in a Catholic boarding school and 'protect them' from their extended family, as their parents could not afford to keep them. On both their mother's and father's sides there were Protestant connections, and the Revd Dunne and John A. Glynn wrote to the Archbishop expressing their fear for the children's faith. In one of the letters Dunne noted: 'I may get the nuns down to £90 a year'.

Fears of proselytism, and actively proselytising

In the folder containing the reports of the free night shelter in Back Lane, there is a piece entitled 'Non-Catholic shelters in Dublin – objectionable lines on which they are run', written by one of the members of the free night shelter committee. The discussion refers to the two non-Catholic shelters in Dublin, the Salvation Army's shelter in Peter Street and the Protestant lodging-house in Poolbeg Street. It claims that both shelters were run 'at a substantial profit' and overcrowded, and most importantly, it highlights the proselytising uses of the shelters:

> even though we meet with many disappointments among the class we deal with, we feel that we were well repaid by our success in the prevention of work of Proselytising Agencies, which are so active at present in our midst. We seek to make them better men and better Christians. The material relief is only a means to an end.[78]

The shelter in Back Lane was not the only way the Society directed its energies towards the 'redemption' of men. In 1925 the subscribers and donors to the Catholic Male Discharged Prisoners' Aid Committee included the Governor-General of Ireland and the manager of Hibernian Bank on College Green. The practice of the committee's members was to meet prisoners on their entry to Mountjoy prison and follow this up with visits to their relatives and family. In situations involving juvenile offenders, the reports state that visitations had been 'most fruitful of good'[79] as parents were encouraged to 'improve their surroundings and exercise proper parental control'. At the end of every report, the committee thanked the prisons board, those who subscribed and donated and 'the Press of Dublin for its valuable reviews of the Committee's work in previous years'.[80] In 1927, the committee's report explicitly stated that it provided assistance 'entirely to young men, first offenders and very exceptional cases'. It appears they were fearful of losing donations for the Society if it was felt they were supporting men past redemption. In order to demonstrate the rhetoric and bias of the Society, as well as its wide-ranging influence on families, the following cases in the 1926 report are reproduced verbatim:

> Gardener, whose wife became a Catholic on marriage. His wife subsequently left him and returned to Protestantism. She left him and had him arrested on his sick bed in Hospital for not contributing to her support. Whilst he was in prison she gave the two children, two girls, to a Proselytising home, going away herself to England. The Committee took up the case, and securing the man's release a month earlier than the termination of his sentence, with the help of the Catholic Protection and Rescue Society, succeeded in getting back the children and placing them in a Catholic Orphanage.[81]

> Information came to the Committee that there was danger of Proselytism of the children, ten in number, of a man awaiting his trial for a serious offence. This prisoner wrote asking the Committee to look after his children. The family was visited, and are still being visited. The great danger in this case recently became apparent. It came to the knowledge of the committee, that a high dignitary of another church was becoming interested in this Prisoner in order to get him to execute a deed.[82]

> A very high class skilled cabinet maker, who used to work on Ocean Liners, was imprisoned for Bigamy. He had two charges of Bigamy against him. His lawful wife [was] with a grown-up family living. There was also a family in both of the bigamous cases. The case looked rather hopeless but his lawful wife was visited and consented to forgive him. He was restored to his family, and the Committee set him up in business at a small cost. This man has been very successful and is leading a good Catholic life. He has made a great fight and remained in Ireland, when he could have got very high wages in England. We consider this the most successful case of the past year.[83]

> Young Dublin man, who had been arrested in England was found to have married a Protestant in a Registry Office there. The Committee sent him to a priest, and the marriage was regularised. Situations were subsequently procured for him and his wife.[84]

These cases demonstrate the SVDP's concern with upholding families by helping and guiding men, and deterring women and children from going to other agencies. As the first case shows, for women this could mean taking a husband back even if he had already set up another family. Throughout, the focus was on the threat of emigration, proselytising and mixed marriages. The answer was always the redemption of men. From 1935 the members of the Catholic Male Discharged Prisoners Aid Committee and the SVDP not only provided material aid and assistance to prisoners, they acted as probation officers for some: 'Men from English prisons, discharged on licence and sent to this country (Free State) are now allowed to report monthly to this Committee, instead of the previous rule of reporting to the police.'[85] This would allow the SVDP to influence both Catholic and Protestant men. In a lecture delivered at Trinity College Dublin in 1944 on probation services in Ireland, Edward Fahy commented on the fact that outside of Dublin, there was no regular probation service. With the SVDP being utilised as an informal probationary service, this is not surprising. Yet again the State gave a Catholic organisation control over a group of vulnerable/minority persons because of its own inability or reluctance to provide the service. In general, it seems the SVDP's actions were primarily driven by a fear of proselytising agencies:

> Amongst the families of the poorer classes of prisoners, we find Proselytising Agencies active, taking advantage of the absence of the father who is in prison, they hold out inducements to the poverty-stricken wife and children to change their faith. Where there is such danger, we spare no efforts to combat the proselytiser's work, and we feel well repaid by our success in this during the past year.[86]

As noted previously, the focus on proselytism was a battle that developed in the nineteenth century, particularly with regard to the care of children. The fears of Catholic organisations appear to have continued after independence, even though Protestant charities and schools were now an even smaller minority. One of the most vocal and active figures with regard to proselytising was Frank Duff, the founder of the Legion of Mary. In its charter, the Legion outlined its role and organisational structure: 'The Legion of Mary is therefore organised on the model of any army – principally on that of the army of ancient Rome'.[87] The Legion actively proselytised, and in letters from Duff to Archbishop Byrne in the 1920s and 1930s he discusses how members of the Legion had made lists of three groups of people: 'converts', 'those who began to take instruction in the Faith and did not continue' and 'those in mixed marriages'. In order to establish contact with the people listed, the Legion held regular socials, and the letter claims they made thirty converts as a result of these efforts. In a subsequent letter Duff requested permission to place an advertisement in Protestant newspapers encouraging those interested in Catholicism to approach the Legion. He argued that he felt it would be less intimidating for those interested in conversion to approach a lay person as opposed to a priest.

The Legion, however, was not without controversy and opposition, both within the Catholic hierarchy and community and outside. In 1929 a petition was sent to Archbishop Byrne signed by a group of Dublin families arguing against the Legion's policy 'of sending young girls out to rural branches'. Fearful for the safety of the girls, the letter described the work being carried out as 'a Legion frenzy'. In response to the critique, and the Archbishop's refusal to grant official approval for the Legion, Duff wrote: 'I respectfully submit to Your Grace that as a worker in this diocese since 1913 (fifteen years of unremitting labour) I am entitled to treatment from my Archbishop which an ordinary parent would give to his child. Indeed, not one kind word has ever come my way.' Not only had the Archbishop reprimanded Duff regarding the petition and the sending out of young girls in the Legion, he expressed concern over the work carried out in 76 Harcourt Street, the Legion's female hostel for wayward girls. As a result, Duff sent a list of the names of sixty-nine girls who had entered Magdalene laundries from the hostel, a list of those who had left and found work, and the names of sixty girls who had been married upon leaving. He also listed twelve girls who had been converted through being in the hostel, and the men converted following marriages to girls. However, there was also a list of thirty-two girls who died in the hostel or in work afterwards, specifically recording whether the priest or curate was present at the death bed, and a further list of thirty women whose children were placed in Catholic orphanages, industrial schools, convents and with foster parents. Byrne refused to acknowledge the Legion officially, yet throughout the period their role in proselytising was very marked.

'Widely praised and much maligned': 'Mammies' and the 'St. Vinnies'

In *Dublin's Lost Heroines*, Kevin Kearns examines attitudes of Dubliners to the SVDP. Highlighting that 'virtually every mother was touched by the St. Vinnies', the testimonies demonstrate that aside from the desperately needed relief, many mothers dreaded the visit of the SVDP man and the demeaning way in which their homes would be examined. One woman interviewed, Mary Murray, described how, even though her family was in dire poverty, her mother refused to take charity from the SVDP men: 'Me mother wouldn't take *nothing* from them. Nothing. *Ever!* She had that much pride.'[88] This scrutiny (one which the men of the house avoided) put much pressure on working-class mothers, and negative attitudes to the SVDP can be understood in the context of class difference and dependence.

Other testimonies about the SVDP recorded situations in which its men would inspect families and turn them down because their flats were clean or they had decent furniture. Margaret Byrne from Thomas Street described how:

> St. Vincent de Paul was good to some people, but they were not good to my mother, even though my mother was a widow with a young family. They visited us and said we didn't need help – but we really and truly did need

help! See, if you had furniture in the place they'd say you didn't need help. You had to have nothing in your room before you'd get help from them.[89]

In these situations, the options open to families were limited. The Salvation Army, a Protestant society, offered assistance to all families, but the decision to take help from the army was a difficult one for a Catholic mother. Dinah Cole's description of her own mother's choice demonstrates the bind:

> I was maybe nine at the time. We were very poor. And she was sick, and really there was no food or anything. And we went to the St. Vincent de Paul for help. But we had a clean home, and they thought if your house is clean, you're well off. So, St. Vincent de Paul wouldn't help us. So we went to the Salvation Army – and they gave us help. She took us down to the Salvation Army on a Sunday morning. And, you know, that was against our religion. And the Legion of Mary (members) were walking up and down saying, 'please don't bring your children in there.' Well we were only going in cause they gave you a parcel of food. But you had to wait for the (semi-religious) service – which was terrible. And my mother was very upset, I remember, and she was crying ... She was a very religious woman.[90]

From Golden Jubilee to Irish Society for the Prevention of Cruelty to Children (ISPCC), 1939–56

In 1939, the year of its Golden Jubilee, all NSPCC branches in Ireland began to use as a subtitle the caption 'National Society for the Protection and Care of Children'. The reasoning was addressed in the Dublin Report:

> This will undoubtedly please many friends who have felt too much prominence has hitherto been given to the word Cruelty in our work. After the prevention of cruelty, all who take an interest in social work know how many other ways the Society is helping children who are suffering and being deprived of the simplest needs of life.[91]

The society founded for the prevention of cruelty had officially begun to acknowledge that this was no longer was its principal aim. Two years prior to this, the North Louth, Monaghan and Cavan branch report stated the purpose of the Society's existence: 'to look after the exceptional child who is not receiving the care and protection that justice and humanity demand'.[92] To mark the Golden Jubilee in 1939 it was decided that the first annual report in Ireland would be reprinted in a commemorative booklet. Notes were placed in the margins regarding the present position of the Society on issues still prevalent, and quotations from writers and philosophers espousing sentimental and romantic notions of childhood were placed at the bottom of each page: 'Children are Travellers newly arrived in a strange country; we should therefore make conscience not to mislead them'; 'A child is a flower with a soul'; 'Be child-conscious'.[93] The report states that in 1938, the Society dealt with 4,450 cases and that from its foundation, 560,000 Irish children had been helped. It argued: 'Fifty years' work and publicity have achieved their object. It is now generally known that it is wrong and illegal to ill-treat or neglect a child'.[94] The report also states that the increase in cases of 'advice sought' demonstrates that 'the bogey of the "Cruelty Man" has been replaced by the "Humane Man".'

When looking at the changes in the Society in Ireland from 1939 to 1956, it is first necessary to address the changes in the British Society. Sherrington has examined the Society in Britain from its foundation to 1883. For the period 1908–48, she explores the changing relations between the Society and the State. While the Society's early innovatory work had become more formalised in the twentieth century, statutory services were expanding into areas originally pioneered by the Society, and Sherrington describes this as a period of 'crisis and change' within its work as it attempted to redefine its role. The Society was now acting as a form of children's police, involving itself in matters of justice more than charity. Following the Second World War, strategies for survival were further developed by the Society, particularly after the publication of the Beveridge Report, which was the *Report of the Inter-Departmental Committee on Social Insurance and Allied Services* chaired by William Beveridge. This report identified five 'giant evils' in society – squalor, ignorance, want, idleness and disease – and went on to propose widespread reform to the system of social welfare in the United Kingdom to address these. It formed the basis for the post-war reforms and the development of the welfare state, which included the expansion of National Insurance and the creation of the National Health Service. Anxious to assuage the fears of those who saw the impending demise of voluntary organisations, the NSPCC discussed areas not covered by the new welfare system, claiming: 'voluntary agencies will be needed more than in the past, for exploring as specialists the new avenues of social service which will open when want is abolished'. These specialised services and issues highlighted included the Women Visitors Scheme and the acknowledgement of battered child syndrome, which became instrumental in the Society's redefinition in Britain after the Second World War.

To what extent was the Irish Society influenced by developments in Britain? In general, the Irish branches of the Society appear to have followed the British Society's redefinition as an advisory agency for families, while also addressing pertinent issues such as desertion, overcrowding, illegitimacy, poor relief and juvenile delinquency. Yet in matters of sexual crime or 'immorality', adoption or fostering, it was almost silent. Aside from one report that requested the banning of advertising of adoptions in the press, adoption, contraception, abortion and sexual crime were not discussed (generally, issues of immorality had been discussed very rarely throughout the period in Irish reports – another difference with the British reports). With regard to the development of welfare reforms after the Second World War, Ireland's neutral stance during the Emergency, but particularly the freeze on wages, allied to increasing inflation and emigration produced a different 1950s economy than that of many other European states. The introduction of children's allowances is addressed elsewhere in this book, but it is worth noting here that the State did consult with the NSPCC on a number of occasions from 1939 to 1944. Other than the allowances, the 1951 'mother and child scheme' debacle would represent the biggest debate on child welfare during the period. That the Catholic Church and medical profession were triumphant is significant, but the lack of input or discussion by the Society officially and unofficially is also noteworthy. It appears from the annual reports, that the Society was appeasing the State, as opposed to introducing reforms to benefit families. In 1951, all branches featured Article 42, Section 1 of the 1937 Constitution at the beginning of their annual reports; this states: 'The State acknowledges that the primary and natural educator of the child is the Family and guarantees to respect the inalienable right and duty of parents to provide, according to their means, for the religious and moral, intellectual, physical and social education of their children'.[95] In 1952, Article 41 was quoted:

> The State recognises the Family as the natural primary and fundamental unit group of Society, and as a moral institution possessing inalienable and imprescriptible rights, antecedent and superior to all positive law ... The State therefore guarantees to protect the Family in its constitution and authority, as the necessary basis of social order and as indispensible to the welfare of the Nation and the State ... In particular, the State recognises that by her life within the home, woman gives to the State a support without which the common good cannot be achieved.[96]

What was the official relationship of the NSPCC to the State? In 1933, £10 9s 0d was recorded as 'not allocated' in the Wexford District branch report. It had been contributed by the Wexford County Board of Health, demonstrating that the Society was in receipt of official funding.[97] That the State was providing the NSPCC branches with contributions is significant. Whether this was the case throughout the period of examination is unclear, but £10 to one of fourteen branches that was not spent could signal quite a significant donation from the State to the Society annually. Together with its central role in court proceedings and with the industrial school system, this funding suggests that the NSPCC was more akin to a semi-State organisation in this period.

With regard to the connections between the Irish and British branches, it appears that by the late 1940s the main connection was that the Society in Ireland was financially dependent on the British umbrella fund. From 1922, donations had decreased, inspectors' wages had fluctuated significantly and the Society was competing with Catholic charities for funds from the public. The returns in reports show that the Society must have been receiving money from the British branch in order to keep running. Was this a significant factor in the renaming of the Society to the ISPCC in 1956? Although it can only be speculated, it appears that the change was more to do with restructuring by the NSPCC after the Beveridge Report than the

Irish Society needing to be independent. In 1953, the Liverpool SPCC, the only independent branch in England, was integrated into the NSPCC. This was symbolic of restructuring in the NSPCC. Although it is not possible to discuss all the changes that the Irish Society underwent before and after the formation of the ISPCC, it is a study that deserves to be told.

From the beginning of the twentieth century child protection became an increasingly professionalised, secular activity in Britain, the United States and other Western countries, marking the waning influence of religiously motivated, charity volunteers. NSPCC inspectors were middle-class men and women, many ex-police officers, who visited and policed families, increasing their role as social workers. In Ireland, the Society's role was significant, but it was not the only social work or charitable organisation dealing with families. The 1920s and 1930s witnessed an expansion in the role of Catholic associations such as the SVDP and the Legion of Mary, as the State allowed the Church to take the lead in the provision of social services, institutional care and educational provision. In his examination of Catholicism, subsidiarity and assistencialism in Ireland, Fred Powell describes how, after independence, as Catholic social philosophy became predicated on subsidiarity (which was profoundly anti-statist), the State took the stance that it should not assume responsibility for social service provision if it could be managed alternatively. As Father Jerome O'Leary, a vocal exponent of subsidiarity stated, 'State intervention should always be regarded as merely a first-aid measure'.[98] Powell outlines how this has provided much power to the Catholic Church, which retained control over most schools, hospitals and social services. In particular, he discusses the role of the SVDP, whose growth and influence in the provision of social services and welfare has previously been addressed.

Conclusion

From 1922 onwards, the principal actions of the NSPCC were divided into three broad areas: the recategorisation and expansion of child neglect; the promotion of the Society as an advisory agency with more 'advice-sought' cases; and its continued involvement in the placement of children in industrial schools. It was also pushing for certain welfare reforms, all which had one common trait – they would help to keep families intact. Highlighting desertion, inadequate poor relief, Dublin slums, illegitimacy and 'deformed children', the Society was willing to address certain acceptable issues. None of these reforms, however, would impinge on the Catholic Church's near monopoly in education, or endorse welfare measures deemed too socialistic or radical. The Society did not discuss single-mother benefits (aside from widow's pensions), children's allowances or welfare payments other than poor relief, and although it discussed the problems associated with industrial schools from the late 1940s, inspectors were, as we shall see, regularly involved in removing children to these schools and prosecuting parents.

As Britain and other Western countries developed State welfare systems, re-evaluated juvenile delinquency and reduced and eventually ended the use of industrial schools and reformatories, the emphasis in Ireland remained on institutionalisation and charity as opposed to welfare. Aside from draconian censorship measures, the prohibition of contraceptives, the ban on divorce, the illegality of adoption and the refusal to legislate for adoption, successive Irish governments resisted the financial support of any family outside the male breadwinner model. Single mothers were particularly affected and stigmatised, as were their children. The extension of compulsory schooling, institutionalisation and prosecution of parents was now sanctioned by the State, but enforced by the NSPCC, which had redefined its role in independent Ireland.

Notes

1. Extract from the Democratic Programme, adopted by the First Dáil on 21 January 1919.
2. Lindsey Earner-Byrne, 'Reinforcing the family: The role of gender, morality and sexuality in Irish welfare policy, 1922–1944', *History of the Family: International Quarterly Journal*, 13:4 (2009), pp. 361.
3. See Sherrington, 'NSPCC in transition', p. 2.
4. Henry A. Mess, writing in 1948, warned of the dangers of social institutions continuing when the need for them was gone. Cited in Sherrington, 'NSPCC in transition', p. 3.
5. For a discussion of social legislation focused on health and welfare, specifically maternity and child welfare, see Earner-Byrne, *Mother and Child*, passim.
6. Maguire, 'Foreign adoptions', p. 397.
7. For a discussion of child neglect in the United States see Gordon, *Heroes of Their Own Lives*, pp. 116–67.
8. Inspector Books for the Wexford District branch, 1925 (ISPCC, Limerick). (Punctuation added for clarity.)
9. Ibid.
10. CF #202 (ISPCC, Limerick).
11. CF #91.
12. CF #213.
13. First recorded from 1922 in the NSPCC branch reports.
14. For a discussion of the mother and child scheme, see Earner-Byrne, *Mother and Child*, pp. 130–45.
15. AR Dublin District branch 1933–34 (ISPCC, Limerick), p. 17.
16. 'NSPCC and child neglect', *Irish Times*, 13 July 1920.
17. The consistency and completeness of the statistics in the annual reports varies greatly and many contain gaps in certain years. These figures are an approximate estimate of the number of cases and children investigated from the surviving and recorded reports. While most reports contain full classification of the offences and the results of cases, some also include details such as whether the child was legitimate, illegitimate, related to the offender or a step-child.
18. AR Dublin District branch, 1931 (ISPCC, Limerick), p. 5.
19. See Annual Report of the Department of Local Government and Public Health,

1932–33, p. 125.
20 AR Dublin District branch NSPCC, 1937–38 (ISPCC, Limerick), p. 8.
21 Ibid., p. 8.
22 AR Dublin District branch NSPCC, 1938–39 (ISPCC, Limerick).
23 Ibid.
24 Kearns, *Dublin Tenement Life*.
25 See Patricia Kennedy (ed.), *Motherhood in Ireland: Creation and Context* (Mercier Press, 2004); Lindsey Earner-Byrne, 'The boat to England: An analysis of the official reactions to the emigration of single expectant Irishwomen to Britain, 1922–72', *Irish Economic and Social History*, 30 (November 2003), p. 57; Earner-Byrne, '"Managing motherhood": Negotiating a maternity service for Catholic mothers in Dublin, 1930–54', *Social History of Medicine*, 20:2 (August 2006), 261–77; Earner-Byrne, '"Moral repatriation": The response to Irish unmarried mothers in Britain, 1920s–1960s', in Patrick J. Duffy (ed.), *To and From Ireland: Planned Migration Schemes c. 1600–2000* (Geography Publications, 2004), pp. 155–73; Earner-Byrne, *Mother and Child*; Paul Garrett, 'The abnormal flight: The migration and repatriation of unmarried mothers', *Social History*, 25 (2000), 330–43; Maria Luddy, 'Moral rescue and unmarried mothers in Ireland in the 1920s', *Women's Studies*, 30 (2001), 797–817; Clíona Rattigan, '"Crimes of passion of the worst character": Abortion cases and gender in Ireland, 1925–50', in M. Valiulis (ed.), *Gender and Power in Irish History* (Irish Academic Press, 2008), pp. 115–40.
26 Mary Daly, '"The Primary and Natural Educator": The role of parents in the education of their children in independent Ireland', *Eire-Ireland* 44:1, Spring/Summer 2009.
27 Dáil Éireann, vol. 14, 5 February 1926, cols 518–19.
28 Ibid.
29 Inspector Book for Wexford District branch NSPCC, 7–30 August 1922 (ISPCC, Limerick).
30 Annual Report, Wexford District Branch, 1936, p. 3.
31 In 1933 the president of the branch was the Revd Dr Codd and the vice-presidents were the Revds Dean Rennison and J. Sinnott. The Revd Dr Codd, the Lord Bishop of Ferns, remained the Society's president until his death in 1938. There was, as with most branches, a Ladies' Committee and a League of Pity (the junior branch of the Society). The branch solicitors were M. J. O'Connor and Co.
32 AR Wexford District branch NSPCC, 1934 (ISPCC, Limerick) p. 2.
33 AR Wexford District branch NSPCC, 1937 (ISPCC, Limerick) p. 2.
34 AR Wexford District branch NSPCC, 1939 (ISPCC, Limerick) p. 2.
35 Two published works by past presidents of the British Society are also worth noting: Parr, *The Baby Farmer* and Benjamin Waugh, 'Baby farming', *Contemporary Review*, 57 (January–June 1890), 700–14.
36 For official reports on the Infant Life Protection Act, 1872, see Hansard: Report from the Select Committee on Infant Life Protection (RSCILP), vol. 9 (1908); Report from the Select Committee on the Infant Life Protection Bill (RSCILPB), vol. 13 (1890); Report from the Select Committee on Protection of Infant Life (RSCPIL), vol. 7 (1871); Report from the Select Committee of the House of Lords on the Infant Life Protection Bill and the Safety of Nurse Children Bill (RSCHLILP), vol. 10 (1896).
37 *Irish Times*, 30 November 1905.

38 The period 1933–50 was chosen in this instance as the reports for this period were complete.
39 CF #34 (ISPCC, Limerick). This does not represent the actual case file number as a confidentiality agreement was signed to ensure no names, or numbers would be used in the publication of research.
40 CF#123 (ISPCC, Limerick).
41 CF #52 (ISPCC, Limerick).
42 CF #12 (ISPCC, Limerick).
43 Sample case, AR Dublin branch NSPCC, 1933–34 (ISPCC, Limerick), p. 9.
44 Sample case, AR Dublin branch NSPCC, 1934–35 (ISPCC, Limerick), p. 10.
45 Linda Gordon, 'Single mothers and child neglect, 1880–1920', *American Quarterly*, 27:2 (Summer 1985), 173–92.
46 Ibid., p. 192.
47 Ibid., p. 191.
48 Earner-Byrne, *Mother and Child*, p. 172.
49 CF #118 (ISPCC, Limerick).
50 CF #67 (ISPC, Limerick).
51 *Irish Independent*, 14 April 1915.
52 *Irish Independent*, 13 May 1931.
53 Parr, *The Cruelty Man*, p. 33.
54 CF #78.
55 CF #55.
56 CF #34, Letter from Garda Siochana, Oylegate, to NSPCC Inspector, 16 May 1939 (ISPCC, Limerick).
57 CF #30.
58 CF #156 (ISPCC, Limerick).
59 CF #217 (ISPCC, Limerick).
60 CF #01 (ISPCC, Limerick).
61 *Irish Citizen*, 4 October 1913.
62 Ibid.
63 Sample case, Annual Report of the Dublin District branch NSPCC, 1933–34 (ISPCC, Limerick), p. 7.
64 Sample case, Annual Report of the Dublin District branch NSPCC, 1931–32 (ISPCC, Limerick), p. 10.
65 Ibid., p. 11.
66 Sample case, Annual report of Dublin District branch NSPCC, 1937-38, (ISPCC, Limerick), p.14.
67 *Carrigan Committee Report*, cited in Mark Finnane, 'The Carrigan Committee of 1930–31 and the "moral condition" of the Saorstat', *Irish Historical Studies*, 32:128 (November 2001), 816–36, p. 531.
68 Jacinta Prunty, *Dublin Slums 1800–1925: A Study in Urban Geography* (Irish Academic Press, 1998); Kevin Kearns, *Dublin Tenement Life; Dublin's Lost Heroines: Mammies and Grannies in a Vanished City* (Gill and Macmillan, 2004).
69 Annual Report of the Society of St Vincent de Paul, 1930 (Dublin Diocesan Archives).
70 The orphanage had on average 150 boys per year, cited in the 1923 Report of the Council of Ireland of the Society of the St Vincent de Paul, Ireland (Dublin Diocesan Archives), p. 6.
71 Ibid., p.6.

72 Ibid.
73 Earner-Byrne, *Mother and Child*.
74 Ibid., p. 25.
75 1930 Report of the Council of Ireland of the Society of St Vincent de Paul, Ireland, Byrne Papers (Dublin Diocesan Archives), p. 12.
76 Ibid., p. 29. The president at this time was John A. Glynn and the honorary secretary was Thomas A. Murphy.
77 1928 Report of the Committee of the St Vincent de Paul Male Orphanage, Byrne Papers (Dublin Diocesan Archive), p. 6.
78 1926 Report of the Catholic Male Discharged Prisoners' Aid Committee, Byrne Papers (Dublin Diocesan Archives), p. 2.
79 1925 Report of the Catholic Male Discharged Prisoners' Aid Committee, Byrne Papers (Dublin Diocesan Archives), p. 7.
80 Ibid., p. 9.
81 1926 Report of the Catholic Male Discharged Prisoners' Aid Committee, Byrne Papers (Dublin Diocesan Archives), p. 2.
82 Ibid.
83 1926 Report of the Catholic Male Discharged Prisoners' Aid Committee, Byrne Papers (Dublin Diocesan Archives), p. 3.
84 Sample Case Q, 1928 Report of the Catholic Male Discharged Prisoners' Aid Committee, Byrne Papers (Dublin Diocesan Archives), p. 13.
85 1925 Report of the Catholic Male Discharged Prisoners' Aid Committee, Byrne Papers (Dublin Diocesan Archives, Dublin), p. 8.
86 Sample Case J, 1928 Report of the Catholic Male Discharged Prisoners' Aid Committee, Byrne Papers (Dublin Diocesan Archives), p. 9.
87 'The Legion of Mary' (Dublin Diocesan Archives), p. 1. With regard to the Madgalene laundries in the Irish Free State, the SVDP retreats and the hostel at Harcourt Street are critical to the debate. The yearly retreats began in 1922, and one was held by R. S. Devane. The report states: 'of the girls obtained, it can be asserted confidently that few, if any, would have presented themselves at a Magdalene Laundry. Most of the girls are now in different Magdalene Laundries, but it is doubtful if any of these would have been there but for the Retreats and the subsequent residence in Harcourt Street.'
88 Kearns, *Dublin's Lost Heroines*, p. 61.
89 Ibid., p. 62.
90 Ibid., p. 64.
91 AR Dublin District branch (ISPCC, Limerick), p. 3.
92 AR North Louth, Monaghan and Cavan branch of the NSPCC, 1937 (ISPCC, Limerick).
93 NSPCC Irish Golden Jubilee Commemoration, 1939 (ISPCC, Limerick), pp. 8–14. In 1939, it was decided by that the first Annual Report in Ireland would be reprinted in a commemorative booklet. Notes were placed in the margins regarding the present position of the Society on the issues raised.
94 Ibid., p. 8.
95 Article 42, Section 1, *Bunreacht na hÉireann*.
96 Article 41, Section 1, *Bunreacht na hÉireann*.
97 AR Wexford District branch NSPCC, 1933 (ISPCC, Limerick).
98 Fr Jerome O'Leary, cited in F. Powell and D. Guerin, *Civil Society and Social Policy: Voluntarism in Ireland* (A & A Farmer, 1997), p. 74.

4

Institutionalisation, the State and the NSPCC

Introduction

> The State shall endeavour to ensure that the strength and health of men and women, and the tender age of children shall not be abused and that citizens shall not be forced by economic necessity to enter avocations unsuited to their sex, age or strength. (Article 45.4, Bunreacht na hÉireann)

One of the principal themes addressed in this book is the use of institutionalisation by the State to deal with children whose parents were unable, or deemed unable, to care for them. Institutionalising children in poverty was not a twentieth-century phenomenon in Ireland. Crossman's recent work on children under the Irish Poor Law has demonstrated that institutionalisation was the main option chosen by Poor Law guardians and the State in Ireland in the nineteenth century, unlike Scotland for example, where the boarding-out system was utilised to a much greater extent.[1] This chapter will elaborate on how this process continued into the twentieth century. Although the establishment of industrial schools and reformatories was a British initiative, and one that was followed in many other Western societies in the nineteenth century,[2] from the 1920s institutionalisation was increasingly criticised in Britain, other European states and the United States, and preference was given to alternatives such as boarding-out and adoption.[3] This chapter will question why successive Irish governments continued to choose institutionalisation, and the extent to which the NSPCC and the Catholic Church were complicit in the maintenance of this system. Although reformatories and juvenile delinquency will also be considered in this discussion, the principal focus is the industrial school system, due to the sheer number of children who were committed to the schools and the direct involvement of NSPCC inspectors in their committal by the courts.

The story of Ireland's industrial schools in the twentieth century has received much attention from the media and a small number of historians and sociologists over the past fifteen years. This attention has focused on the abuse and neglect suffered by past residents. In 1996, the documentary *Dear Daughter,* which described Christine Buckley's experiences in Goldenbridge industrial school, represented a first look at the abuse suffered by past residents in Ireland. Following on from this in April 1999, the Irish television station RTÉ aired a three-part series, *States of Fear*, that documented the experiences of former residents of the industrial school system in Ireland.[4] The programme caused widespread debate on the schools, and in the weeks that followed, the media was filled with stories from former residents. On 11 May 2009, the Irish State issued a public apology to 'the victims of childhood abuse', while also announcing the setting up of a commission to investigate allegations made by victims. Also in 1999, Mary Raftery and Eoin O'Sullivan's seminal book *Suffer the Little Children*,[5] succeeded in illuminating a very recent chapter in modern Irish history, one which has yet to be fully addressed. Throughout this period and up to the present time, the public disclosures and personal testimonies of those who were resident in these institutions have had far-reaching implications for the Catholic Church and to a lesser extent the State. In May 2009, the Report of the Commission to Inquire into Child Abuse (the Ryan Report) described the emotional, physical and sexual abuse that occurred in the industrial schools as 'systematic' and 'endemic'.[6] Since the publication of the report, Bruce Arnold's *The Irish Gulag: How the State Betrayed its Innocent Children*[7] has shed further light on the State's role. This work and others raise the central question of culpability with regard to the schools. On the whole, Arnold argues that 'the real culprit was and is the State, which is still floundering over child protection'.[8]

In this discussion, the analysis will focus primarily on the involvement of the NSPCC in recommending and facilitating the removal of children to State institutions, as well as the State's use of industrial schools. The Society's responsibility is one which has not been fully discussed in the historiography, although the Ryan Report states that 'it played an important role in committing children to Industrial Schools'.[9] The Society's role as a virtual semi-State body is also critical, as the Society's officers were allowed to informally and formally act as school attendance officers in areas where they were not in place (principally outside of Dublin). Following an outline of the development of the industrial school system from the nineteenth century, the chapter will centre on a number of key questions: what was the attitude of the State to the use of industrial schools and reformatories after independence? What were the findings of the Commission of Inquiry into the Reformatory and Industrial School System (Cussen Committee)[10] in 1936? What was the NSPCC's official policy with regard to industrial schools? What was the attitude of the Society and the State to juvenile delinquency? Why were alternatives such as boarding-out and adoption rarely chosen? Finally, testimony from past residents of their experience of the NSPCC inspectors will be discussed.

Industrial schools in the nineteenth century – child protection or social control?

Harry Hendrick argues that the establishment of reformatory and industrial schools in the mid-nineteenth century was representative of a more comprehensive process that had been developing since the end of the eighteenth century in which the criminal justice code was being 'reordered'.[11] The justifications Hendrick points to are similar to those that have been put forward with regard to the industrial schools and reformatories in Ireland in the twentieth century. Justifications such as poorly trained staff, voluntary staff (or, in the Irish context, individuals ordained as priests and nuns, not always as teachers), under-funded schools and 'unruly' children ignore the enormity of the situation and the culpability of many different influential forces. In order to address these influences it is necessary to look at the establishment of the system, and in particular the connection of the Irish industrial school system with the prison system generally.

Hendrick argues that in Britain and Ireland in the nineteenth century, industrial schools and reformatories represented a system of control of the working class, as well as a means of managing poverty and destitution in working-class, urban families and rural labouring families. Prior to establishment of these schools, the workhouse was the primary institution catering for destitute children. By 1853, 77,000 children below fifteen years were living in workhouses.[12] Although proposals were put forward to give contributions directly to families, the workhouse and Poor Law system were repeatedly chosen, as they maintained the stigma attached to the 'charity' of the State. In reference to the industrial schools, reformatories and other institutions, alternative systems such as the boarding out of children and outdoor relief were never preferred by the Poor Law guardians or the State, perhaps due to the fact that institutions represented a more effective method of social and religious control.[13]

Initially, reformatories were set up by voluntary organisations to cater for 'juvenile delinquents' and, following the 1868 Industrial Schools Act, residential schools for vagrant and neglected children were also opened. By the 1880s these schools included those children who had been abused or labelled 'truants', and over the following years the expansion of the categories of children included would continue to grow.[14] The first reformatory in Ireland was established in 1858,[15] while the first industrial school[16] was opened in Sandymount, Dublin, in 1869. By 1875 there were fifty industrial schools, and the highest number was reached in 1898, when there were a total of seventy-one schools of which sixty-one (fifty-six schools for Catholics and five for Protestants) were in what would later become the twenty-six counties of the Irish Free State. At its height in 1898, the population in the industrial schools was 7,998, compared with 6,000 in the same year in the workhouse.[17] That the number of children in industrial schools had outnumbered those in the workhouse is significant, and demonstrates that the schools did have an effect on the placement of children in the workhouse. The word committal is also key to the differentiation between workhouse (later County Homes) and industrial schools. 105,000 children were committed to industrial schools by the courts between 1868 and 1969, with 15,899 children committed to reformatory schools in the same period.[18] With regard to the relationship between industrial schools and reformatories, from the 1920s, the distinction between both would be increasingly highlighted by those in government, and the decrease in numbers being sent to reformatories would result in an increase in those being sent to industrial schools. Again, it appears that industrial schools were more politically palatable than the reformatories or the workhouse.

With regard to administration, in the original Reformatory Schools Act, it was provided that 'the office of Inspector of Reformatory Schools must be held by one of the Directors of Convict Prisons, or one of the Inspectors-General of Prisons, or such Special Inspector as the Lord Lieutenant might appoint'.[19] In Ireland, the first Industrial Schools Act (1868) directed that the Inspector of Reformatories should also be the Inspector of Industrial Schools. From the establishment of the reformatory system in 1858 until 1927 (with the exception of the period 1890 to 1906) the Inspector of Reformatory and Industrial Schools also held a position in the prison service. In 1890 it was decided to appoint an inspector with a focus on education and punitive measures, but in 1906 the connection with the prison service was again resumed. In 1924, the general supervision of the system was transferred to the Minister for Education, and in 1928 the connection with the Inspectorate of the Prison Service ceased. Two inspectors, one male and one female, were appointed. What is noteworthy is the continuing association of the industrial school system with the prison system. Also, with regard to the NSPCC, in a letter from the Inspector of Reformatory and Industrial Schools in 1917, it is interesting to note that the offices were located on 19 Molesworth Street, Dublin. This was right next door to the offices of the NSPCC, and the Children's Shelter, at 20 Molesworth Street.

Juvenile delinquency, reformatory schools and borstals

Before looking at the specifics of the juvenile justice system in Ireland, it is necessary to establish the theoretical arguments on the concept of juvenile delinquency. In his article on juvenile justice in Ireland, Eoin O'Sullivan examines the construction and ideology of the juvenile justice apparatus from the 1850s. He argues that the objective of the system was 'to correct and reform the children of the dangerous and perishing classes',[20] and its role was 'firstly ... a function of the intersecting structures and purpose[s] of the adult criminal justice and child care systems, and secondly as an element in a steady expansion of State control over the working class young'.[21] Through the development of reformatories, industrial schools, borstal institutions and the Children's Court, children convicted of minor offences were ushered into a punitive, repressive and prison-like system of institutions. Theoretically, Anthony Platt argues that the juvenile justice system represented part of a general movement directed towards developing a specialised labour market and discipline under corporate capitalism.[22] With regard to the child welfare movement, Christopher Lasch contends that the system represented the creation and maintenance of the child welfare movement apparatus, comprising the formalisation of control by one group over another.[23] Included in this group were teachers, social workers and doctors, all forming the controlling group and exercising their will over the working classes. As a result of both, however, the family was undermined, and the professional experts substituted parents. These measures were not unique to Ireland, but as institutional measures introduced in the late nineteenth century were removed or reformed in Britain and the United States in favour of specialist homes and an emphasis on the psychology of adolescence by the 1930s, the nineteenth-century institutional approached remained. In order to examine why and how this occurred, the British developments will be briefly addressed.

By 1921 the juvenile crime rate in Britain had decreased, yet, as Hendrick notes, there remained 'an intense interest' in the problem of juvenile delinquency. In 1925 the Departmental Committee on the Treatment of Young Offenders investigated the juvenile court system.[24] The Committee unanimously agreed that the 1908 Children Act was insufficient to deal with the issue of juvenile delinquency, and distinctions would need to be made to differentiate the treatment of children from adults in the court system. Even withstanding the aims of the committee, the central issue of 'justice versus welfare' remained unresolved. This issue is crucial when assessing both Britain and Ireland. As early as 1917, the Penal Reform League in Britain had called for psychological studies of children classed as juvenile delinquents. Similarly, from the 1920s, medical, legal and child-study journals had begun to address the issue of psychology in reducing the prevalence of juvenile delinquency. The period was heralded as one of transformation of the issue of punishment in relation to children, with the amalgamation of industrial and reformatory schools into 'approved schools', and an emphasis on reinstating 'order' in society. One of the central elements of this debate was the issue of child neglect and parental responsibility. In 1927 the Report of the Departmental Committee on the Treatment of Young Offenders specifically addressed the issue of 'neglected' children. The Committee looked at people who were 'the victims of cruelty and other offences committed by adults and those whose natural guardianship proved insufficient or unworthy of trust'.[25] The result was the 1933 Children and Young Persons Act. In effect, the act brought three groups of children together: offenders, neglected children and child victims of offences. The concept of neglect had been developed and expanded and was now seen as an aspect of crime in the broadest sense. As Harry Hendrick argues, 'the term "protection" hardly referred to protecting children from "cruel" treatment by parents; rather, it referred to "protecting" children from the criminal and moral consequences of parental "neglect".[26] The distinction meant that neglect now referred to exposure to conditions that could lead to criminality or immorality; or, in many cases, that parents seen to be neglectful were now contaminating children.

With regard to the 1933 act and the amalgamation of industrial schools, the legislation did not radically alter daily conditions in the institutions. What it did do, however, was increase the inspection powers of the Home Office and increase the use of boarding-out to deal with children sent to the juvenile courts. In general, Hendrick argues that from the late nineteenth century to the late 1940s juvenile institutions in Britain did not change dramatically, and it would not be until the Curtis Committee Report in 1948 that a new era of child care for the 'public' child would emerge. Yet in Ireland, the State repeatedly chose to adhere to the nineteenth-century institutional approach to child care. The disparity in the Irish and British situations did not go unnoticed. In 1939 Deputy James Dillon addressed the Dáil on the issue of Children's Courts, stating:

> If the conditions surrounding juvenile delinquency in this country were known in Great Britain or in America, we would be scandalised. In the worst and most backward city in America conditions such as we have in this country would not be tolerated for a house. In no part of England would such conditions as at present obtain here be present for an hour.[27]

The issue of children's courts was continuously addressed by the NSPCC, in the Cussen Report and in the Dáil, yet the situation remained unchanged. The principal issue was that outside of the juvenile court in Dublin, children who were being committed to industrial schools, tried with minor offences such as simple larceny or even more serious offences, were forced to stand up in an adult court with a (primarily) adult audience. While the State had been so careful to protect fathers in incest cases and maintenance cases, it seems that 'juvenile delinquents' did not deserve the same sensitivity. In 1938, Deputy Dillon had previously addressed the issue of juvenile delinquency in the context of parental responsibility:

> The matter of juvenile delinquency should be approached, in my submission, from one point of view and one point of view only, and that is, are the parents able to look after the child? If, after ample inquiry, it appears that the parents are wholly incapable and that the child will go to the devil unless taken out of their hands, then, and only then, should the State take over the child.[28]

In 1927 the Public Safety Act in Ireland placed liability on parents or guardians for certain young offenders. In response, the Women's International League for Peace and Freedom recorded their conviction that 'such coercive legislation, by increasing the difficulty of constitutional legislation ... increases the danger of recourse to violence'. Similarly, William J. Cosgrave, a Justice of the Peace, urged the government to 'give some attention to the poor people'.[29] Extraordinarily, from a bureaucratic perspective, the Children's Courts, reformatories and borstals all came under the Department of Justice, while places of detention for juvenile delinquents and industrial schools came under the Department of Education. What this meant was that departments could regularly defer responsibility on matters relating to the institutional apparatus. In 1937 three principal issues arising from juvenile delinquency were addressed in the Dáil: the need to abolish the trying of juvenile delinquents in the courtroom, the exclusion of the public from proceedings conducted before the children's district judge, and the inclusion of the press. At the same meeting, Deputy Dillon drew attention to the need for probation officers in other urban areas apart from Dublin. He also requested the abolition of reformatories and borstal institutions. Interestingly, with regard to the Report of the Commission of Inquiry into Reformatory and Industrial Schools, the deputy stated that he could not find the report: 'it is not in the Library so that one is rather handicapped in examining the question.'[30] While the Cussen Report was published, the lack of availability of the report to the deputy suggests that the government was not eager to go through the conclusions – particularly as many of them pointed to a lack of resources and training and to generally inhumane conditions.

In general, what emerged from debates in the 1930s was the financial concern of the Departments of Education and Finance in the running of reformatories and special homes. As with industrial schools, institutions only appear to have been seen as redundant when the number of children in them outweighed the grants being provided. That this approach existed at State level explains much with regard to the religious orders actively seeking children for the industrial schools in particular. The Department of Education did come under scrutiny by some deputies in the Dáil, particularly Deputy Dillion. In 1937 he stated in the Dáil:

> I said yesterday, when referring to the Department of Justice Vote, that in regard to this matter of juvenile delinquency, the Department of Education was dead from the neck up. I wish I thought that was not true, but I must say that my experience of the Department of Education in connection with this whole matter is that they are antediluvian in outlook. They think of this whole problem in terms of 40 years ago, and they allow their whole judgement to be vitiated by the representations of the Department of Finance. If they would take a bold line in the matter of juvenile delinquency, they could blow the bottom out of the representations of the Department of Finance without slightest difficulty.[31]

Aside from a critique of the Children's Court, borstal institutions and reformatories, Deputy Dillon referred to the 'mentally affected' children in need of specialised medical and psychological care. That these children were being placed in punitive institutions as opposed to specialist facilities was labelled outrageous by the deputy. In contrast to Dillon, most deputies continued to argue for increased funding for reformatories and borstals. Deputy Gerard McGowan, in particular, repeatedly brought up the fantastic operation of Glencree institution, lamenting its need for increased funding from the Department of Finance.

The highlighting of the benefits of Glencree at this stage was not as popular as it would have been previously. In his recent work on the Clonmel borstal, Conor Reidy has demonstrated the changing attitudes to juvenile delinquency and borstal institutions in Ireland and Britain from 1906 to 1956. Placing the establishment of the borstal in the context of penal measures and developments from the end of the eighteenth century, Reidy states the book's intention as an institutional history of Clonmel borstal, not 'a comprehensive analysis of juvenile crime and its punishment'.[32] He also states that until more work has been done on 'the juvenile delinquent' and the institutional provision for young offenders, comparisons should not be made between treatment in industrial schools, reformatories and borstals. Yet one of the significant factors in the story of the borstal in Ireland is the after-care received by inmates, due to the borstal association of Ireland. It appears that unlike industrial schools, this group did have a positive effect on past residents, although the similarities of the conditions in the borstal to that of prisons can never be underestimated. In order to further address these issues it is necessary to look in more detail at the discourse surrounding juvenile delinquency in the press and by the NSPCC.

Discourse on juvenile delinquency

The discourse surrounding juvenile delinquency was not only limited to the Oireachtas. Throughout the 1930s particularly, the press carried a variety of stories on the issue. While much of the *Irish Independent*'s coverage centred on the clergy and the connections being made between the cinema, dances, motor cars and juvenile delinquency; the *Irish Times* regularly reported the views of the NSPCC and international trends in treating the perceived problem of juvenile delinquency. In 1936, in an article entitled 'The failure of democracy: The increase of juvenile delinquency', a sermon by the Revd P. L. Cannon was cited:

> It was certain that juvenile delinquency to-day was definitely on the increase. Instances of perfectly appalling depravity, callousness, and almost bestial brutality were before the Courts, where the culprits were still in their teens. And, in general, young boys and girls just out of school were more inclined, since the Great War, to run amok. This was more marked in the case of young girls.[33]

In an article in the *Irish Independent* in 1938, the rise in juvenile delinquency was attributed by the Recorder of Derry to 'unemployment, dance halls and the cinema'. Again in 1939, the *Irish Independent* covered a sermon by R. S. Devane, examining how far the cinema was responsible for juvenile crime. In 1937, at a meeting on juvenile delinquency and probation held by the Society of Friends at Eustace Street, Mary Kettle said that 'most countries had improved their methods of dealing with juvenile delinquents, but in the Free State they had a long way to go'. She continued to compare Ireland and Britain, arguing that while Britain may have had more money at its disposal to spend on social services, 'social services were not national extravagance – they were national economy'. Highlighting the lack of probation officers, and the lack of a Women's Police Force, she quoted the Minister for Justice who had suggested that the NSPCC could act as such a force, and voluntary workers could be used as probation officers. In response she stated: 'anyone dealing with the problem knew that they must have paid and trained officials for efficient service'.[34] That the Minister seriously suggested such a course demonstrates the attitude to juvenile delinquency. As noted in Chapter 3, the SVDP was already visiting the families of juvenile offenders to encourage parents to take responsibility for their actions, as well as acting as probation officers to those prisoners who had lived in Britain. Now the minister was suggesting that there should be more posts for NSPCC inspectors, who were already acting as school attendance officers in many rural areas, children's police in all areas and court representatives in cases involving removals to industrial schools. This is one reason why the NSPCC was so critical to the debate on delinquency.

From the 1920s, in keeping with trends in the SPCCs in Britain and the United States, the NSPCC began equating the situation of the neglected child with that of the delinquent child. However, while this occurred outside Ireland, there was now a structure of special homes in place in Britain and the United States, and a greatly reformed children's court. This was not the case in Ireland, and young boys in particular continued to be pushed through an adult system into reformatories, borstals and industrial schools. For many, NSPCC inspectors' recommendations brought them and their parents to the attention of the court under a new category of neglect, 'failure to exercise proper guardianship'. From the 1930s, this category appears prominently in both the Society's reports and case files. In a case in 1938, the adopted parents of a ten-year-old boy were investigated for 'neglect'. The inspector recorded: 'the boy is illegitimate and undoubtedly drifting into a life of crime'. After numerous supervision visits the parents were asked to maintain the boy, but in 1939 they approached the inspector, claiming he was staying out and stealing money. The inspector recorded: 'the boy appears to be utterly out of control and parents are not firm with the lad.'[35] Although they continued to request his removal to an industrial school, eventually the parents agreed to hold onto the boy. In many instances, however, inspectors encouraged parents to send children to schools for reformation. As with the committal of children to industrial schools, the Society was involved in institutionalising children. While this was far from their aim or possibly preferred option, as the State continued to drag its heels on issues of child protection, the Society assumed the roles it could in independent Ireland. By 1965, most committals to industrial schools involved a charge of lack of proper guardianship – demonstrating the NSPCC's influence in this regard.

In 1963, the number of juveniles convicted for indictable offences was 3,268, or 41 per cent of the total number convicted of juvenile offences. This slowly decreased over the coming years, and in 1967 the figure was 2,963, or 31 per cent of the total.

Irish over-reliance on industrial schools

With regard to the initial years of the industrial school system in Ireland, the Cussen Report states that the system was at first 'imperfectly understood'. In 1870, addressing the Statistical Society of Ireland, the Lord Lieutenant drew attention 'to the advantages and to the social order which would soon follow on the establishment of the Industrial Schools'.[36] He continued by highlighting the fact that in Ireland, the number of criminals other than vagrants and tramps known to the police was less than half the number in an equal proportion in England and Wales; while the relative number of tramps and vagrants under sixteen years was the reverse. The Cussen Committee argued that this increased the opinion among the public that the schools were for young criminals. Table 4.1 further demonstrates the greater use of the schools in Ireland early on, signifying that the Irish reliance on industrial schools for the care of children was not a twentieth-century phenomenon and reaffirming Crossman's analysis of children under the Irish Poor Law. It is also worth noting that both the workhouses and industrial schools were under the control of local boards and authorities. Their responsibility will be addressed at numerous points in this analysis. Also, it is worth noting the fact that there was much concern by the turn of the century regarding the numbers of children in Irish industrial schools.

In the year under examination (1881), 472 boys and 730 girls were placed in industrial schools and 231 boys and thirty-eight girls were placed in reformatories.[37] As Raftery and O'Sullivan have shown, this unequal distribution of girls and boys in both institutions continued to be a consistent trend throughout the twentieth century.

Table 4.1 Number of children in industrial schools in Ireland, England and Wales in 1881

	Ireland	England & Wales	Difference
Total number under detention	7,288	2,677	4,611
Under detention at beginning of year	6,086	2,019	4,067
Received during year	1,202	658	544
Disposed of during year	1,009	584	425
Under detention at end of year	6,279	2,093	4,186

Numbers for England and Wales are given for a proportion of the population equal to the population of Ireland. Figures taken from the Criminal and Judicial Statistics for Ireland, 1882 (C3355), 75, p. 243.

Table 4.2 Number of boys and girls committed to reformatories in 1881

	Boys	Girls	Percentage boys	Percentage girls
Total committed	231	38	100	100
Illegitimate, deserted, or one or both parents destitute or criminal	83	17	36	45
Under control of parents, other than above	81	9	35	24
One parent dead	31	8	13	21
Total orphans	36	4	16	10

Figures taken from the Criminal and Judicial Statistics for Ireland 1882 (C3355), 75, p. 243.

Table 4.3 Breakdown by sex of those sent to industrial schools and reformatories in 1881

	Men and boys	Women and girls	Total	Percentage
Industrial schools	2,414	3,486	5,900	38.6
Reformatories	936	213	1,149	7.4

Figures taken from the Criminal and Judicial Statistics for Ireland 1882 (C3355), 75, p. 243.

With reference to the grounds for committal, in a subsequent report in 1899, of the 955 children committed to industrial schools, the 'cause' of over half of the committals was either 'found begging or receiving alms' or 'wandering and not having proper guardianship'.[38] In the reformatory returns for the same year, seventy-four of the 122 committals were for larceny and petty theft. The figures suggest that in both industrial schools and reformatories poverty was the primary factor in children's placement. In reference to the greater use of schools in Ireland, the 1882 report states:

> It appears that in Ireland the persons held in confinement for punishment or reform under the law, are more numerous than in the corresponding portion of England and Wales ... the proportion of children in Industrial Schools is 53.6 per cent, as compared with 23.7 per cent in England and Wales. As there is no other form of compulsory education in Ireland except industrial schools, these institutions are made much use of.[39]

Again the notion that the industrial school system had been 'imperfectly understood' in Ireland is apparent. However, if, as the report states, the lack of compulsory education was the primary factor in the extensive use of the schools in the late nineteenth century, why did this situation continue through to the late twentieth century when compulsory primary education was in place? Ironically, legislation put in place to ensure that all children received a primary education resulted in many being placed in schools where they did not receive one.

From 1929, the School Attendance Act (1926) in conjunction with the Children Act (1929) would be used by the courts to commit children to industrial schools for non-attendance at primary school. In principle, the School Attendance Act was supposed to ensure that all children up to the age of fourteen years received a primary education, in keeping with international trends in education in the period. In reality, there were economic reasons why many children were not sent to school, and because legislation was introduced without compensating parents for the loss of a wage in an urban context – or a worker in a rural context – parents were criminalised for their poverty, while children were punished. Many families relied on the contributions of eldest children in particular, as without social welfare and with high poverty levels many families could not survive on one smaller wage or, in cases of unemployment, no wage. Although families in rural districts often managed to avoid 'discovery' by the NSPCC, this was not the case in Dublin, which had five inspectors and five school-attendance officers. What was so perverse about the use of the act to commit children was that, as Arnold states, 'in no educative sense were these institutions "schools".'[40] The use of institutionalisation as a solution to perceived social problems extended beyond the industrial schools to lunatic asylums, workhouses, reformatories, borstals, Magdalene laundries and prisons. Throughout the nineteenth and twentieth centuries the State consistently chose institutionalisation over support for the family. This does not mean that it ignored families, but it acted in a way that separated, as opposed to assisted, families in poverty. Even with corporal punishment still legal, the brutality many children faced daily in the industrial schools was unjustifiable, as the Ryan Report has demonstrated, and as it was the State that had ultimate financial and regulatory control, its role will now be assessed.

Institutionalisation and the State in independent Ireland, 1920–40

> in the main, as far as Industrial Schools are concerned, the problem is one not of criminal tendencies, but of poverty.[41]

The following quote from Joseph E. Cavanan's review of the 1927 *Report into the Relief of the Sick and Destitute Poor* sums up the mentality of many of those in influential positions with regard to children in poverty in the first decades of independent Ireland: 'by utilising both the system of boarding out and the Industrial Schools, the Report provides well for the children of the destitute poor who are not entitled to Home Assistance.'[42] The fact that home assistance was not enough to maintain a family or that boarding-out was very rarely chosen left only the industrial schools for most parents in poverty. When discussing the increasing use of industrial schools from the 1920s, two significant changes must be addressed. Firstly, the State's abolition of the Poor Law meant that the workhouse would no longer be the chosen option for families in poverty to seek temporary respite. Although the county homes were basically the workhouses renamed, there was a significant decrease in the numbers seeking aid from the 1920s, due both to the stigma attached and the regulations in the homes. Secondly, international discourse surrounding the rights of children and changing conceptions of delinquency began to permeate official discourse, with the result that the reformatories were now viewed as a less desirable option. Over the coming years, the numbers being sent to reformatories decreased, as the numbers entering industrial schools increased. Yet while this discourse on delinquency in Britain resulted in legislation to reform industrial schools and set up specialist, more humane provision for children and families, in Ireland, debates on industrial schools were almost exclusively focused on the financial aspect. In the Oireachtas debates, aside from a few dissenting voices, concerns centred on the trades that children were being taught, whether agriculture was being sufficiently catered for, and how much should be spent on the schools. Before looking at these debates, the administration and management of the schools from 1922 must be addressed.

In 1924 the industrial school system came under the control of the Minister for Education. At this time the 1908 Children Act was the principal legislation covering the committal of children to schools. As noted, the act was a landmark in the history of child protection, and in Ireland many of its clauses would remain in force until the Child Care Act of 1991. Under the 1908 Act, the Minister for Education had the following functions: the certification of schools; the withdrawal of certificates from schools; approval of school rules; approval of alterations to buildings etc; the conditional or unconditional discharge of a children from detention; discharge from supervision; the transfer of a child to another industrial school; the amount of government contribution to schools (subject to the Department of Finance); remission of payments ordered to be paid by parents and the making of various orders and regulations. With regard to the grounds for committal, the 1908 Act (and later the 1926 School Attendance Act and 1929 Children Act) covered numerous situations, ranging from children under fourteen years found begging, destitute, orphaned, without a parent or guardian, in the company of a reputed thief, etc, to 'a daughter, whether legitimate or illegitimate of a parent who has been convicted of an offence under the Criminal Law Amendment Acts 1885 to 1935' (as stated in one clause). In general there were very few instances, if the case was argued, in which a child could not be sent to an industrial school. This would be particularly relevant with reference to the evidence of NSPCC inspectors in the courts. Also, the fact that the 1926 and 1929 acts extended and strengthened the grounds for committal demonstrates the intentions of the first Irish Free State government with regard to the schools. With respect to the management of the schools, in 1934 six of the senior boys' schools were run by the Irish Christian Brothers, one by the Presentation Brothers, two by the Order of Charity and two by the Committees of Management (Board of Governors), the managers of these being priests. The girls' schools were managed as follows: one by the Poor Clares; twenty-two by the Sisters of Mercy; four by the Sisters of the Good Shepherd; four by the Sisters of Charity; one by the Sisters of Our Lady of Refuge; one by the Sisters of Saint Louis; and two by the Sisters of the Presentation Order. Three of the junior boys' schools and the mixed school for girls and junior boys were run by the Sisters of Mercy, while the Irish Sisters of Charity and the Sisters of Charity of the St Vincent de Paul each ran one junior boys' school.

Committee to inquire into the reformatory and industrial school system (1934–36)

From the establishment of the Irish Free State, there had been calls to investigate the reformatory and industrial school system. In 1934, this was finally addressed with the setting up of the Commission to Inquire into the Reformatory and Industrial School System. The chairman was George Cussen, a senior justice for the Dublin District Court. The committee comprised: the Revd Joseph McArdle, Mrs Mary Hackett, Mr Joseph Hanna from the Department of Finance, Dr Patrick MacCarvill, Mr Seamus O'Farrell, Mrs Angela Russell, and Mr Prionsias Ó Tighearnaigh, the deputy chief inspector of the Department of Education. All members were resident in Dublin. The committee sat for thirty-eight days to hear evidence and consider the report. Twenty-seven witnesses were examined. Special invitation for evidence was given to a number of groups, most notably: probation officers (only in place in Dublin), the Christian Brothers, the Industrial School Managers Association, the NSPCC, the SVDP, the Catholic Rescue and Protection Society of Ireland, the Dublin Trades Council, the Irish Women Citizens' and Local Government Association, Dublin Corporation and the Departments of Education, Justice and Local Government and Public Health. While evidence was received from numerous interested parties, and a report and questionnaire was required from each of the schools along with a visit, much of the emphasis appears to be on Dublin. Also, as the visit to the schools was scheduled, it is difficult to accept all findings as regular or normal.

The report is extensive, covering eighty-two pages including appendices. The fifty 'principal recommendations' provide a glimpse at the committee's findings. The recommendations included: wider discretion for Justices and the Minister for Education with regard to committals; the abolishment of the term 'Committal Order' to 'Admission Order'; the establishment of children's courts outside of Dublin; more variety of diet in the schools; more contact of pupils with the outside world; proper recreation periods; better medical attendance; better standards of education and properly trained teachers; and legislation dealing with the 'general problem of mental defectiveness'. It appears that one of the principal reasons for the investigation was the association of industrial schools and reformatories with the prison system. A change of name was therefore suggested: industrial schools would be renamed 'National Boarding Schools' and reformatories would become 'Approved Schools'. The committee acknowledged the inadequacy in education and training in some schools, particularly farming training, which was of concern to them as the pupils in the schools were there to be trained in skills that would be beneficial to the country. It acknowledged the low pay levels of teachers, the fact that many were not qualified as teachers and the need for better inspection of schools. In reference to the NSPCC, the report stated that better cooperation between schools and charitable organisations should be enlisted in the work of after-care. It was the responsibility of schools to provide after-care, although evidence in the Ryan Report has shown that in most schools, after-care consisted of pupils being transferred to unpaid manual labour.

Interestingly, boarding-out and alternatives to industrial schools weressimil mentioned only briefly in one paragraph of the report. It stated:

> Evidence was given in support of the system of boarding out children as an alternative to their committal to Industrial Schools, and we consider the system capable of extension in suitable cases. We suggest that where a child who has been boarded out with foster parents attains the age of 5 years and the foster parents are suitable persons and desire to keep the child, a payment which, we think, might be at the rate of 11s per week should be made to the responsible Local Authority to the foster parents until the child reaches the age of 10 years, such payment to cease if at any time it is shown to the satisfaction of a Justice that it would be in the child's interest to send it to an Industrial School. We consider that expenditure by the Local Authority under this head should be subject to recoupment to the extent of 50 per cent by the State.[43]

There are a number of issues to be addressed concerning this recommendation. Firstly, the fact that payment stopped at ten years would not entice foster parents to continue to keep a child, given the economic situation for families in the period. Secondly, the amount given to schools per child was roughly 11s per week. This shows a commitment on the part of neither the State nor the local authorities to increase the number of children being boarded-out. While the report was welcome, as the Kennedy Report and later the Ryan Report would demonstrate, the recommendations on diet, pupil numbers, teacher qualifications, after-care, holidays, etc, were never implemented. In fact, it appears that from the 1930s, the conditions in schools continued to degenerate.

While punishment, abuse and neglect were not addressed, some of the committee's findings should perhaps have sparked greater attention. With regard to recreation, the report stated:

> In many schools (particularly girls' schools) at the time of our visit playing fields were not provided. In one school for girls near the City of Dublin we found that although there were several areas of grazing land (the prop-

erty of the School Authorities) surrounding the school, the girls were not allowed to play in the fields save on Church holidays, and had to take all their recreation in a flagged or concrete yard; and although the school was convenient to the sea, the children were never brought to play on the strand ... in some schools monotonous marching round a school yard took the place of free play at the time of recreation.[44]

The sections of medical inspection and care were even more worrying. The report cited the pay of four school medical attendants in 1935. In School A, the medical attendant was paid £4 10s a year to care for eighty-nine children. In School D, the doctor received £11 for the year. As the report states: 'we consider he could not be expected to provide adequate medical attention at the rates of remuneration at present'. Yet the Minister for Education had ultimate control over rates of pay. It is not possible in this chapter to elaborate on the other sections of the report, particularly those dealing with training and education, but in 1970 when the next report on industrial and reformatory schools was published (commonly known as the Kennedy Report), it became very clear that even the small changes suggested by the Cussen Committee were not put in place. Whether there was any opposition in the Dáil or Seanad will now be addressed.

Oireactas debates

From 1922, there were a minority of dissenting voices in the Dáil and Seanad on the issue of industrial schools, most notably Deputies J. Dillon, S. Moore, T. Johnson and A. Byrne. These did not cause great change or uproar, but their investigation reveals much about the attitude of successive Ministers for Education to the schools. In 1923 Deputy Johnson questioned the then Minister for Education, Professor O'Sullivan, on how the capitation grant for each child in the industrial schools was being spent. He compared the breakdown of expenses he was requesting to the costing submitted by the managers in Dundrum Asylum. The following was O'Sullivan's response:

> We have no direct control over this institution. Dundrum Asylum is different; it is a State institution. Every item of expenditure is sanctioned by Government authority; scales of pay and clothing allowances are sanctioned by the Treasury. These schools are independent bodies, which carry on their work in their own way, subject to inspection and general regulations, but they are not subject to financial control. They simply received the grants fixed a considerable number of years ago, which they now allege to be insufficient.[45]

The grants to which the minister was referring were quite substantial at the time, averaging roughly £100,000 per year. Each child was to be kept on 11s per week, almost twice the home assistance given to whole families. That no one considered giving this money directly to families is significant, considering that it was accepted that poverty was the principal reason for children's committals. It also demonstrates that while the financial aspect of the schools remained the State's concern, the State was not willing to support families in poverty as an alternative, as this would have meant the closure of institutions now run solely by the Catholic Church. The alternative of institutionalisation, boarding-out, was dealt with on a small number of occasions in the Dáil, as was the decreasing number of children being sent to reformatories, and the increasing number being sent to industrial schools. In 1922, Deputy O'Connell stated:

> Industrial Schools are very largely agencies for the keeping of children who might otherwise be destitute and who in former days to some extent were kept in the Workhouses. There is a sort of controversy going on between boarding-out and the conduct of Industrial Schools on enlightened lines. In some parts of the country, as far as my own experience went, the boarding-out system was exceedingly successful. In other parts of the country the boarding-out system has been the reverse of successful and it has been thought it would be very much better to use Industrial Schools. For that purpose the Industrial Schools ought to be separated entirely from the Reformatories if Reformatories are continued, and the whole Association ought to be ended. That is a thing I think is agreed upon and will be accomplished before long.[46]

What the Oireachtas debates demonstrate is awareness that there were problems associated with placing children. However, discourse did not surround the closure of schools; instead, it centred on the decreasing reliance on reformatories and increasing use of industrial schools. Consecutive Ministers for Education remained stalwart in their backing of the schools. In 1927, Deputy Johnson pushed the Minister for Education to consider issues surrounding the schools:

> I do not want to press the Minister now on this matter, but I would suggest that he should take advantage of the opportunity when the new Estimate comes forward to give the House some information as to the policy regarding industrial schools, and whether there has been any change in the administration, any new policy adopted regarding committals. I would also like him to compare the figures at the present time with the figures, say, pre-1916, perhaps even pre-war, within this area. I think it is important to have some information of that nature, because the whole question is an important one. I hope that there will be an increased interest in this question of industrial schools and the policy of committals, and, further, an interest in the kind of education and training that is given in them. I do not want to press the Minister at this hour, but I would like him to be prepared for a future discussion on this matter.[47]

The subject of inspections also emerged sporadically. In 1931, the following debate took place between Deputies S. Moore, P. Little, R. Anthony and the Minister for Education, Professor O'Sullivan, during a meeting of the Committee for the Finance of Reformatory and Industrial Schools:

Mr. Moore: Is there any inspection of these schools, and is there any report from them to the State in respect of the grants obtained? Does the State determine what trades are to be taught there, and whether agriculture is taught or anything of that kind?

Professor O'Sullivan: The schools are fully inspected.

Mr. Moore: There is no provision in the Estimates for inspection.

Professor O'Sullivan: There are individuals who carry out the inspection. There is actually a lady inspector, [1925] and the chief executive officer does a certain amount of inspection of industrial schools.

Mr. Little: Is there any system of report from the industrial schools?

Professor O'Sullivan: Yes.

Mr. Little: Would such report not state how the pupils who had left the schools were getting on?

Professor O'Sullivan: If the Deputy looks up the report of the Department he will see that a considerable amount of space is devoted to the industrial schools. He will see there are plenty of statistics. The different trades to which the pupils are attached are also set out. I have no evidence that the people, on whose shoulders the responsibility of supervision lies, namely, the managers, are neglecting their duty.

Mr. Little: I am not suggesting they are.

Professor O'Sullivan: There is no duty imposed on us to follow the pupils so far as their after life is concerned; the duty is on the managers.

Mr. Moore: Does the State suggest the curriculum for the schools or interfere with it in any way?

Professor O'Sullivan: We interfere very little with the schools. The curriculum is under debate at the moment between the industrial schools and ourselves. Some of the industrial schools are quite willing to accept the position that less trade work should be done at certain stages, at all events, during the period when the pupils are attached to the schools. Some of the others find a difficulty in changing their present programme. They are essentially the people who will decide the running of the schools. We interfere to a certain extent, but only to a certain extent.

Mr. Moore: Is agriculture taught in these schools?

Professor O'Sullivan: Yes, in quite a number.

Mr. Anthony: Deputy Moore should be aware, as a member of the Committee of Public Accounts, that so far as this question relating to the aftercare of the boys leaving industrial schools is concerned it has been already gone into. He should be satisfied that there is very rigid inspection up to the age of eighteen years. I know of at least one school, the

> Greenmount Industrial School in Cork, and long after the boys leave that school and are apprenticed, or sent out to farms, there are very frequent reports as to how they are getting on. I do not know what Deputy Moore has in mind.
>
> Mr. Moore: It might be necessary to remind Deputy Anthony that what takes place at the Committee of Public Accounts is confidential.
>
> Mr. Anthony: Yes, but the Deputy should know what took place there, and he should not ask the Minister such a question.[48]

What echoes throughout the debate is the Minister for Education's lack of knowledge about the schools and eagerness to pass responsibility to the religious orders. This attitude of 'non-interference' may have appeared the easiest option for the minister and the State, but the schools were funded by the State and the children inside were the State's responsibility. Not only that, most had been committed by the courts. It is very unlikely a similar stance of 'non-interference' could have been taken with regard to prisons; how was this acceptable in relation to industrial schools? One of the other few questions in the Dáil regarding the schools related to the number of parents/children being prosecuted under the 1908 Children Act. In January 1938, Deputy Archie Heron asked the Minister for Justice, Dr Ryan, if he could state the number of prosecutions brought by the courts over the previous seven years under this act. He also asked for the number of such prosecutions that resulted in convictions, and those of offences covered by the act that did not involve cruelty to children. The Minister responded with a table of offences. In total, there were 1,030 prosecuted cases of cruelty to children, resulting in 387 convictions, and 462 cases in which the charge was proven and no conviction made. The table also shows seventy-eight 'other offences' under the act, which resulted in fifty-five convictions and nine cases where the charge was proven but no conviction made.[49]

The State's attitude to voluntarism is also important in this context. In 1939, at the NSPCC's Golden Jubilee celebrations in Dublin, the Minister for Finance Seán MacEntee, paid tribute to the humane work of the Society which he described as 'indispensable and irreplaceable'. Expanding on this point, the minister highlighted the value of voluntary charity; which is 'particularly important at a time when people are apt carelessly to cast upon the Government the burden of carrying out all social work'.[50] He also observed that 'Bureaucracy must act according to rules and regulations, and cannot take the place of the warm heart and helping hand of voluntary effort'.[51] What the Ryan Report has demonstrated is that voluntary charity as espoused by the minister offered neither a 'warm heart' nor a 'helping hand' for many families and children in institutions. The control of the schools by the Catholic Church, the use of this 'unpaid' workforce by the State and the referral of children by the NSPCC inspectors could have benefited from the watchful eye of the bureaucratic structures in the Department of Education. In 1940, in the parliamentary debates on the Children's Bill, the attitude of the Department of Education was equally revealing. Upon the suggestion by Deputy Dillon that the presentation of medical and psychological reports of children to the District Justice before committals should be compulsory, the Minister for Education Tomás Derrig stated:

> It is really painful to hear the case made that there is some psychological disease or other in the city of Dublin just because clinics have been established in Chicago or Detroit or some other city. Where is the comparison between conditions in the Catholic city of Dublin and the city of Chicago? There is no comparison. I am quite sure that Justices will scout examination of every child brought before them, but if Justices in particular cases feel that they should have some medical report, that they would like to have the benefit of medical advice, I feel certain that that is a matter which the Department of Justice would consider.[52]

Interestingly, when Tomás Derrig was in opposition in 1929 during debates on the 1929 Children Bill, his opinion on the industrial schools was very different:

> This Vote gives an opportunity of which I would crave the kindness of the House to allow me to avail in order to call attention to the general position in regard to industrial schools. Last autumn I called attention to the necessity for reform in connection with the Borstal Institution for which the Minister is responsible. I got no reply on that occasion. This, however, is a much greater problem because, as the House will observe, according to the Estimate, there are in industrial schools 5,883 children as well as 112 in the reformatories, and to all intents and purposes the Dáil is the guardian of these children. We are responsible for them. We have taken them over in the name of the State, and periodically we ought to revise the position in regard to them in order to see how they are being treated and whether proper facilities are given to them to enable them to take their place in the world. We ought also find out whether improved conditions can be made for them. If that is so, as I believe it is, we ought to impress on the Minister for Education, who is responsible, the necessity for taking up this problem and dealing with it.[53]

He continued to discuss how, since the foundation of the industrial schools in 1868, 'there has been no improvement in the conditions or regulations governing these establishments'.[54] The speech by Derrig also highlighted the issues surrounding the stigma attached to industrial school education, and the fact that most of the children in industrial schools were 'quite respectable'. He made particular note of the conditions in Daingean Reformatory, which the Ryan Report has demonstrated was a particularly degenerate institution. He also acknowledged the large number of children placed with farmers after leaving the schools, stating that he believed the conditions in this instance to be 'very bad'. In reference to the after-care of children placed in industrial schools, he argued that no proper effort was being made for such provision, certainly not for the expenditure of £114,000 being made by the State. He suggested that if employment could not be obtained, the

State should 'follow the lines of recent reforms in England and provide money to enable them to enter as apprentices whatever occupations or trades they wish'. This subsidy was suggested by an English Departmental Committee in 1927, demonstrating Derrig's awareness not only of the issues surrounding the schools, but also of the developments and discourse in Britain on industrial schools. With regard to the capitation grant provided by the State, he argues that the 12s per week per boy or girl was 'quite insufficient'. Interestingly, he did point out that the instalments to schools were usually not given until the end of the year. This could signal why religious orders were withholding certain basic needs from children at times, putting further blame on the State for their administration of the system. He again referred to the situation in England, where payments were given quarterly to schools, ascertaining that at the least, schools should have resources at their disposal in the early part of the year. All of Derrig's points in this debate are issues that have emerged in the debates since the airing of *States of Fear* in 1999. Children were not being adequately provided for at times; inspections were not being carried out by the State; religious orders and managers were not receiving funding until the latter part of the year and after-care was, in many cases, a very pointless and degrading experience for those leaving the schools.

In response, the Minister for Education Professor O'Sullivan countered with a denial of the responsibility of the State, aside from financially, for the schools. Yet even on the financial responsibility, he stated that the House was not primarily responsible for financing 'these schools', which were the primary responsibility of local authorities. He even went on to urge deputies 'to devote some of their attention to try to induce local authorities to give more money'. He stated that he could not accept Deputy Derrig's description of the industrial schools, and that a full programme of primary education was being provided in the industrial schools. He conceded that 'attention to routine work in the institution might interfere with the general education, but on the whole [he could] not accept in any way the description given by the Deputy as applicable to the industrial schools as they now exist[ed]. In fact one pupil became a teacher'. With regard to accusations that children's education was stopped at fourteen years of age and they were sent to work, he denied this allegation.[55]

What the debate highlights is that there was an awareness of the conditions in schools, and that successive ministers for Education were willing to ignore this knowledge and tow the party line once in power. One of the most revealing actions taken by the State, and significant action in the context of the last debate, was the recertification of the old rules for industrial schools by the first Fianna Fáil Minister for Education Tomás Derrig in 1933. By that year, whereas Britain had moved to a greatly reformed system with short sentences, reduced corporal punishment, strict inspection and accountability, the first Fianna Fáil government had chosen to leave the rules unchanged and recertify the draconian measures of the nineteenth century. Arnold highlights how Derrig could have chosen to lift the 1923 and 1933 regulations from Britain, but instead 'wilfully chose to introduce rules that allowed Irish child prisoners to be whipped without limit'.[56] In 1936 the Cussen Commission would comment on the perception that the schools were 'prisons for children', arguing that a change of name could alter this perception.

Was there any critique outside the Dáil chamber? In 1935, the Irish Labour Defence League began to petition for support for the parents of a boy who had died in Artane Industrial School. The following is a letter written about the case to Hanna Sheehy Skeffington:

> A few weeks ago a boy names John Byrne lost his life in Artane Industrial School following a beating by a teacher named Lynch. This terrible tragedy calls for an investigation. There is every reason to believe that the authorities intend to let the matter pass and take no action. The boy's parents (he was their only son) are endeavouring to take the matter into the Courts and to make a claim for compensation for the death of their son. But this cannot be done without financial help. £5 is needed at once to enable the solicitor to proceed. All just minded people are asked to come to the assistance of the parents of the dead boy and enable them to make a fight for justice to ensure that such inhuman recurrences will no longer happen in these institutions.[57]

The correspondence ends here. The case was covered in the *Irish Times* and *Irish Independent*, and the boy appears to have died in suspicious circumstances. But in the subsequently published Cussen Report, Artane was the only school singled out. In the section on care of children, the report states:

> In our opinion the best results can be obtained only where the number under any one Manager does not exceed 200 pupils. We think that in no case should the number exceed 250. It is necessary in this connection to refer specifically to the case of Artane Industrial School, which is certified for 800 boys and where there are on average about 700 boys. It is in our view impossible for the Manager in an institution of this size to bring to bear that personal touch essential to give each child the impression that he is an individual in whose troubles, ambitions and welfare a lively interest is being taken. We strongly recommend, therefore, that Artane should be divided into separate schools, the pupils being segregated according to age and attainments.[58]

The reformatory schools, borstals and probation services did receive some academic investigation, although not without some resistance. In 1940, when Edward Fahy of Trinity College Dublin was researching reformatory schools, borstal institutions and probation services in Ireland for a series of lectures, the Department of Justice refused to supply statistics, copies of the probation rules, and returns of the Chief Probation Officer, information on the terms and conditions and any other relevant information. The department's reply focused solely on the juvenile offender and Garda statistics of crime: 'the reason assigned appears to suggest that the Probation System in Éire is being used only in respect of young offenders.'⁵⁹ In his lecture Fahy went on to point out that of the paltry six probation officers in Ireland, all were based in the city of Dublin. He criticised the Irish system's dependence on voluntary workers, and concluded:

> [I]t must be frankly admitted that nothing approaching a comprehensive account of the working of the Probation System can here be given. This very regrettable state of affairs is due to the fact that since the birth of our State no official investigation of the Probation System has ever been conducted, and to the further fact that the closest official secrecy is maintained regarding that System.⁶⁰

In another lecture on the borstal system he asserted: 'it is fair and accurate to comment that, in essentials, the Borstal and Prison Systems of Éire are not two distinct systems. With a few unimportant differences, they are really one System – the Prison System.'⁶¹ With regard to the reformatory schools and the farms in which boys were supposedly being trained in agricultural practices he claimed: 'The farms fail, however, to achieve their primary object. They do not serve to train the boys in farming. The boys are little more than juvenile labourers.'⁶² Speaking about Daingean reformatory, Fahy argued: 'It is the system which perpetuates this relic of a bygone age which is being attacked. That system must be destroyed if the blunders of the past are not to be continued.'⁶³

While the lectures only touched on the industrial school system and were more focused on conceptions of juvenile delinquency, they highlight the State's lack of concern for those in the institutions, and the measures undertaken in Britain and internationally in the same period that were being ignored in Ireland. As the only child protection agency in operation in the period in Ireland, the NSPCC's role will now be assessed, as will individual cases that resulted in removals to industrial schools.

The NSPCC and the industrial schools

> During the year we have had to arrange for the placing of a large number of children in industrial schools chiefly because their parents were unable to maintain them ... The whole question of the treatment of 'deprived' children in this country calls for investigation, such as it has received recently in England ... It is not surprising that many of our more experienced officers try to avoid the easy course of committal, even when the task of bringing about suitable home conditions seems almost insuperable.⁶⁴

This statement, from the NSPCC in 1948, is revealing for a number of reasons: first, the recognition children were being committed to industrial schools due to their parents' poverty; second, the lack of alternatives to the industrial schools; and third, the recognition that England had moved far from institutionalisation as the answer to poverty in families while in

Ireland this had remained fixed. This was not the first time the NSPCC had discussed the schools in their reports. From the early 1890s, the Dublin reports contain numerous discussions of the 'controversy surrounding industrial schools' with the Society denouncing their use unconditionally in 1894. However, it appears that it was forced to roll back on this in the following and subsequent years. In 1895, the Society reiterated that while it did not endorse the sending of children to industrial schools, in cases where provision was not available in the form of relatives (particularly when parents were convicted and imprisoned) they could be sent temporarily. In 1900, the report stated:

> [T]hey fully understand that there are circumstances under which it is better for the child to be removed from the influence of the parents, and under such circumstances they are prepared to avail themselves of the Industrial School System, or of any other suitable one the presents itself. We do not wish to enter into the controversy that has been raised over the Industrial Schools question. Our position in regard to the system is a simple one. We believe in the absolute responsibility of enforcing parental responsibility. We do not think that it is good for the individual, or just to the public who are taxed, that any persons should be lightly relieved of the duty of supporting his children in order that they should be brought up at the public expense. That this has been too often done in the past we know from experience.[65]

Why this shift in perspective? Was it possibly due to the realisation that the schools were the favoured option in Ireland – or the only option? Or more specifically, a recognition of the power of the Catholic Church as the principal providers of education and management of schools? Perhaps the issue was also related to the problems the Society had in opening and maintaining temporary shelters?

Initially, the Society's principal arguments against industrial schools were that children should not be maintained at public expense and should, where at all possible, be kept within the home. This argument benefited the Society in a number of ways: in the first instance, by emphasising that the Society kept children within the home, it was tactically gaining public approval, and maximising its influence. However, more importantly, in order to endorse middle-class ideals of domesticity and 'redeem' working-class homes, children needed to remain in the home (the removal of illegitimate children was obviously outside this remit as one-parent families were not the nuclear ideal and the removal of children from 'immoral surroundings' was widely accepted). Louise Jackson's examination of child sexual abuse in Victorian England discusses the involvement of the Society in removing children from the home and placing them in institutions in the late nineteenth century. Examining cases of sexual abuse or 'immorality', she acknowledges the Society's awareness of the controversy surrounding child custody from the beginning of the twentieth century and argues that welfare workers in schools and homes, 'were more than simple cogs in a bourgeois mechanism that aimed to mould the lower orders into humble and obedient servants'.[66] Taking a similar stance in her study of industrial schools and children's homes in nineteenth-century Scotland, Linda Mahood maintains that historians should break away from the 'social control' paradigm influenced by Foucault's work on institutions and focus on issues of initiative, agency and resistance on the part of child clients and their parents. However, in the Irish context, it is difficult to view the widespread neglect, physical abuse and sexual abuse that occurred in industrial schools in the twentieth century without focusing on the 'social control paradigm'. Initiative, agency and resistance are also difficult concepts, as even those parents that requested their child's placement appear to have done so due to an inability to support them, and a lack of understanding of their parental rights. While a later chapter will focus on how working-class mothers used the NSPCC and voluntary organisations to gain financial aid through requests for advice and in situations of desertion, many seemed unable or unsure of their rights when it came to their children's committal to schools. Similarly, families in poverty were rarely in a position to pay for legal representation, and if a justice was faced with a testimony from an NSPCC inspector, school-attendance officer or garda, it is likely that opposition from a parent would not have been successful. This is not to diminish the role of families and society in the committal of children to schools, but to emphasise the lack of choice and power for many families in poverty.

Officially, from 1922 until 1940, the NSPCC in Ireland did not involve itself in discussions of the industrial schools, or the need to protect the family and support alternatives such as fostering and legal adoption. This is one of the starkest contrasts between the Irish and British branches in the 1920s and 1930s, and the conclusion must be drawn that as a pressure group its influence was greatly reduced in independent Ireland. In fact, it appears in the reports to be appeasing the State throughout the 1920s and 1930s. As mentioned in Chapter 3, in 1951 all branches cited Article 42, Section 1 of the 1937 Constitution at the beginning of their annual reports.[67] In 1952, Article 41 was quoted. When looking at the State's control and interference in families from the 1920s, both articles seem almost farcical. Far from recognising or protecting the family, by removing children to industrial schools, and not granting financial support to families, the State was jeopardising the family, in all its forms. While the extent to which the NSPCC inspector was involved in removing children to industrial schools and reformatories in the twentieth century may never be known due to insufficient documentation, observations can be made from the existing files and the testimonies of residents in the Ryan Report. Table 4.4 details the number of children in the Wexford District sent to industrial schools for the period 1937–40 on the recommendations of the NSPCC inspector following neglect investigations. Table 4.5 charts the schools to which they were sent.

In 1937 alone, eleven per cent of the neglect cases investigated resulted in removals,[68] a statistic that demonstrates how far the Society had moved

Table 4.4 Number of children sent to industrial schools as a result of investigations in Wexford by the NSPCC, 1937–39

Year	Cases	No. of children	Boys	Girls
1937	14	25	7	18
1938	6	11	3	8
1939	9	17	3	14

Table 4.5 Classification of schools to which children were sent as a result of investigations in Wexford by the NSPCC, 1937–39

	1937	1938	1939
St Michael's, Wexford	8	7	12
St Aidan's, New Ross	10	1	1
Artane Industrial School, Dublin	3	2	1
St. Kylan, Rathdrum	4	1	1
St Michael's, Cappoquin	0	0	1
Total	25	11	16

away from its initial policy of protecting children within the home and had changed its policy on institutionalisation. Similarly, in the Waterford and District branch in 1939, thirty-four of the 490 children dealt with were placed in industrial schools, while in 1940 this figure was forty-three out of 527 children involved in cases with the NSPCC. This is not a criticism of the Society in isolation, as it was enforcing a policy supported by the State, but an examination of the files reveals much about the families involved in these situations and the biases of the inspector. In 1929, a sister in St Michael's industrial school in Wexford wrote to the inspector regarding a mother 'who had turned up at her doorstep' looking for her daughter:

> the mother of K is here, just crossed from Wales – wants to take K back this evening. She, the mother has not seen her husband. What is to be done? Would it be well to ask one of the Guards to call up and explain the law to her? She seems reasonable but wants the child.[69]

The police were called and the mother was told her rights by the police and the convent. It was a clear case in which, upon signing the committal form, a parent had not considered, or perhaps been coerced into thinking, that this was the best place for their child.

It was, however, not always the convents and schools that did not agree to the return of children. In 1930, a sister in the same school wrote to the local NSPCC inspector requesting advice regarding the release of a young girl in the school: 'I should not regret this child's departure from the School but *there is a soul in question*' (emphasis mine). The inspector replied,

> The parents of M detained in your school are well known to me. The father is a man of very low mental standard and has neglected his family for years. The mother is not morally good. In my opinion it would be a grave error to discharge or release on licence the said client.[70]

In an even more revealing case, the following extract divulges not only the inspector's distrust of the boy's parents and relatives, but the idea of the child being a commodity of the State:

> The boy, who is now 10 years old, is due to be transferred to Carriglea Industrial School and with the necessary training at the end of six years he will be an asset to the State. In view of the information disclosed by the inquiry I cannot recommend that the boy be discharged from School (at this stage) and returned to the relatives … who are said to be mentally deficient.[71]

The extent to which the Church, the State and the NSPCC collaborated in the removal of children is difficult to assess. However, the following letter reveals one particular aspect of and attitude towards the placement of children in religious institutions. The letter, written by Sister X in St Michael's, Wexford, to the local inspector demonstrates her attitude not only to the welfare of destitute children but also to their religious denomination and faith:

> My messenger, ___ had some business in the Co Home Enniscorthy on Monday last. She said something of the women and children of that institution and from her description of the place and inhabitants, I could not think of sending the little ___ children there – if permitted to keep them we shall keep them in the school without any renummeration [*sic*]. The Almighty will provide the means. A few years ago we took in two English Protestant children who were abandoned by their step-mother, the father being dead. They were brought over from Wales and left in an old shed near Wexford – We were asked to admit them. We did so and kept them for some years. They are now Catholics and work in a Convent Laundry … Since that time we have not known want in this Institution so we shall trust to the Grand God to help us in the ___ case also – Thanking you very much for many favours and for your letter of Thursday.[72]

While many institutions expected donations from the parents of the children being admitted, and legally justices could enforce this, if a school was not filled to capacity this 'donation' was not a necessity, as the following passage reveals: 'A few lines to let you know that we would be glad to get the Browne children you mentioned some time ago. We could take them anytime. I would defray any expenses with them.'[73] Dated two days after the arrival of the children, the same sister wrote to the inspector stating that one of the children who 'was let out to her aunt for the day' had not returned. Unfortunately this is where the file ends, so it is not possible to know whether the child was found and brought back to the school, although it is highly likely that this was the case.

Although the policy of maintaining children within the home was reiterated by the NSPCC in its annual reports, the correspondence in the case files reveals another side to the issue, and perhaps, as the 1948 Dublin report addressed, it was easier for inspectors to partake in the incarceration of children in the schools. Some testimonies have suggested that certain NSPCC inspectors received money for children – but to date I have very limited evidence. In numerous letters from those in charge at St Aidan's Industrial School for Girls, Wexford; St Michael's Industrial School for Girls, Wexford, and St Michael's Industrial School for Boys, Waterford, references are made to the need to protect the souls of Catholic children and maintain the numbers of children in the schools. Overall, the language used by both the inspector and those working in the institutions is instructive, and at times detached. In 1938, one Sister of Charity wrote to the inspector regarding a child that was to be committed: 'I hope she is healthy and normal.'[74] Similarly, in his own writings on his experiences as an NSPCC inspector, Robert J. Parr's description of a mother and her two children demonstrates his own attitude to neglect cases:

> 'I do wish one could put the "smell" of that case into a book!' Mrs Inspector spoke feelingly. Mrs. Barley and two of her children had recently paid a visit to the Local Office, and the smell of them lasted for an hour afterwards in spite of opened doors and windows. No word picture, however complete, can accurately portray a case of real 'Neglect' as our men discover by the thousand every month ... Each will accept the description in a comparative way, and each determine the depth of the evil by his or her own experience ... The yearning of the child for mother – and father-love, the aching pangs of hunger, the bitterness of the cold wind upon the shivering form, the 'smell'.[75]

As well as from the NSPCC, the SVDP and the Legion of Mary, the police and the courts played a considerable role in children's committal, as will now be considered.

Relationship between the courts, the gardaí, the NSPCC and the religious orders

> The role of the courts was central to the way in which the system operated. It was they who committed the children, passed the information on to the Department of Education and relevant local authority, who then between them funded each child by way of a capitation grant which was paid to the religious order running the particular industrial school in which the child was detained.[76]

As the above quote demonstrates, the relationship between the courts, the NSPCC inspectors and the Catholic management of the institutions was crucial in deciding which children were committed. Once children were brought to court, be it by the NSPCC inspector, the school-attendance officer, the SVDP, the gardaí or the Legion of Mary, they were never given representation, even though they were being committed for a 'crime' they did not commit. It appears from survivor testimonies that this situation was understandably confusing, frightening and harrowing, and one of the pivotal memories from the industrial school experience. Yet the respect that each of the institutions and agencies appear to have had for one another contrasts starkly with the descriptions of those investigated and committed by the courts.

In the cases dealt with by the Ryan Report, thirty-seven per cent of committals were as a result of the NSPCC inspectors' involvement. While the cases I have examined reveal roughly twelve per cent, this sample is much smaller than that documented in the report. The report states that 'the general public perception at the time was that the Society was heavily involved in committing children to Industrial Schools, hence the apprehension in the minds of the public associated with the "cruelty man".'[77] The report goes on to quote Frank Duff of the Legion of Mary in response to a letter by Archbishop McQuaid of Dublin:

> I profoundly distrust every word and action of one of the Society's Inspectors, Mrs X. I go further and I say that I regard her as a danger. She is quite capable (by which I mean she has already done it) of distorting facts by trying to suit any point of view she is trying to make. She exercised an ascendancy over ex-Justice Y, and between them they simply shovelled children into Industrial Schools.[78]

Taking into account Duff's own bias as the president of the Legion of Mary, his choice of the only female NSPCC inspector in Dublin, and his previous distrust of any British influence in Ireland, his identification of a connection between the courts, the NSPCC and religious orders is not unfounded. In fact Duff and Archbishop McQuaid were two rare opponents of the industrial schools.[79] Eoin O'Sullivan has described Duff as 'one of the more interesting commentators on the industrial school system', as he believed that the breaking up of families went against the Catholic Church's belief in the sanctity of the family. According to O'Sullivan, Duff wrote numerous memos to the Department of Health about the industrial schools.[80]

In the NSPCC files, three separate letters from the mother superior in St Michael's, Wexford, to the NSPCC inspector reveal the personal relationships that existed between these institutions of influence in the State in cases of child welfare. In the first in 1928, the sister wrote to the inspector: 'If Mr. 'X' is not presiding at Court on the 24th I shall not send the "Connor" children down but defer committal to another day'. In a subsequent letter in 1929 regarding the committal of a young brother and sister, there is a small note to the inspector with the following scribbled on the bottom: 'I mentioned the other matter to Mr 'X' and he was not at all pleased as like myself he appreciates all the help you always give in children's cases.'[81] In a final letter in 1928, she includes a note from the local priest to the inspector stating that a particular mother had consented to the committal of her child if the inspector would like to follow up the case. The familiarity that existed between the inspector, the local clergy, the managers of the religious orders, the courts and the gardaí is very complex and difficult to assess. However, with a capitation system in place in industrial schools in Ireland, a child living in a home deemed 'immoral' by the inspector could quite easily be placed in a school if the incentive was there. The lack of regulation of inspectors discussed in Chapter 3, and the class of the mostly male inspectors who were in place must also be considered in this context. Finally, from the reports of the Society it appears that the NSPCC inspector was receiving on average £250–£300 a year. This was quite a substantial sum when you consider that the assistance the inspector was sometimes able to acquire for families was 6s per week.

Each inspector in the branches was answerable to a local committee 'of interested persons'. As the majority of cases were reported to the inspector by the general public, the letters to the inspector referring him to families are important to assess. In 1939 a man wrote a letter drawing attention to a twenty-year-old mother 'fond of reading novels'. In the files, aside from 'morals doubtful', there are a number of other 'moral' complaints: 'girl is drifting', 'parents mentally incapable/defective', 'girl (15) is going to the pictures and staying out late', 'quarrelling over domestic affairs'. Also, in addition to the derogatory language used to describe parents, there is a complete disregard for their rights. In a case in 1928, in which a nurse child was placed in a school by the inspector, the mother superior wrote:

> regarding the case of E, unless it is necessary for the father to appear it may be so well that Mrs M take the child to court. The woman with whom the child lived recently has been here on 2 occasions to see her – crying over her – and wishing to have her back – E seems quite unmoved and not anxious to remain many minutes … Of course if the father wishes to take his child to court on the 22nd I shall not object.[82]

The relationship between the courts, the inspector and the religious can be further seen in the following two notes. In the first the sister mentions a particular family to be investigated, asserting that 'both cases are cases that should pass in court I think'.[83] In another case sent on a Tuesday morning to the inspector, the hastiness of the sister is apparent: 'regarding the three ____ children, would it be too late now for application to Next Wednesday's court?'[84]

Although the role of the religious orders in charge of the schools has been discussed with respect to the NSPCC and the State, it is important to deal with their position separately. The following letter is significant as it was written in 1920, prior to independence.

Dear Inspector L,

Many thanks for kind letter. I am happy to say the two children arrived today. The Police were busy. Thanking you most sincerely for your kindness to us. If you have any more children you won't forget St. Aidans.

I am dear ____

Yours gratefully,

Mother Superior.[85]

In the available NSPCC files in the period, most of the correspondence is between the inspectors and nuns in schools in Wexford, Waterford and Cork, and the tone of the above letter is common. The idea of children being an asset to the school or a commodity of the State is prevalent and can be observed in the correspondence. As previously mentioned, the system of capitation grants should not have continued as long as it did, as it created a situation in which institutions were competing against each other and against alternative child-care options. The structure of Catholic religious orders must also be considered – particularly with regard to the hierarchy of power.[86] Sisters were answerable to the mother superior, the local bishop and beyond. The need to keep the different schools operating, a type of survival instinct, has been discussed by Raftery and O'Sullivan with respect to the 'Poor Law children' sent to schools in the 1950s. In the NSPCC annual reports, the sample cases often state that children committed to industrial schools are 'doing splendidly', yet there is no evidence in the case files that the inspectors did follow up cases after committal. Nor is there any correspondence relating to children in the schools after their entry. It appears that once children were placed, unless family members kept in contact, they were left to the 'care' of the system.

In 1939, the mother superior in St Aidan's wrote to the inspector concerning a phone message from the matron in the County Home requesting the school to take two children. She explains in her letter that she refused due to the understanding from him that one of the children 'was subject to fits'.[87] However, she goes on to state: 'we are under obligations to these nuns who are kind to our children and who refused to admit a consumption case lately in order to give beds to our children.'[88] The position of the County Home in relation to the industrial schools is an interesting one, and a far more complex one than can be addressed in this discussion. Here, it is worth noting that the County Home did allow families to remain intact in certain circumstances. Children were not automatically separated from parents, and women were not committed for a number of years, as was the case with the industrial schools and Magdalene laundries. Likewise, those in the County Home were not used by the institution to work in the fields and laundries. In a case in 1934, a girl of seven was documented by the NSPCC inspector. The file states that the girl's mother refused to send her to school and told her 'if the Guards found her on the road they would kill her.'⁸⁹ The case file describes how the young girl had to look after the younger children, fetch water from the well and chop wood for the fire. The inspector wrote, 'she was in bits when we found her', as 'her mother used to beat her often'. She was placed in the county home, and the last detail recorded is a statement from the child.⁹⁰ On being asked where she would like to stay, she told the inspector: 'I will not go back to my home. I would like to stay here as I am quite happy and the Sister lets me play with the other children.'⁹¹

The unofficial stories: the families and the abused

> I am doing the best I can for my children, my earnings are small and I find it hard to make ends meet.⁹²

Throughout the NSPCC files, some of the most emotive letters are those sent by mothers and fathers asking if their children can be taken into industrial schools and reformatories as they could not provide for them. Whether they believed the schools would afford a better future for their children, as many did at the time, or whether they were coerced by members of the clergy or the NSPCC inspector, the letters are heartrending pleas which were intended to spark sympathy.⁹³ However, not only do the files contain requests for the admittance of children, they also contain requests for their return. In 1938 one mother wrote numerous letters to the New Ross Industrial School, the government and the local NSPCC inspector requesting the return of her ten-year-old boy. Following this she employed a solicitor whose letters are included in the file. As with many similar cases, her 'bad' character was cited as the reason for the rejection of her requests.⁹⁴ In another case, the local priest wrote to the inspector:

> Dear Sir, Another case to trouble you. A young lad A., Ballymorris, Galbally, aged 6 years, illegitimate; mother wants to go to work, hampered by child – as in the case I told you about a few days ago. Will you kindly get this lad sent to an Industrial School.⁹⁵

From the late 1930s, the NSPCC began to justify the sending of children to industrial schools more and more through the use of the sample cases in the reports. In the 1935–36 report of the Dublin District branch, the inspector records the case of a widower, the father of 'two nice children' who had 'come to the end of his resources and called on the inspector for advice'. The man's income was a 10s weekly pension and the house was described as 'only one room in a poverty stricken condition' but 'clean and tidy'. The report states the inspector 'succeeded in getting both children placed in school within the city area, where they can be visited by the father, who is most grateful for the Society's help'.⁹⁶ The inspector's sympathy for the father is clear, particularly with regard to the fact that a school in Dublin city was chosen in which to place the boys. Often children were placed in schools far from home. The reasoning for this cannot be fully ascertained, but I would suggest that in some instances authorities believed that separation from the family would be the best option for the child. In another case cited in the same report, the attitude of the inspector to the children's father was very different. The man is described as 'addicted to drink' and the mother 'slovenly and lazy, [who] spent the greater part of her time gossiping in neighbours' houses'. A local doctor was called in and the children were treated for symptoms of severe neglect. Both parents were prosecuted and five of the six children were sent to industrial schools with the father ordered to pay 1s 6d per week for each child towards the cost of maintenance. In this situation, the fact that the father was earning 44s weekly was highlighted by the inspector. To be in poverty and neglectful was understandable, although the outcome was the same, but to be earning and neglectful was severely criticised.

Of particular interest are requests to admit children under the age of six to schools (the minimum age for committal). In this situation, mainly mothers appealed for babies and children of six years and under to be placed in mother-and-baby homes, many to no avail. In 1939, a young mother repeatedly asked the inspector to arrange to place her baby in a Catholic Home. The inspector refused, continually telling the woman to find relatives to take the child. It is possible that this attitude was based on the fact that the mother was pregnant again when requesting that the child be placed. While one illegitimate birth could be dealt with, being seen to 'make the same mistake twice' led to the mother being described by the inspector as the 'giddy and irresponsible type'.[97] With respect to cases in which families were split up, it is interesting to note which children were left with the parent or parents. In 1939, a father who had been widowed three months previously approached the inspector for advice. The ten children in his care were aged between three months and eleven years. The four youngest girls were sent to industrial schools while the eldest daughter and five boys were kept, including the three-month-old baby. In a similar case in 1939 a widower, the father of six children, agreed to the committal of the two youngest girls aged six and seven years, keeping the eldest daughter and the boys. From the limited number of case files available, it appears that the pattern was to keep the eldest girl and the boys.

What alternatives could have been pursued by the State? In the annual report of the Dublin NSPCC branch in 1948, the following extract relating to illegitimate children is interesting in the alternatives offered:

> The position, as put to us by many mothers, is briefly: 'I can't support my child unless I go to work. But if I go to work I cannot look after my child. What am I to do?' The answer is either to find a foster-mother, generally an impossible task, or an industrial school. Either way the child loses the mother's care, and the mother loses an incentive to keep straight in the future. In other countries the provision of nursery schools goes a long way to solve this difficulty. Yet beyond one small model nursery centre dealing

with three dozen children, all, incidentally, of married mothers, and the two small crèches, one of which specifically refuses illegitimate children, there is not provision ... The financial aspect discloses a similar picture to the case of the children dependent on social service allowances, in the model centre, the cost of keeping each child during working hours is 7/8 per week, of which the mother pays 2/6, yet if any of the children had to be committed to industrial schools they would cost the State 15/-. The cost to the rates of the odd 5/- or so per head of the children accommodated in such centres if set up by local authorities would be amply justified.[98]

Single mother benefits had been introduced in the United States from 1910, but the Society in Ireland never called for their introduction under the period of examination. In fact, unmarried mothers' allowances were introduced only in 1973 in Ireland. Equally, aside from a few extracts similar to the one above, the Society did not push for child-care supplements or highlight the cases in the files in which women and men needed help in caring for children. They tip-toed around the issues but, unfortunately for those in industrial schools, continued to work with the system.

The abused

> That night I began to identify myself with the Christian Brother. I found myself behaving in almost the same manner as Brother Vale. It was then that I began to think of sadism as a terrible and contagious disease.[99]

In 2008, Diarmuid Whelan edited and published the account of a man, Peter Tyrrell, who had been resident in Letterfrack Industrial School in the 1920s and 1930s. Tyrrell's account exemplifies the anger and bitterness carried into adulthood by many children abused in industrial schools. The story is harrowing, in the details he recorded and the life and death that was described in Whelan's introduction, but it is a clear concise account of life before, during and after Letterfrack Industrial School – one which ended when he took his own life in 1968. The cycle of violence and problems endured by those in the schools after release is dealt with skilfully by Tyrrell, with many connections being made between his experiences in Letterfrack and people and places in the world afterwards. In the chapter on his return home, he recounts the story of a tailor who worked with him and had been in a school in Salthill twenty years earlier:

> When he heard I had been to Letterfrack he asked me if the Brothers still took the boys' trousers off. When I answered yes, he told me that he was in jail during the 1921 trouble and had a far better time than at school. This man's name was Maye. He was married with three children, and his wife had often taken him to court for drunkenness and beating her, and non-maintenance. Another tailor in the town also from Salthill, called Duggan, was a heavy drinker who neglected his wife and kids and eventually left them to be a tramp.[100]

What is interesting is not only the drunkenness and the abuse the men inflicted on others later in life, but the fact that this man's testimony refers to abuse on-going in the early twentieth century. Jane Barnes has examined the industrial school system in Ireland in the late nineteenth century, but what has not been addressed is the extent to which the punitive regime depicted by survivors in the twentieth century was the same prior to this. Referring to Harry Hendrick's early quotation on 'the incarceration of children and young adolescents in the certified schools in the mid-nineteenth century', even without the testimonies of survivors, the industrial schools never appear to have provided the education or care needed by children. Although undoubtedly the schools degenerated in Ireland from the 1920s on, particularly in the lack of education being provided to children, their history throughout is one of incarceration. In 2002, speaking to a journalist in the United States, a former resident of the Artane Industrial School, Jim Beresford, discussed his and others' abuse: 'What eventually stopped them abusing me was that I had parents, and I was articulate. Most of the other children were inarticulate and illiterate because they had spent their whole life in the institution.'[101] In 1939, twin girls born to a single mother in Cork were placed in Clonakility Industrial School. For the three years prior to this the girls were in the workhouse where 'Annie' recounts they were being looked after by 'a tiny little lady ... a kind of mother who made pretty dresses'.[102] Once in the industrial school, she recounts memories of beatings, bed-wetting and humiliation. With regard to her education she states: 'The classroom was a place of punishment. It was where we watched people being sadistically beaten. If we were ambitious to study, they did not like that.'[103] Annie's story has so many commonalities with other testimonies from former residents of schools – the beatings, the bed-wetting, the fear, the starvation, the cold, the abuse, the humiliation, the degradation. So overwhelming and specific are the details, it has become more and more difficult for those trying to discredit these testimonies to do so.

Peter Tyrrell's committal was not ignored by society, and was in fact recorded in an article in the *Irish Independent* in 1925:

> A shocking story of child neglect was deposed to at Ballinasloe District Court by Miss Monnelly, N.S.P.C.C., in support of her application to have seven children of one family, named Tyrrell committed to and industrial school ... Their 'home' was a shed without windows, and the rain was coming through the roof. When she visited the place at 1 o'clock in the day she found the father and mother in bed, and the children, half naked, sitting round the spark of fire ... When she remonstrated with the father for being in bed at that hour, he jumped out of bed and chased her into the street threatening to take her life ... She had visited the whole country, including Connemara, and a case of such utter neglect and destitution she had never met before.[104]

The path to the Kennedy Report

In 1969, a leading psychiatrist stated with regard to the Kennedy Commission and the industrial schools, 'We must go back to the roots. Can our present services give children adequate care? If not let us scrap them. Let us not say we have an institution and we must keep it. The children must not be there to serve the agencies. I am told "you are attacking the clergy". I am not attacking any clergy, but if there is a defect in the system I will attack it.' His awareness of the conditions many children from deprived backgrounds lived in, and the effects of such conditions was progressive and revealing. He continued with a discussion of corporal punishment and a critique of teachers inflicting severe punishment on vulnerable children: 'a child who lives under appalling stress, who is neglected and hungry, cannot concentrate and to treat him like other children is grossly unrealistic. If the teacher beats him, you complete the cycle and he becomes anti-social and delinquent.' While today these sentiments are taken for granted for the most part, in late 1960s Ireland it was a refreshing stance – particularly since corporal punishment would remain legal until 1984.

The critique was not isolated. In the *Irish Times,* Michael Viney's articles on young offenders were particularly cutting – highlighting all the inadequacies of the children's courts, Daingean, probation officers and treatment of young offenders generally by society. He demonstrated that juvenile delinquency was in no way being addressed sufficiently and by trained persons. With regard to Daingean he stated: 'The current grants are merely a reflection of what the orders can screw out of the Department of Education and the Local Authorities.' His description of the children's court was particular insightful.

> The children's court in Dublin is a disarming chamber of justice, functional and mellow as an old village schoolroom, with a turf fire burning in the grate. Nobody wears uniform and there is no dock for the accused. But a mere appearance in this court allots a child his role in a formal drama. Up to now his relationships with the adult world have been fluid, malleable and fairly spontaneous. Now all the players, including him, take up a ritualised position. The policeman accuses him of wrong and refrains from comment … The probation officer contributes a brief Greek chorus on his home and school background. His mother, somewhat diminished by the setting offers her defence 'He's a good boy at home' or rejection 'I can't do a thing with him'. What the boy himself may say is expressed in the non-committal formulas 'I dunno sir'. Only the justice seems free to improvise – but even he is tied, eventually, to ritualised alternatives of justice.

Previous to this in 1965, Mary Maher's discussion of Artane demonstrated a distinct awareness of the fact that institutionalisation was not the best option – 'if it is not a penal institution or a workhouse, neither is it a home, not in any true sense a training school designed to prepare children for the future. It is a place to keep alive in from the age of eight to 14 or 16. Luckily at eight or even 14 or 16, injustice is still an abstract concept, and futility is a word on a spelling list.' The reference to industrial schools being a place to 'keep alive in' may have appeared extreme – while we now know that it was nowhere near extreme.

This type of analysis was a sign of the times, the 1960s being somewhat progressive in discussions of many social issues. For most commentators then, the 1970 Kennedy Report signalled a triumph for child welfare and children in care. The problems had been acknowledged and (aside from the issue of starvation and extensive sexual, physical and mental abuse), discussed. However, the Kennedy Report also ignored many issues and did not effect change to the extent that history has recorded. In fact, as Nell McCafferty pointed out in 1971, the Kennedy Report achieved very few of its aims. Children were still being held in certain industrial schools and reformatories; Justice Kennedy was still sending them there through the children's court; abuse was still occurring in both the industrial schools and the new residential homes. Poverty was also not being tackled in any real way. In June 1972, the Campaign for the Care of Deprived Children (CARE), published a memorandum on deprived children and children's services in Ireland. The aims of the organisation were to 'promote the welfare of deprived children in Ireland ... to look for improvements in children's services and to emphasise that children should be maintained in their own family where at all possible and that services should be based on this principle'. More specifically, it stressed the importance of the social and emotional environment of the developing child, adequate assessment of medical, psychological and educational problems and reform in the legislation affecting children, especially child offenders. Finally, it aimed to encourage the raising of standards in child care and the development of training and professional services. CARE was a sign of new times many hoped.

With regard to the ISPCC, in 1970 the following was the breakdown of new cases brought to their attention – 1,116 cases of neglect (3,996 children), 106 cases of assault or ill-treatment (379 children), 26 cases classed as 'beyond control' (69 children), 6 cases of abandonment (28 children), 19 cases of other abuse (47 children), and 650 cases of aid or advice sought (2165 children). The year 1970 is indeed a landmark in the history of reports into child welfare. Whether it signalled a dramatic change is yet to be proven.

Conclusion

> We are overcrowded with applications and I must keep vacancies for children whose faith is in danger as this is the object for which we were founded.[105]

The industrial school system was a nineteenth-century British construction endorsed by successive Irish governments until the late-twentieth century. Representing one of a myriad of institutions kept in place to deal with perceived social problems, it was accepted then and now that the principal reason for children's removal to industrial schools was poverty in families. While from the 1920s Britain, the United States and most other Western countries had begun to move towards developing a welfare State to deal with this poverty, in Ireland the Church and State retained control of families through the continued use of institutions. This was not the only option, nor was it the cheapest option, yet even a cursory glance at the other alternatives (social welfare, single-mothers' allowance, legal adoption, nurseries, fostering, and more generally, the legalisation of contraceptives and abortion) demonstrates the tension that would have existed between the Catholic Church and the State if they had been pursued. Maintaining a structure of 'charity' as opposed to one of social welfare set Ireland apart internationally, particularly in the inter-war years, yet it enabled the Church and State to retain an enormous amount of social control. This control spread past the separation of undesirable families and the reluctance to support families through welfare. Both the industrial schools and Magdalene laundries provided the Church and State with an unpaid workforce. That this did not emerge in debates at the time demonstrates the State's lack of inspection of the schools and the class and gender bias towards those placed. Yet the State did not act alone, and the role of the NSPCC was central to the maintenance of the industrial schools. Not only did inspectors choose the families that would be subject to investigation, they acted as a semi-State workforce in bringing children to court, accompanying them to the schools and corresponding with all the actors involved in the industrial school system. Nothing represented a greater move away from the motto of 'protecting children within the home'.

Notes

1 Crossman, 'Cribbed, contained and confined?', pp. 37–61. Crossman states that 'the slow take-up of boarding out was a consequence of the misgivings of local guardians, not the poor law commissioners', p. 50. For a discussion of boarding-out in Scotland, see Helen J. MacDonald, 'Boarding-out and the Scottish Poor Law'. For a discussion of nurse children in Ireland and baby-farming, see Buckley, 'Found in a dying condition'.
2 The industrial school system in Britain was based on a Continental model, and by the 1850s, Germany, Switzerland and the Scandinavian countries had over a hundred institutions catering for criminal and destitute children.
3 There had developed a growing critique of institutionalisation in the United States and other Western societies from the late nineteenth century. In 1886, W. P. Letchworth in the United States referred to children becoming 'institutionalized', yet in Ireland this option would be repeatedly chosen (Bremmer, *Children and Youth in America*, vol. 2, p. 296).
4 *States of Fear*, narrator, Áine Lawlor; writer, producer, director, Mary Raftery,

RTÉ, Ireland 27 April 1999.
5 Mary Raftery and Eoin O'Sullivan, *Suffer the Little Children: The Inside Story of Ireland's Industrial Schools* (New Island, 1999).
6 The report of the commission was published on 20 May 2009. The commission was set up in 2000. For a copy of the report, see www.childabusecommission. ie. From here on the report will be referred to as CICA or the Ryan Report.
7 Bruce Arnold, *The Irish Gulag: How the State Betrayed its Innocent Children* (Gill and Macmillan, 2009). Arnold argues that 'during the greater part of the twentieth century the Irish State owned and managed a prison system for children spread across the whole of the Republic', p. 2. He also pinpoints how the Irish system remained unchanged and unreformed.
8 Ibid., p. 304.
9 CICA Report, vol. 5, chapter 1, p. 9.
10 Report of the Commission of Inquiry into the Reformatory and Industrial School System (1934–36) (Dublin, 1936). This will be referred to throughout as the Cussen Report, as G. P. Cussen was the chairman of the committee.
11 Hendrick argues: 'The incarceration of children and young adolescents in the certified schools from the mid-Victorian years onwards is often presented as a programme of humanitarian reform, struggling against poorly trained staff, mean-minded officials and inadequate funding, and occasionally marred by the brutality of individuals. This comfortable and reassuring myth bears little resemblance to the true situation.' Hendrick, *Child Welfare: Historical Dimensions*, p. 121.
12 CICA Report, vol. 1, chapter 2, p. 35.
13 Crossman's examination of the Poor Law system and children has demonstrated that institutionalisation was chosen from the nineteenth century. Crossman, 'Cribbed, contained and confined?', pp. 37–61.
14 With regard to legislation, the Irish Industrial Schools Act was passed in 1868. The Act provided for the establishment and regulation of industrial schools in Ireland. The Prevention of Crimes Act (1871) and the Industrial Schools Amendment Act (1880) further extended the classes of children who could be sent to the schools. In 1903, under the Employment of Children Act, a child could be sent to an industrial school for a second or subsequent infringement of the bylaws of the act.
15 Although reformatories were established first, industrial schools soon surpassed them both in numbers of schools and numbers of pupils. Of the ten reformatories opened from 1858 to 1865, by the end of the century only seven of the original reformatories survived, and by 1922 only five survived. For a discussion of the industrial schools in Ireland from 1868 to 1908, see Jane Barnes, *Irish Industrial Schools, 1868–1908: Origins and Development* (Irish Academic Press, 1989). By the time the Cussen Committee was investigating reformatories and industrial schools in 1934, only two reformatories remained – the reformatory at Glencree run by the Oblate Fathers and the reformatory at Limerick run by the Sisters of the Good Shepherd; see Cussen Report, p. 7.
16 Section 44 of the Children Act, 1908, states: 'The expression "industrial school" means a school for the industrial training of children, in which children are lodged, clothed and fed, as well as taught'.
17 See Barnes, *Irish Industrial Schools*, p. 69.
18 Figures taken from Raftery and O'Sullivan, *Suffer the Little Children*, pp. 20,

27.
19 Cussen Report, p. 7.
20 Ibid., p. 71.
21 Ibid.
22 Christopher Lasch, *Haven in a Heartless World: The Family Besieged* (W. W. Norton, 1977).
23 Anthony Platt, *The Child Savers: The Invention of Delinquency* (1969; University of Chicago Press, 1977).
24 Hendrick, *Child Welfare: Historical Dimensions*, p. 114.
25 Ibid., p. 115. For a discussion of the 1927 juvenile offenders committee and the 1933 Children and Young Persons Act, see pp. 114–24.
26 Ibid., p. 117.
27 Deputy James Dillon speaking in the Committee on Finance for Prisons, *Dáil Éireann*, vol. 74, 16 March 1939.
28 Deputy Dillon speaking on the issue of juvenile delinquency, *Dáil Éireann*, vol.70, 24 March 1939.
29 Letter from William J. Cosgrave Esq. J. P., s5486 (NAI, Dublin).
30 Deputy Dillon speaking on the issue of juvenile delinquency and the children's courts, *Dáil Éireann*, vol. 66, 31 March 1937.
31 Ibid.
32 Conor Reidy, *Ireland's Moral Hospital: The Irish Borstal System, 1906-1956* (Irish Academic Press, 2010), p. 5.
33 'The failure of democracy: Increase of juvenile delinquency', *Irish Times*, 9 March 1936.
34 Mary Kettle, cited in the *Irish Independent*, 13 July 1937.
35 CF #45 (ISPCC, Limerick).
36 Cussen Report, p. 7.
37 Ibid., p. 32.
38 House of Commons Parliamentary Papers, *Criminal and Judicial Statistics for Ireland 1889* (C5/95) 85:241, pp. 160–1.
39 Ibid., p. 48.
40 Ibid., p. 5.
41 Edward Fahy, Public lecture at Trinity College Dublin in 1942. 'Reformatory Schools in Ireland', *Hermathena*, 60 (November 1942), p. 61.
42 Joseph E. Cavanan, 'The Poor Law Review', *Studies*, 16:4, 1927, 631–44, p. 633.
43 Cussen Report, p. 19.
44 Ibid., p. 23.
45 *Dáil Éireann*, vol. 3, 25 June, 1923.
46 *Dáil Éireann*, vol. 1, 18 October, 1922.
47 *Dáil Éireann*, vol. 18, 25 February, 1927.
48 *Dáil Éireann*, vol. 38, 27 May, 1931.
49 *Dáil Éireann*, vol. 69, 13 January 1938.
50 AR Dublin District Branch NSPCC, 1940 (ISPCC, Limerick).
51 Ibid.
52 Fahy, 'Reformatory Schools in Ireland', p. 65.
53 *Dáil Éireann*, vol, 29, 17 April, 1929.
54 Ibid.
55 Ibid.

56 Arnold, *Irish Gulag*, p. 15.
57 Letter signed by Lawrence Wright, Secretary of the Irish Labour Defence League, 16 May 1935.
58 Cussen Report, p. 21.
59 Ibid., p. 79.
60 Edward Fahy, 'Probation of offenders', *Hermathena*, no. 62 (1943), 61–82.
61 Edward Fahy, 'Borstal in Ireland', *Hermathena*, no. 58 (1941), 70–85, p. 80.
62 Ibid., p. 71.
63 Ibid., p. 66.
64 AR Dublin Branch NSPCC 1948–49 (ISPCC, Limerick), pp. 5–6.
65 AR Dublin Branch NSPCC, 1900–1, p. 15.
66 Louise Jackson, *Child Sexual Abuse in Victorian England* (Routledge, 2000), p. 133.
67 Article 42, Section 1, *Bunreacht na hÉireann*.
68 There were 133 cases of neglect investigated by the inspector in 1933, with fourteen cases resulting in committal to industrial schools. AR Wexford District Branch, 1937 (ISPCC, Limerick).
69 CF #99.
70 CF #221.
71 CF #65.
72 CF #02.
73 Ibid.
74 CF #13.
75 Parr, *The Cruelty Man*, chapter 2.
76 Raftery and O'Sullivan, *Suffer the Little Children*, p. 56.
77 CICA Report, vol. 5, p. 5.
78 Ibid.
79 Frank Duff to Archbishop McQuaid, cited in Arnold, *Irish Gulag*, p. 128.
80 Ibid, p. 172.
81 CF #77.
82 CF #189.
83 CF #60.
84 CF #104.
85 CF #117.
86 For a discussion of nuns in Ireland in the nineteenth century, see Caitríona Clear, *Nuns in Nineteenth-Century Ireland* (Gill and Macmillan, 1987).
87 CF #143.
88 Ibid.
89 CF #71.
90 CF #36.
91 CF #61.
92 NSPCC case file, 1039. CF #148.
93 CF #88. The mother of an illegitimate boy is described by the local priest and the inspector as 'of loose morals ... lives by prostitution'. It was suggested that the boy be removed to an industrial school, but the mother refused her consent.
94 CF #12.
95 CF #101.
96 Sample case, AR Dublin Branch NSPCC, 1935–36 (ISPCC, Limerick), p. 8.

97 CF #155.
98 CF #136.
99 Peter Tyrrell, *Founded on Fear: Letterfrack Industrial School, War and Exile*, edited by Diarmuid Whelan (Irish Academic Press, 2006), p. xxiii.
100 Ibid., p. 105.
101 Jim Beresford in an article by Jane Yellard in the *Huddersfield Daily Examiner* (19 December 2002), cited in Arnold, *Irish Gulag*, p. 171. Jim has been a vocal proponent for the need to remove the criminality attached to those who were placed in the industrial schools.
102 Ibid., p. 158.
103 Ibid., p. 159.
104 'Father Sent to Prison', *Irish Independent*, 10 February 1925.
105 Letter to the NSPCC inspector from a Sister of Mercy, St Michael's Industrial School Wexford, 1929. Case files of the NSPCC (ISPCC Limerick).

5

Incest and immorality

Introduction

1884, the Recorder of Dublin[1] commented with regard to the case of a fifty-year-old man charged with 'assault to ravish his daughter':

> [T]his was one of the worst cases ever proven in a Criminal Court. On submitted evidence this man was proven to have committed an act of violence, an unnatural offence on his own child, a girl of fourteen. The circumstances were unspeakably shocking. The prisoner should have been sentenced to penal servitude for life.[2]

The man received two years' imprisonment in separate confinement; but the case is notable for four primary reasons: the judge's reaction; the father's defence; the role of the girl's mother; and the girl's attempts to resist. While the shock and horror of the judge is apparent in the above statement, his comments later also demonstrate Victorian attitudes to respectability and femininity, as he discusses the effect of the incident on the 'decency and morality of the girl and her sisters, and the respectability of the man's wife'.[3] In examining the father's defence, the lack of any remorse – a feature common to most cases involving incestuous abuse – is evident. Initially, the defendant referred to his twenty-five years of service in the army, and following this, he moved to blaming his wife's actions for the incident:

> When in India I unfortunately married a soldier's widow when I was young and foolish, which has been my drawback ever since. Her former husband poisoned himself with drink, she has taught the children as they grew up to dislike me. She also has kept me in perpetual torment and disgrace by running away from me and the children.[4]

In many cases of incest, the absence of a wife/mother for short periods of time resulted in the eldest girl being forced to take over domestic duties. In this instance, the man intimates that the daughter should also have taken over marital duties, providing a perspective on perverse attitudes towards the female child in a patriarchal family structure. The girl did, however, attempt to resist the abuse; the report stated, 'on one particular occasion he tried to induce the girl to sleep with him. Suspecting his intentions she refused and went to stay with her little sister; he came to her bed and she rose and attempted to dress herself as he was attempting to ravish her'.[5] Prosecuted in 1884, the case was tried twenty-two years before incest was made a criminal offence in Britain and Ireland. Prior to 1908, offences could be prosecuted criminally as carnal knowledge or rape of a daughter or sister. Yet, as will be argued in this chapter, legislation did not always ensure greater protection for victims of incest or better rates of detection. In fact, the provision of hearing cases in camera placed greater barriers to prosecution.[6] Once this impediment was realised, and following intense debate in three separate committees on sexual offences, in 1922 British legislation was amended. This was followed swiftly by legislative change in Northern Ireland in 1923. Yet in the southern State, these changes did not occur until 1995, with the result that incest remained a misdemeanour and cases continued to be heard in camera until then. The reasoning behind this seventy-year lag will be addressed in this chapter, particularly with regard to the treatment of sexuality and sexual 'morality' after independence, the role of the family in Irish society, and the powerlessness of victims of incest whose paths of resistance were limited. The NSPCC's role is critical here also. The need to protect the sanctity of the family, and the moral power of the Catholic Church in society, would act as bulwarks to any interference in the family unit that would cause disruption. Revelations of incest would surely have done just this.[7]

First, this chapter will trace the debates surrounding incest from the 1880s to the introduction of the 1908 Punishment of Incest Act. Changes to the act in Britain and Northern Ireland in the 1920s will then be addressed, to highlight the failure of the Irish State to protect victims legislatively, as will the issue of in-camera proceedings. With regard to the State, the silence in parliament and in the press surrounding incest and sexual offences against children after independence will be discussed, as will the report on venereal disease (1926), discourses on 'evil literature' (1927) and the Carrigan Committee (1931–32). A discussion of the role of the National Society for the Prevention of Cruelty to Children (NSPCC) in Ireland in identifying 'immorality' then follows. Finally, examples from the NSPCC case files and the courts will be examined, highlighting the restricted choices available to victims of incest – principally emigration, institutionalisation and drawing outside attention to the situation. As many cases came to the attention of the police as a result of pregnancy or infanticide, how girls were treated by the courts will also be addressed.

'A working-class crime': the 1908 Punishment of Incest Act

Historically, incest was an ecclesiastical and not a criminal offence, and this interpretation of incest as a moral crime remained dominant throughout the nineteenth century. As late as 1885, incest was spoken of euphemistically in medical journals as 'things done in secret',[8] and in Ireland, debates were couched in this euphemistic language until the emergence of second-wave feminism in the 1970s. Following an examination of the housing conditions of the working classes in Britain in 1883–84, social reformers began to acknowledge and represent incest as a vicious male and implicitly a working-class crime. As with debates on cruelty to children and wife-beating, they pursued their agenda through the use of environmentalist language and, in particular, through the perceived connection between incest and overcrowding. The effects of this contextualisation would reverberate throughout the twentieth century in Ireland. From the beginning of the twentieth century, the Dublin slums became the focus of vigilance groups and campaigners, as the relationship between overcrowding, sanitary conditions and immorality among the working classes was regularly referred to in official reports and the press.[9] As late as the 1940s, this connection was still prevalent in Dáil debates.

In a 1979 article on the creation of the 1908 Punishment of Incest Act, Bailey and Blackburn outline the circumstances that led to the decision to legislate. They highlight the notion that incest was not viewed as a crime as it was not legislated for, the fact of its being a subject of taboo in Victorian Britain, and the lack of statistical evidence of its prevalence, which led to ideas that incest remained 'an area of morality' into which the intervention of the criminal law 'did not seem appropriate'.[10] Addressing the rediscovery of incest in the late nineteenth century, and the social context in which criminalisation occurred; Bailey and Blackburn begin the examination with the Royal Commission on the Housing of the Working Classes (1884–85). Following this, the National Vigilance Association (NVA) and the NSPCC are referred to, as both campaigned for the moral protection of children through 'legal threat and legal action', highlighting increasing numbers of immorality cases. While two initial legislative attempts were defeated, in 1908 the Punishment of Incest Act was passed, with two notable amendments – the prevention of prosecution without the sanction of the Attorney General or Director of Public Prosecutions; and all proceedings to be held in camera.

In general, the 1908 act was a product of a distinctive social movement, which combined preventative work in the cause of child protection with a demand for social purity. Unfortunately, without the public acknowledgement of incest, the statutes themselves were more significant for the NSPCC and NVA than for victims, in particular with regard to the holding of cases in camera.[11] The ineffectiveness of the acts was an issue in the British legislative change in 1922, as it became apparent that the continuation of the in-camera proceedings was not suitable. In Ireland, the 1908 legislation was not amended until 1995. The Irish State's failure to amend the 1908 legislation is significant, particularly in regard to the in-camera proceedings. As censorship of sexual matters in Ireland became a constant from the late 1920s, the question of whether incest cases prior to the 1908 were reported sensationally, or dealt with in an objective manner, is critical. In 1918, the chairman of the committee to examine the Criminal Law Amendment Bill and Sexual Offences Bill in Britain addressed this issue:

> before that Act was passed, the very large majority of cases of carnal knowledge of children under 13 were cases of incest and those cases were invariably heard in public; and as far as the reports in newspapers were concerned I can say I have seen a very great number of them and generally they are three lines: 'So and so, by a serious offence on his own daughter, aged 7, seven years penal servitude', and that is all; there are no details given at all. Then when the Incest Act came the same cases were tried under the Incest Act, and they are not reported at all except in the same way ... I do not think criminal cases are indecently or suggestively reported in the newspapers.[12]

Interestingly, during debates on the Illegitimate Affiliation Order Bill in Ireland in 1930, in both houses of the Oireachtas a number of ministers mentioned the in-camera proceedings. In particular, the Minister for Justice Mr Fitzgerald-Kenney repeatedly argued against the in-camera proceedings in maintenance cases, with Mrs Wyse Power on the opposing side. Senator Wyse Power flagged the opinions of the clergy and social workers on this issue, who were both in favour of in-camera proceedings. The motivations of each are worth considering. For the clergy, in-camera proceedings protected the pure image of Irish men and women, and kept debates on unmarried mothers and putative fathers away from the press. For social workers, the motivation may have been similar, although more centred on gaining maintenance for the woman involved.

In Britain in 1922, legislation reclassified incest as a felony as opposed to a misdemeanour, leading on from the recommendations of the 1918 British committee to examine the Criminal Law Amendment Bill and Sexual Offences Bill, who stated: 'it is far better that there should be the right to go in and hear justice administered than have justice administered in secret'.[13] In Ireland the secrecy was protected. Even at this stage, the divergence of British and Irish opinion on child protection and particularly child sexual abuse was apparent, and would only become more pronounced from the 1920s on. In relation to the second provision in the 1908 act, the authority of the Attorney General or Director of Public Prosecutions, in 1912 a letter was written to the Chief Constable of the Borough Police by the Secretary of State regarding a man who was arrested and charged with incest without communicating with the Director of Public Prosecutions. As a result, the man's indictment was quashed. The letter states: 'in no case should a prisoner be arrested or a charge preferred under the Punishment of Incest Act unless the authority of the Director of Public Prosecutions or the sanction of the Attorney General has been first obtained.'[14] This leads to serious issues with regard to the actual detection of incest and the charging of persons alleged to have committed the crime. As with notification of most crimes, the more difficult it is to arrest and charge suspected perpetrators, the less cases will be brought to the attention of the police and the courts, and the fewer victims will come forward to report crimes. This will become more relevant when looking at the courts, but by and large, although campaigns on sexual matters between 1880 and 1925 did succeed in bringing legislative changes, they merely channelled victims through a 'totally unsympathetic criminal justice system' which was ill-prepared to deal with the nuances of sexual cases.[15] If anything, as acknowledged by the 1918 British committee, the introduction of incest legislation curbed the number of cases being brought to court. The following section will look specifically at Ireland after 1922, particularly official debates on the Criminal Law Amendment (CLA) Acts (1885–1935) and sexual offences.

Morality and 'the sanctity of the family' in the Irish Free State, 1922–50

> We have the power to legislate if we have the will to put power on the legislature.[16]

The move towards Irish independence was 'disruptive'[17] for a number of reasons: the suffrage campaign which had threatened gender roles and provided a demand for women's new role in the Irish Free State, discussions of sexuality and sexual morality which had emerged from the suffrage and labour press, and the 'politicisation of prostitution and venereal disease'[18] by nationalists and feminists. Prior to independence, the *Irish Citizen* newspaper was central to feminist activity in Ireland. Published from May 1912 to August 1920, it produced seven volumes and was the political and radical newspaper associated with the Irish suffrage movement.[19] With regard to sexual crime, the work of women such as M. E. Duggan, the Honorary Secretary of the Watching the Courts Committee,[20] made readers of the paper aware of the 'unpleasant'[21] cases of child abuse that were occurring in Dublin, a radical departure at a time when the press reported very few if any such cases.[22] As Duggan wrote in 1915 with regard to the removal of women from the courtroom during sexual abuse cases:

> When will men realise that women are part of the public; that they are fully entitled to be present at all cases open to the public, and that there is nothing unusual nowadays (or, indeed, at any time in Ireland) in women interesting themselves in political cases? There is something quaintly Early Victorian in the attitude that, while welcoming women as nurses on the battle-field, as doctors in charge of military hospitals at the Front, still regards it as 'unwomanly' for them to be seen (save in the dock, of course: no one disputes their right to be there) in Green Street or in the Police Court.[23]

Lindsey Earner-Byrne's work demonstrates how, in the period after independence, there emerged an 'ideal' vision of Irish society, one which would involve a partnership between the churches, the voluntary and charitable organisations, the State and the family. In essence, this partnership would 'protect' the family unit and portray a moral image of Ireland internationally. However, as Earner-Byrne shows, this vision emerged at a time when the

Irish family was being challenged by a low marriage rate, poverty, modernity and fears of immorality.[24] How these fears and anxieties manifested in legislation and welfare policy is critical, as are comparisons with Britain and Northern Ireland, particularly in official debates. As will be demonstrated, incestuous abuse in the family unit lay far from the ideal official image of a moral, Catholic, traditional society.

Debates on sexual crime and children in Britain and Ireland from the teens to the late 1920s can be identified through an examination of six specific reports, which will be referred to by year and short title. In Britain, the published report on the CLA Bill and Sexual Offences Bill (1918); the report on the Criminal Law Amendment Bills (1&2) and the Sexual Offences Bill (1920); and the report on Sexual Offences Against Young Persons (1925). In Ireland, the unpublished report on Venereal Disease (1926) and the report on the Criminal Law Amendment Acts (1880–85) and Juvenile Prostitution (commonly known as the Carrigan Committee report). In November 1918, the committee report of the CLA and Sexual Offences Bill was entered unfinished, due to the dissolution of parliament. It had considered the bills put before it, most notably on the age of consent, penalties for wilfully transferring venereal disease, the recommendations of the 1916 Royal Commission on Venereal Disease, the presence of children in court, incest proceedings, prostitution, and various other issues. In 1920, another committee was formed to look at the bills and a further bill on the CLA Acts. It was decided they would amalgamate the three and the result was the 1922 CLA Act. In contrast to Irish reports in the 1920s, issues such as incest were discussed in detail, as was the use of 'honest defence' with regard to age of consent in cases of indecent assault. While the changes proposed by both committees would result in a change to the CLA Acts, in Ireland this legislative change did not occur until 1935 and to a far more diluted extent.

In 1925, the British report of the Departmental Committee on Sexual Offences against Young Persons was published. The committee had initially emerged from a debate in a Home Office vote in July 1923. From July 1924 to July 1925,[25] the eight committee members met forty-eight times and interviewed seventy-five witnesses.[26] Their aim was 'to collect information and to take evidence as to the prevalence of sexual offences against young persons'.[27] With regard to incest, the report stated:

> A conviction of incest may deprive the family of the support of a father or brother for many years and there are may be no source of income, other than Poor Relief, during the time he is in prison. It is therefore readily admitted by official and other witnesses that the number of incest cases reported to the police can only be a small proportion of those that actually occur.[28]

The report included statistics on children who had died from venereal disease (VD), stating that: 'from the evidence of legal and medical witnesses, a certain number of cases of gonorrhoea in these young girls is due to the superstition that connection with a virgin will cure a man'. In the Irish report on VD from 1917 to 1923, produced in 1926, it was stated that 177 infants under the age of one year died from congenital syphilis, while only six infants were recorded as dying from other venereal diseases. Due to the lack of official statistics these figures could possibly have been much larger, yet incest was rarely mentioned in any of the Irish reports, and especially not in relation to venereal disease, which can, in the case of gonorrhoea, be an indicator of incest. This is important when we look at cases in the courts, where prosecutions were often successful as a result of the child having contracted a sexually transmitted infection or disease, demonstrating medical awareness of how VD was contracted.

The Interdepartmental Committee to examine the issues surrounding venereal disease in the Irish Free State was set up in December 1924 and consisted of three members of government: Percy McDonnell, Medical Inspector in the Department of Local Government, Colonel Higgins, Director of Medical Services in the Department of Defence and John Duff, a barrister in the Department of Justice. It held fourteen meetings in Dublin and one each in Cork and Galway and examined twenty-four witnesses, with written statements from others. With regard to the 'moral situation' mentioned by some witnesses as explanation for rising VD rates, the report states: 'while this contention may be accurate, we felt that were it accepted it may lead us outside the subject with which we were appointed to deal'.[29] Continuing this point, and also passing responsibility to different agencies, the report states: 'we may remark that the extent to which the State can interfere to promote morality is strictly limited: we feel that the only hope of any marked improvement in this respect lies in the activity of moral agencies.'[30]

The committee made a number of observations in its report, such as the fact that a number of the sufferers were innocent persons, especially women and children. The evidence from the army demonstrated that while prostitution was an issue, '90 per cent of the men who acquired the disease were infected by women who were not prostitutes'.[31] It also commented on how the recommendations of the 1916 Report of the Royal Commission on Venereal Disease had not been adopted in most counties in Ireland, and the 'lack of interest of the medical profession' evidenced in the insignificant number who sought training in treating the diseases. Some of the recommendations made to the committee were that notification of venereal disease should be compulsory, but that the sufferer should remain anonymous; that it be made a crime to wilfully and knowingly infect another with venereal disease; that steps be taken to educate the public; and that in dealing with girls charged with soliciting the punishment should be reformative rather than punitive.

Evidence to the committee varied greatly, from social worker Frank Duff's suggestions of 'State or state-encouraged action', and in particular the legislative curbing of indecent literature, to Dr Moorhead's statement that 'education of the public by public lectures is undesirable'.³² The evidence also noted lack of police powers with regard to brothels, prostitution and indecent assaults, as well as considerations of the effect of immoral behaviour on children. In comparing the report to the Royal Commission in 1916 and the three British reports of the 1920s, there are a number of similarities: the recognition of the need to focus on VD as a public health issue, the suppression of prostitution by the removal of the fine on first offence, and the discussion surrounding making it a crime to willingly infect another with VD.³³ However, there are also contrasts. Unlike the British reports, the Irish reports rejected recommendations for women police, were overtly focused on morality; contained limited statistics on VD; and failed to examine a possible connection between venereal disease and incest. The next time these issues would be examined officially was in 1931 by the Carrigan Committee.

The Carrigan Committee and sexual offences against young persons (1931)

A Department of Justice memorandum regarding the Carrigan Committee Report, dated 27 October 1932, stated:

> It is understood that many competent authorities have grave doubts as to the value of children's evidence. A child with a vivid imagination may actually live in his mind the situation as he invented it and will be quite unshaken by severe cross-examination.³⁴

The Carrigan Committee was set up in 1931 to examine the 1880 and 1885 CLA Acts and the 'problem of juvenile prostitution'. As previously addressed, in Britain and Northern Ireland the CLA legislation had been changed in 1922 and 1923, and by the late 1920s new CLA legislation in the southern Irish State was 'overdue and unavoidable'.³⁵ The chairman of the committee was William Carrigan, K.C.; on 20 August 1931, after seventeen sittings, twenty-nine witnesses and eight resolutions, including memoranda from a range of national and international sources, the final report was submitted to the Minister for Justice. Incest was referred to only twice – in the evidence of the Garda Commissioner General Eoin O'Duffy, who provided statistics for incest cases reported to the police, and by the district judge Dermot Gleeson, who stated his belief that late marriages resulted in incest cases. The emphasis on the mind and the psychology of young girls was provided by women working in the medical profession and was in keeping with developments in Britain in the inter-war years, in which adolescence was highlighted as a period of vulnerability for young girls. Generally, the Carrigan report reflected many of the suggestions of the women witnesses. The evidence from the eighteen women reporting to the committee had followed two decades of lobbying and feminist consciousness-raising, highlighting the following imperatives:

that the age of consent be raised from 16 to 18, with further protection up to the age of 21 against employers or guardians who might exert pressure to obtain consent; repeal of a proviso in the 1885 CLA Act that permitted a defence in unlawful carnal knowledge cases that accused had 'reasonable cause to believe' a girl was aged between 13 and 15 years of age; and the raising of the statutory time limit for initiating unlawful carnal knowledge cases from six to twelve months after the offence had occurred.[36]

Following Fianna Fáil's accession to power in 1932, a committee composed of government ministers was set up to consider the Carrigan Committee's report. After extensive consultations with the hierarchy a 'watered-down version' of the initial Carrigan report was proposed.[37] In response to the recommendations of the committee, the National Council of Women of Ireland passed a motion in favour of the age of consent being raised to eighteen years minimum. It also agreed that solicitation laws should be equally applied to women and men, and female police officers needed to be introduced into the Garda Síochana. All of these items had been recommended by the Carrigan Committee, and an identical resolution was passed by the United Council of Christian Churches and Religious Communions in Ireland. Both were sent to the Minister of Justice and both were rejected. With regard to the influence of Catholic organisations, it appears they had an effect on the ministerial committee and the final legislation passed; however, it also appears that the State was attempting to impose its own moral ideal and protect men from being 'falsely accused' of sexual impropriety. Sandra McAvoy's examination of the committee's actions demonstrates that the evidence of female witnesses was representative of lobbying by feminists before and after independence, as well as Catholic and Protestant moral purity campaigners throughout the 1920s.[38] McAvoy questions the decision not to publish the report, arguing that while the desire may have been to conceal information on serious socio-medical problems in the Irish Free State, most of this information had been in the public domain for the previous two decades. She continues: 'Might a more pressing reason have been a possibility that a CLA Bill would fail, or be rendered ineffectual, had a full discussion of the age of consent and 'reasonable clause' provisions been permitted?'[39]

On the wider issue of child sexual abuse from the late-nineteenth-century, Eoin O'Sullivan argues that the interest in the sexuality of children from the 1880s was part of a broader concern with 'redefining childhood' associated with the latter half of the nineteenth century.[40] Citing various moral panics in the nineteenth and twentieth centuries, O'Sullivan pinpoints the debates surrounding the age of consent and the CLA Act (1885); the 'problem' of the unmarried mother and immorality in the 1920s; as well as the Carrigan Committee and the CLA Act (1935). With regard to the 1885 Act, O'Sullivan discusses how legislation 'failed to provide adequate protection against sexual abuse within families', in that where a girl had passed the age of sixteen, the law could not be utilised retrospectively to punish ongoing incest.[41] After independence, the discussion focuses on the rigorous debate on sexual abuse that took place, 'couched as it was in various euphemisms', with the unmarried mother representing the principal concern. Tracing the development of special homes in the 1920s, O'Sullivan examines R. S. Devane's influence and writings, particularly surrounding the age of consent.[42] Following this, the emphasis is placed on the Carrigan Committee, and the 1935 CLA Act. Overall, O'Sullivan contends that our understanding of child sexual abuse is socially and legally constructed, rather than an everlasting truth.[43] The following section will address the NSPCC's role in this construction from the 1880s.

The NSPCC and 'immorality'

From its foundation, the NSPCC pushed for legislation to criminalise incest, while also acknowledging its occurrence through the removal of children who were victims of 'immorality' from the home to industrial schools. Aside from the Society's official reports, in the 247 case files that have survived up to 1940, there are a small number of references to incest – albeit euphemistically termed. Also, from 1889 to 1906, of the 1,227,786 children dealt with by the NSPCC, 25,478 were described as 'morally outraged'.[44] This figure includes both Britain and Ireland, but it is a substantial number of children in a seventeen-year period. Due to the vagueness of the term 'morally outraged', assumptions should not be made that all these cases involved sexual abuse, but a considerable figure more than likely did. Louise Jackson has examined the Society's use of the term 'immorality' in cases of child sexual abuse, and ascertained that it often referred to cases of incest, while the term 'juvenile prostitution' usually alluded to cases of child sexual abuse.[45] That 'juvenile prostitution' was included in the terms of investigation for the Carrigan Committee indicates the continued use of euphemisms in Ireland after independence in discussions of sexual crime against children. In the case of the NSPCC, from 1920 the term 'immorality' was replaced in the Irish NSPCC reports by the euphemisms 'immoral surroundings', 'moral danger' and 'other wrongs'. With regard to how cases of immorality were treated, in 1895 the Dublin branch stated that while it was opposed to the use of industrial schools as a rule, this was not the case in investigations of immorality. In these instances, children should be transferred to industrial schools immediately. Yet aside from this, there is little discussion of immorality except for figures in the annual reports of the Irish branches. These figures will now be addressed.

As Table 5.1 shows, between 1930 and 1941, there were 133 cases of 'immoral surroundings/moral danger' investigated by the Dublin branch of the NSPCC, and 623 cases classed as 'other wrongs'. In Cork there were fifty-one cases of 'immoral surroundings' and 698 cases of 'other wrongs'. Yet throughout all twelve other branches from 1933 to 1950, there were only twenty-nine cases of 'moral danger', twelve of these coming from

Table 5.1 Number of investigations of immoral surroundings or moral danger and other wrongs in NSPCC annual reports, 1933–50

	Immoral surroundings/ moral danger	Other wrongs
Dublin	133	623
Cork	51	698
Limerick / Clare	12	85
Remaining branches	17	84

ISPCC, Limerick.

the Limerick/Clare District branch, and 169 'other wrongs', with eighty-five of them from the Limerick/Clare District branch. As there was more policing in urban areas than in rural areas, the figures are not surprising. However, the limited number of cases prosecuted in the courts poses questions surrounding how the inspector dealt with situations of 'moral danger'.

From the Society's beginnings, it was acknowledged that children in situations of 'immorality' would be removed from their homes and placed in industrial schools. From the case files it is difficult to assess whether this policy was pursued throughout the period of examination, but it most likely was. Although it can only be speculated from the available evidence, it is probable that placement in an industrial school or Catholic home would have been the preferred choice of both the NSPCC inspector and the family involved. As testimonies in court records will demonstrate, incestuous abuse was never disclosed and acted on voluntarily. The reasons may lie in the answers to the following three questions: aside from escaping the abuse, what recourse did victims have? With attitudes to children's evidence and uncorroborated evidence, why would victims face an unsympathetic court system? With the continuation of in-camera proceedings, and no press coverage of incest, did many victims know that legally their rights were being violated? Before addressing individual cases and common themes in the files, it is necessary to address the situation in the courts.

Watching the courts

From the sample of incest cases retrieved from the court records, there are a number of interesting observations that can be made. Of the twenty-five cases prior to 1920, the average sentence was just under seven years, although the majority of offenders were given sentences of penal servitude. From 1920 onwards, of the twenty-four cases located, the average sentence was two years (again, however, this was an average of two years' imprisonment, as penal servitude was chosen very rarely in the period). As previous cases could be prosecuted under the crime of rape, perpetrators could be sentenced for up to twenty years, while the 1908 act identified incest as a misdemeanour.

This carried a maximum sentence of seven years. With regard to official figures of cases investigated from 1922, from Eoin O'Duffy's evidence to the Carrigan Committee in 1935 it appears that forty-four cases of incest were investigated by the Gardaí from 1927 to 1935.[46] Similarly, from 1939 when the figures were first recorded, to 1949, twenty-one convictions of incest resulted in prison sentences. The above facts all demonstrate that although incest was not being directly addressed by the State, the medical profession, the legal profession or to a large extent the press, it was a fact of Irish life.

How, then, did these cases come to the attention of police or the gardaí? In general, the discovery of incestuous abuse was as a result either of a girl's pregnancy (or in some cases infanticide or attempted infanticide) or of the perpetrator being 'caught in the very act'. Prior to the criminalisation of incest and the introduction of in-camera proceedings in 1908, many cases of carnal knowledge of children under thirteen reported in the press were incest cases. Drunkenness was a common defence put forward by the perpetrators. In 1890, the *Anglo-Celt* newspaper in Donegal carried an article on the Father Matthew Centenary. In his speech to the congregation, the Revd J. McNulty spoke at length on the evils of drunkenness. His sermon, entitled 'Lower than the Beast', argued that drink 'should be avoided altogether' and cited the case of Lot in the Bible as a warning. As the paper recorded:

> The crimes the result of drunkenness were then shown, and as an example that it caused the downfall of the holiest the preacher mentioned the case of Lot, who under the influence of wine committed incest with his own daughters. It was also impossible that a drunkard could be a Christian man and his hopes of heaven were very small.[47]

Again, as with cruelty to children and wife-beating, alcohol consumption and intemperance were put forward as the cause of incest. That Lot was 'the holiest' further added to the tale, as it implied that any man could commit such a crime under the influence of drink.

The cases

While there appears to be a difference in the sentences imposed by the courts before and after 1922, it is difficult to assess this due to changes in the appliance of penal servitude and imprisonment for offences, as well as legislative changes. This section will therefore look at a number of cases from the NSPCC case files and the courts throughout the seventy-year period, highlighting common themes. It will address the use of institutionalisation to 'deal' with victims (particularly after 1922), the treatment of incest victims accused of infanticide, and the paths of resistance available to victims, primarily emigration and running away. First it will look briefly at cases prior to 1908.

In August 1895, a man received ten years of penal servitude for the carnal knowledge of his daughter, a girl under thirteen years.[48] While concrete evidence was often needed to convict in incest cases, this sentence of ten years was not unusually long, as prior to 1922 cases of rape and carnal knowledge were severely punished by the courts. This is an interesting observation when one considers that legislation was enacted in 1908 to function as a greater deterrent. Again in 1905, a thirty-nine year old farmer was charged with the rape of his thirteen-year-old daughter. He was sentenced to five years of penal servitude. However, during the trial it emerged that the police had believed he had committed a similar offence with another daughter, but 'no evidence could be procured on that occasion'. The testimony appears to have affected the jury's decision to convict, and the judge's urging of a long sentence.[49] As with cases even today, the urging of a judge for either leniency or punitive sentencing was often critical.

In contrast to the previous cases, in 1914, a forty-year-old man who had pleaded guilty to incest received only three years' penal servitude at the Belfast General Assizes. Aside from the length of the sentence, however, there are similarities, most notably the absence of the girl's mother 'owing to a quarrel', and the perpetrator's persistent explanations. In his deposition he claimed:

> I was arrested on the 14 Feb 1914 and charged with attempt to commit an indecent assault on my daughter ... [N]ow my Lord my wife was away and left me with 6 children for 3 weeks and the youngest was only 6 months old and me and my daughter and the baby boy had to get up 3 or 4 times every night to make the baby a bottle of milk and I had to rise every morning at 5.30 to go to work and my daughter had to mind the baby and she left me in Feb 1914 and got me arrested and charged as above ... [T]he doctor said that he had examined my daughter and he said in reply to ____ solicitor ... it could have occurred through a hurt[;] he did not say that I had anything to do with her.[50]

The case illustrates not only the man's lack of remorse but also the girl's final act of desperation. There were numerous previous assaults before she felt she could leave him. Two other prevalent aspects of investigations into child sexual abuse in the period are contained in the case – the reluctance to believe the girl involved, and the need for a medical examination. If the physical evidence had not been satisfactory, the case would not have gone to trial as the Attorney General or the Director of Public Prosecutions had control over what cases made it to court and the evidence needed to be compelling.

There were very few options for victims, and for those who did not run away, the outcome could be pregnancy. At the City Commission of Dublin in 1915, a man was tried for unlawful carnal knowledge of his daughter. She had given birth to a child, but the child had died in a case of suspected infanticide.[51] Although the judge had threatened to prosecute her, she was instead sent to a Magdalene laundry. Her father received only a short sentence. While the judge had shown sympathy in not prosecuting the girl, she was seen to have been tainted, and in need of repentance. In 1932,

Incest and immorality

another case involving infanticide was heard at the Central Criminal Court in Dublin. The girl was charged with the manslaughter of her son in March 1932. She received a twelve-month suspended sentence and a recognisance that she would go to the Good Shepherd Convent in Cork for two years. The circumstances surrounding the case are quite shocking. The incestuous abuse had begun in 1924 but was only discovered after she gave birth in 1931 and the subsequent infanticide charge. Her father was sentenced to ten years' penal servitude on two counts of incest. While this was a severe sentence for the time, the girl endured numerous years of abuse and was then forced to enter a Magdalene laundry.

While the 1920s, 1930s and 1940s saw a complete lack of reporting of crimes of sexual assault or incest in the press due to censorship and the State's unwillingness to deal with child sexual abuse, the NSPCC made a small number of references to incest. In the 1930s, with regard to proposed changes to the Children Act (1908), the Society included a number of sample cases in its annual reports. The following case, entitled 'Difficulty in removing children in danger from an unnatural father', illustrates the Society's concern with needing the permission of a father for the removal of a child to an industrial school. This was a genuine issue that the Society was addressing.

> A father of four children, three boys and a girl, ages ranging from 7 years to 1½ years, of the tramp class had been sent to prison for two years for a very serious offence against his own daughter, a child of 5½ years. The mother sought for some months to get the children into schools as she was only a poor pedlar ... To get the children into schools it was necessary to get the consent of both parents under the law as it stands ... The father was seen by the inspector in the prison and emphatically refused, saying 'let them go to the workhouse'.[52]

The case demonstrates three primary issues: the economic situation for families when the breadwinner was imprisoned, the lack of support for single mothers and their children, and the idea that removing obstacles to institutionalisation was the primary concern of the NSPCC. Obviously, it was undesirable for the man to maintain rights to his children after such a violation, but the automatic response of the NSPCC and the State in choosing institutionalisation did not alleviate the suffering of victims. Separation from the remaining family members and their mother could not have been the best option. As previously addressed, the NSPCC had always maintained that victims of incest, or 'immorality', could be sent to industrial schools. However, both the NSPCC case files and the court records show that many older girls were also sent to Magdalene laundries. In 1938, a widower, the father of six, was investigated for neglect and starvation by the Society. He was described as being 'fond of drink and undignified' and 'very violent when drunk'. The report elaborates, stating: 'Since the death of his wife – is drinking and neglecting his family. Some say that he assaulted his oldest daughter Mary aged 18 years and turned her out of home. The girl is now in an institution in Tramore, Co. Waterford'.[53] In this case the younger children were left with the father. The girl was sent to a Magdalene Home, lending weight to the argument that she was being sexually abused by her father. What is significant is that the inspector did not follow up the claim by visiting the girl or consider removing the other children. If abuse had occurred, the risk to other girls in the family could have been quite great.

Attitudes to gender and 'moral criminality' must be considered. In a case in 1935, the inspector visited a family in Gorey after a complaint was made about a fifteen-year-old girl. The case is significant in that the girl, who had been a victim of her father's incestuous abuse, was the one under investigation. At the time of investigation she was living with her mother, her one-year-old sister and an elderly couple who were not related. Her father had been arrested and sentenced for the crime of incest in December of the previous year, and the inspector was checking that the girl was not 'going astray'. The implication was that because of the abuse she had suffered she was in some way tainted. This double standard based on a gender bias, and a reflection of Catholic social teaching governing 'moral' criminality issues was applied to many other women, not only victims of sexual abuse.

In 1935 the Kane family in Wexford were visited by the NSPCC inspector, after a report by the gardaí concerning the father's conduct and violence.[54] The inspector recorded that on New Year's Eve 1934, Mrs Kane, the mother of the five children, left the house to visit to friends in Dublin. Upon her departure, Mr Kane 'assaulted and terrified' Maureen, the eldest child aged 14 years. The entry in the inspector book describes how he came to her bed, pulled her out and tried to drag her to the other room. She managed to run outside and hide, sleeping in a fowl house at rear of house.

Sibling incest is another interesting theme in the files. It appears the courts were more lenient in cases where they felt it was more innocent. On 6 April 1920, for example, the County Commission in Dublin heard the cases of a brother and sister both charged with incest. Both received a verdict of nolle prosequi. However, in 1941, a man received six calendar months for the indecent assault of his sister, aged thirteen years.[55] That he was much older and the nature of the incestual relationship appears not to have been reciprocal was a factor in the sentence. In a previous yet similar case on 15 January 1935, a man received twenty-one calendar months with hard labour for three counts of incest against his sister at the Dublin Criminal Circuit Court.

With regard to parental incest, often the sentences were quite lenient, particularly when the man pleaded guilty and demonstrated remorse. In April 1923, a man pleaded guilty to the carnal knowledge and indecent assault of his daughter, who was at the time 13 years and 2 months old. He was imprisoned for six months with hard labour.

In 1926 at Cork Criminal Circuit Court, a man received eighteen calendar months for the assault and carnal knowledge of his daughter.[56]

'What has become of the girl?'

In many of cases that have been cited, the figure of the child is often overlooked. In 1928, in a case in which a 52-year-old man fathered his sixteen-year-old daughter's child, the Inspector-General asked 'What has become of the girl?' Owing both to the stigma attached to being an unmarried mother in Ireland at the time and the added stigma of being a victim of incest, the girl was forced to emigrate to England to stay with an uncle.[57] The child was given to an orphanage. What is also missing from the cases is incestuous abuse involving boys as victims. In this study, there were no cases involving boys, except those in which they were implicated in sibling incest. In fact it would not be until 2009 that legislation in Ireland was amended to make it a felony for a mother to perpetrate the crime of incest. This demonstrates another incongruity in perceptions of gender with regard to sexual abuse in the family.

How could the situation for victims have been improved? On an official level, children's courts could have been opened; the evidence of children could have been taken as strong enough to produce a committal – even if it was uncorroborated; legislation could have been passed to have cases heard 'otherwise than in public' and for the offence to be treated as a felony, not merely a misdemeanour. On a wider level, concern for girls and women could have trumped concerns for male protection from 'false accusations', particularly since it was unlikely that false accusations would have been an issue, as accusations of incest carry so much stigma even today.

Conclusion

Discourses surrounding incest suffered most from class and gender bias. From its initial 'discovery' by reformers in the 1880s, both perpetrators and victims were portrayed in equally moralistic and iniquitous terms – working-class men as demonic perpetrators, working-class girls as both victims and threats. Framing incest as a working-class crime along with cruelty to children and wife-beating, reformers stigmatised victims instead of trying to save them. By demonising incest and legislating for it as a working-class crime, reformers could separate incest from their conception of 'home' and the middle-class family. With regard to the criminalisation of incest in 1908, as with the 1908 Children Act, legislation pursued under the banner of children's rights did not always result in a better situation for victims. As the court records demonstrate, in most cases the victim was the least relevant, and the discovery of incest could create further struggles. Revelations of their abuse categorised victims as threats and for most institutionalisation or emigration was the consequence. Although incest was ignored by the press, in the Oireachtas and by the medical profession through much of the period of this study, its presence was alluded to euphemistically, and notwithstanding in-camera court proceedings, its existence was very real and among other immoral issues, should have been acknowledged.

For the NSPCC, incest had remained an imprisoning offence, and from its foundation girls were automatically sent to industrial schools. While the Society was central to the criminalisation of incest in 1908, without an acknowledgement of why or how incestuous abuse occurred, the act simply pushed victims through an unsympathetic legal system. By 1922, Britain had changed the legislation, classifying incest as a felony as opposed to a misdemeanour. In the following years, the issue of child sexual abuse would be addressed in a less punitive manner also, due to the influence of psychological and sociological discourses which broadened understandings of the causes and the effects of incest. In Ireland, legislation remained unchanged until 1995, and as late as 2009 incestuous abuse by a mother remained a misdemeanour. Aside from the courts, the denial of incest by the medical profession, social workers, the press and the State created an impossible bind for victims of incest, and no incentive to disclose abuse. Yet officially, 'morality' and 'immorality' were being addressed by the State, as the investigations into venereal disease and the CLA acts show.

With regard to family and power, probing the topic of incest reveals a variety of power structures and dynamics. On a micro level, these reveal the powerlessness of victims in a patriarchal society, and on a macro level, the power of the State to protect the sanctity of the family as opposed to the individuals in most need of protection. Yet unlike many other power relations, for victims of incest in Ireland resistance was more a rarity than an actuality.

Notes

1 The Recorder of Dublin was a senior judge in the area, appointed by the Crown. Typically, the appointment would be given to a senior and distinguished practitioner at the Bar, and it was, therefore, usually executed part-time only by a person whose usual practice was as a barrister. It carried a great deal of prestige.
2 CRF/1885/Mc26 (NAI, Dublin).
3 Ibid.
4 Ibid.
5 Ibid.
6 *In camera* is the legal term attached to cases heard in private, or 'otherwise than in public'. This became law in 1908 with the passing of the Punishment of Incest Act.
7 For a discussion of incest in Ireland, see Sarah-Anne Buckley, 'Family and Power: Incest in Ireland, 1880–1950', in *Power in History: from Medieval Ireland to the Post-Modern World, Historical Studies XXVII* (Irish Academic Press, 2011).
8 *The Lancet*, 1885.
9 *Report of the Departmental Committee into the Housing Conditions of the Working Classes in the City of Dublin* (CD 7273), Parliamentary Papers, vol. 19 (1914). See also Christiaan Corlett, *Darkest Dublin: The Story of the Church Street Disaster and a Pictorial Account of the slums of Dublin in 1913* (Wordwell Books, 2008).

10 V. Bailey and S. Blackburn, 'The Punishment of Incest Act 1908: A case study of criminal law creation', *Criminal Law Review*, 685–744 (November 1979), 708–18, p. 709.
11 Ibid., p. 716.
12 Report of the 1918 Committee to investigate the CLA Acts (1880 & 1885).
13 Ibid.
14 Letter from Edward Troup, British Home Office, 20 March 1912, file 44F/CRIM/1/276 (British National Archives, London, 1912).
15 C. Smart, 'Reconsidering the recent history of child sexual abuse, 1910–1960', *Journal of Social Policy*, 29 (2000), 55–71, p. 63.
16 Revd Devane, Evidence to the Committee on Evil Literature, 1927. File JUS7/1/2 (NAI, Dublin). Devane's publications include: 'The unmarried mother: Some legal aspects of the problem. Part I – The age of consent', *Irish Ecclesiastical Record* 23 (January–June 1924), 55–68; 'The unmarried mother: Some legal aspects of the problem. Part II – The legal position of the unmarried mother in the Irish Free State', *Irish Ecclesiastical Record* 23 (January–June 1924), 172–88; 'The unmarried mother and the Poor Law Commission', *Irish Ecclesiastical Record* 31 (January–June 1928), 561–82; 'The dance-hall,' *Irish Ecclesiastical Record* 37 (January–June 1931), 170–94; and 'The legal protection of girls', *Irish Ecclesiastical Record* (January–June 1931), 20–40.
17 Maria Luddy, *Prostitution and Irish Society, 1880–1940* (Cambridge University Press, 2007).
18 Ibid.
19 For an examination of the papers involvement in the suffrage movement and the fight for votes for women, see Louise Ryan, *Irish Feminism and the Vote: An Anthology of the Irish Citizen Newspaper, 1912–1920* (Folens, 1996).
20 The committee was initially set up in March 1915 to show by their presence in court that women demand to be admitted to the administration of justice on equal terms with men, and also to collect evidence bearing on the previous demand, and on any other legal or legislative reforms needed for the protection of women and children. The committee was absolutely non-sectarian and non-partisan, and agreed that there would be no demonstrations by members in court. Members were divided thrice yearly into three groups to watch the Four Courts, the Assizes and the Recorder's Court. Mrs Hanna Sheehy-Skeffington was among one of the first women to sit on the committee.
21 The committee members and any women present in the courtroom were asked to leave when a case the court deemed 'unpleasant' was being heard. However, legally they had no right to force women to leave, so the women from the committee would assert their right to stay, much to the disapproval of many of the legal counsels.
22 The committee recorded one incest case, which had been held in Green Street on 6 August 1915. However, as these were held *in camera*, they could report only that it was taking place. *Irish Citizen* (14 August 1915).
23 *Irish Citizen*, 19 June 1915.
24 Earner-Byrne, 'Reinforcing the family', p. 360.
25 The committee was delayed due to the death of its chairman, Sir Ryland Adkins, and committee member Mr Henry William Disney, at the end of 1924. They were replaced by Mr J. C. Priestley, KC, as chairman and Mr T. W. Fry, OBE. The other committee members were Miss E. H. Kelly, Miss Clara Martineau, Dr A. H. Norris, Mr R. J. Parr, Mrs Rackham and Sir Guy Stephenson.

26 The witnesses were principally made up of legal witnesses, judges, chief constables, medical witnesses, government officials, social workers and 'others'.
27 *Report of the Departmental Committee on Sexual Offences Against Young Persons* (Stationery Office, London, 1925), p. 2.
28 Ibid.
29 Ibid. p. 1.
30 Ibid., p. 4.
31 Ibid., p. 5.
32 Ibid., Appendix E., p. 32.
33 This discussion was particularly interesting in the 1918 Report.
34 NAI, Minutes of Evidence, the Carrigan Committee, file Jus/90/4.
35 S. McAvoy, 'Sexual crime and Irish women's campaign for a Criminal Law Amendment Act, 1912–35', in Maryann Gialanna Valiulis, *Gender and Power in Modern Ireland* (Dublin, Irish Academic Press, 2009), pp. 84–99, p. 85.
36 Ibid., p. 86.
37 James M. Smith, 'The politics of sexual knowledge: The Origins of Ireland's containment culture and the Carrigan Report (1931)', *Journal of the History of Sexuality*, 13:2 (2004), 208–33.
38 McAvoy, 'Sexual crime'.
39 Ibid., p. 97.
40 Eoin O'Sullivan, '"This otherwise delicate subject": Child sexual abuse in early twentieth-century Ireland', in Paul O'Mahony (ed.), *Criminal Justice in Ireland* (Institute of Public Administration, 2002), pp. 172–202.
41 Ibid., p. 183.
42 O'Sullivan points out how R. S. Devane's submissions to the committee on the Criminal Law Amendment Acts (1880–85) and Juvenile Prostitution were 'typical' of the majority of the submissions decrying 'the apparent loosening of public morals over the previous decade'. However, he continues to discuss the testimony of Eoin O'Duffy, who emphasised the number of offences against young children, many the result of parental neglect. The police statistics provided by O'Duffy are only one of two mentions of incest in the committee's evidence.
43 O'Sullivan, 'This otherwise delicate subject', p. 198.
44 *NSPCC Annual Report 1907* (ISPCC, Limerick)
45 Jackson, *Child Sexual Abuse in Victorian England*, p. 23.
46 Memo from Thomas J. Coyne, Secretary in the Department of Justice to R. C. Geary in the Department of Industry and Commerce on Juvenile Crime, 14 May 1936 (NAI, Dublin).
47 'The Father Matthew Century in County Donegal', *Anglo-Celt*, 18 October 1890.
48 Bills 11, 12, 13 and 14, August 1895, Crown Books, Dublin, 1C-28-7 (NAI, Dublin).
49 Ibid.
50 CRF/1916/L5 (NAI, Dublin).
51 Bill 5, City Commission of Dublin, 4 August 1915, 1C-51-80 (NAI, Dublin).
52 Sample case, AR Dublin District Branch NSPCC, 1938–39, p. 11.
53 CF #118.
54 Inspector Book, Wexford District Branch, 5 January 1935 to 11 October 1935 (ISPCC, Limerick).
55 V15-21-30 (NAI, Dublin).
56 Bill 5, 17 June 1926 at the Cork CCC (NAI, Dublin).
57 CCC Files, Cork, 1928 (NAI, Dublin).

6

Gender, familial problems and the NSPCC

Introduction

The importance of gender to the development of child welfare and the actual treatment of families in Ireland has been referred to in different aspects of this book, as has the supervision of mothers and fathers by voluntary agencies, the NSPCC and the State. This chapter will further expand on issues surrounding gender, parental responsibility and State interference in the family. Following this, it will address problems within families, in particular desertion and wife-beating. While it may not appear to be as integral to a discussion of the NSPCC as previous chapters, gender was central to its campaigns and activities. For most of the period under investigation inspectors were men – 'masculine' men as endorsed in the *Inspector's Directory* – while women were restricted to fundraising positions. With regard to the Society's official publications and investigations, from its foundation the virtues and shortcomings of working-class mothers and fathers were addressed regularly but to varying degrees. In the early years, in the Society's attitudes to mothers, criticism was directed at the physical condition of home and children, as inspectors compared working-class living conditions to their own middle-class ideals of cleanliness and order.[1] From 1922, this situation appears to have shifted, as did discussions of mothers in the Society's reports. To a large extent this was a result of the actions of mothers in utilising the Society for material aid and the increase in cases of 'advice sought'. However, there also appears to have been a change in the inspector's attitudes to mothers and fathers. For fathers, this resulted in an increasing emphasis on masculinity and financial support for the family, as this chapter will address.

In the courts there was another interesting situation in terms of which parent was deemed culpable for child neglect and cruelty. While prior to 1922, mothers represented the primary parent prosecuted, constituting 70 per cent of convictions in one sample, from 1924 to 1950 this situation appears to have been reversed, with fathers constituting the largest category of offender. Attitudes to fatherhood are central to this shift. Although they had always been criticised by the Society for not providing materially, after 1922 'putative' fathers and 'deserting' husbands were increasingly highlighted in the annual reports. In contrast, although domestic violence or 'wife-beating' is present in the records, it was acknowledged to be a private matter – not one which affected the public finances. Looking at both desertion and domestic violence in this period therefore reveals a multitude of attitudes in Irish society.

Gendering blame? An examination of gender in cases involving offences against children in Ireland, 1900–50

This section will probe the handling of mothers and fathers by the courts, the State and its agencies in the period 1900–50, in cases involving offences against children. The question to be asked here is why, prior to 1924, mothers represented the principal 'offenders' in cases of child neglect, begging, child abandonment and cruelty to children, and the reasons behind this change in independent Ireland. It will also examine why fathers were more likely to be prosecuted for failure to provide under the Irish Poor Law, than convicted under the 1889 Prevention of Cruelty to Children Act or, later, the 1908 Children Act. Overall, it will question whether, in the period after independence, a renewed focus on the father as male breadwinner and an emphasis on women within the home resulted in a change in the gender make-up of prosecutions. As there is still much work to be done on masculinity and fathers in twentieth-century Ireland, this analysis will provide tentative and speculative conclusions.

An investigation of offences against children in the courts from 1880 to 1950 suggests a number of interesting observations with regard to the treatment of mothers and fathers. As mentioned previously, before 1922 mothers were significantly over-represented in both convictions for offences against children and transfers to the State Inebriate Reformatory in Ennis. There are a number of reasons for this over-representation. Mothers were viewed by voluntary agencies and the State as responsible for the upkeep of the home and of the children in it; therefore when neglect was investigated according to nineteenth-century procedures, mothers were the target. Also, men were usually better positioned to pay fines, so in cases where fathers were prosecuted, they could often avoid prison sentences. Judges were also less inclined to send the primary breadwinner to prison in this period. While a mother's work in the home could be done by an older daughter, or by paying a nurse or local woman, or by relying on extended family, without a wage families would have to rely on poor relief.

Next it is necessary to examine which offences parents were being prosecuted for. Prior to the passing of the 1889 Prevention of Cruelty to Children Act, parents could be prosecuted in a number of ways for neglecting to provide for their children, or harming them physically. Under the Poor Law, fathers could be prosecuted for 'neglecting to maintain family', while the courts could prosecute mothers, fathers or guardians for a variety of crimes – from attempted infanticide to abandonment, concealment of birth, exposure or begging. Interestingly, Ireland had a much higher rate

Table 6.1 Class 1 offences punishable by trial by jury in 1881: comparison between Ireland, England and Scotland

	Ireland: offences in 1881	England: proportionate numbers for same population in 1880	Scotland: proportionate numbers for same population in 1880	Difference between Irish and English figures	Difference between Irish and Scottish figures
Total of more serious offences	7,745	4,477	5,615	3,268	2,130
Infanticide	27	15	14	12	13
Murder	40	12	15	28	25
Manslaughter or culpable homicide	82	51	54	31	28
Offences against life of infants, other than infanticide	118	41	48	77	70
Attempts to murder or do bodily harm, other than infants under two years of age	265	147	98	118	167

Figures taken from the *1882 House of Commons Report into Judicial Statistics in Ireland*, House of Commons Parliamentary Papers.

of prosecution for serious offences, particularly offences against children, than England and Scotland, as demonstrated in Table 6.1. The Irish figures for more serious offences were almost twice those pertaining to a proportionate number of the population of England. With regard to the greater offences against children, there are three probabilities: first, that the stigma attached to illegitimacy in Ireland resulted in more cases of infanticide or attempted infanticide; second, that the Irish courts were particularly sensitive to offences against children; or third, that the greater poverty of many Irish families resulted in higher cases of cruelty to children and neglect.

What is certain is that in cases involving offences against children, parents and guardians were frequently represented, demonstrating that prior to the large number of legislative reforms from 1889, the courts were already prosecuting parents and guardians for severe cases of ill-treatment of children.

Table 6.2 Number of persons tried at the Assizes and Quarter Sessions for offences against children and nature of indictable offence, 1880–1908

Year	Cruelty to children	Abandoning children under five years	Child stealing	Procuring abortion
1880	—	14	0	0
1881	—	5	0	0
1882	—	11	1	0
1883	—	10	2	0
1884	—	9	1	1
1885	—	13	0	1
1886	—	11	2	1
1887	—	10	1	2
1888	—	9	1	0
1889	—	11	0	0
1890	—	12	4	0
1891	—	8	0	6
1892	—	8	0	0
1893	—	12	0	2
1894	—	14	0	0
1895	11	4	2	0
1896	10	3	0	0
1897	8	6	2	0
1898	12	3	0	0
1899	3	3	0	0
1900	7	2	0	2
1901	30	4	1	1
1902	16	8	0	3
1903	20	6	1	0
1904	17	3	0	0
1905	8	4	0	0
1906	10	2	0	0
1907	15	1	0	0
1908	15	2	0	0
Total	182	208	18	19

Figures taken from the *Criminal and Judicial Statistics for Ireland*, House of Commons Parliamentary Papers, 1880–1908.

Not only that, on the whole, prosecutions for severe cases of ill-treatment did not rise dramatically after legislative reforms, even with the increasing categorisation of offences instituted through the 1894 and 1908 acts.[2] What did increase was the number of parents being prosecuted for children's non-attendance at school, and those being prosecuted and fined summarily for cases of child neglect, as Table 6.2 shows.

In conjunction with this, one of the NSPCC's initial arguments for the introduction of legislative reforms was the reluctance of Poor Law guard-

Table 6.3 Number of persons proceeded against summarily under the Poor Law Acts for 'neglecting to maintain family', 1880–1908

Year	Number
1880	173
1881	192
1882	272
1883	123
1884	133
1885	117
1886	141
1887	343
1888	395
1889	363
1890	377
1891	373
1892	380
1893	319
1894	319
1895	51
1896	51
1897	79
1898	81
1899	110
1900	86
1901	129
1902	88
1903	114
1904	106
1905	100
1906	61
1907	73
1908	40
Total	5,189

Figures taken from the *Criminal and Judicial Statistics for Ireland*, House of Commons Parliamentary Papers, 1880–1908.

ians to prosecute parents. As Table 6.3 demonstrates, prosecutions under the Poor Law for 'neglecting to maintain family'[3] did decrease significantly after 1895 as a result of the 1894 legislation.

Another issue to be addressed is the question of who was being prosecuted in the courts. Were mothers or fathers being tried for cruelty and neglect of their children? The issue was important to the NSPCC in the early years, as the annual reports included lists of offences divided by gender. In the first report of the Dublin Aid Committee, of the thirty-five penalties

Table 6.4 Number of persons sent to trial at the Assize Courts and the Quarter Sessions for the indictable offence of 'Cruelty to or neglect of children', 1895–1917

Year	Total	Female	Male
1895	11	3	8
1896	10	6	4
1897	—	—	—
1898	12	6	6
1899	3	1	2
1900	7	6	1
1901	30	24	6
1902	14	7	7
1903	20	15	5
1904	14	8	6
1905	8	7	1
1906	11	11	0
1907	15	14	1
1908	15	14	1
1909	23	21	2
1910	17	13	4
1911	25	21	4
1912	14	12	2
1913	10	7	3
1914	8	6	2
1915	9	8	1
1916	2	2	0
1917	6	3	3
Total	284	215	69

Figures taken from the *Criminal and Judicial Statistics for Ireland*, House of Commons Parliamentary Reports, 1895–1918.

listed, seven were against fathers, two against both parents, one against a nurse and the remainder were brought against mothers. Most cases involved intemperate mothers, another significant point as it demonstrates the early focus of the Society on mothers and intemperance. In the courts, as Table 6.4 shows, from the judicial and criminal statistics for Ireland contained in the House of Commons Papers up to 1917 (the last year for which returns were published before the establishment of the Irish Free State), women represented 76 per cent of those prosecuted for indictable offences of cruelty to or neglect of children. This figure holds even more resonance when one takes into account that in almost all other crimes, men significantly outnumbered women in prosecutions. Aside from prostitution and offences against children, women were far more likely to be the victims of crime than the perpetrators. In particular, changing views on motherhood and intemperance can be seen in the sharp rise in female prosecutions from 1900 to 1914, a period in which the State and charities focused much attention on the reformation and rehabilitation of working-class mothers with the opening of the inebriate reformatories – which I will look at it in the next section of the chapter.

In the context of the broader debate about which parent was deemed culpable for cruelty to children or child neglect, figures for the period 1885–1917 suggest an entirely different situation from that shown by the figures for the period 1924–40, as men represent 70 per cent of those prosecuted for cruelty to or neglect of children and cases summarily tried under the 1926 School Attendance Act. The emphasis on fathers as the 'providers' and 'breadwinners', and women as 'mothers' and 'home-makers' in this period is also in keeping with the lower prosecution rates for women, as explained below.

In the nineteenth century, the idea of reformation and rehabilitation in inebriate reformatories, lunatic asylums and other institutions was pursued and often focused on mothers. In the inter-war years, fathers were the focus of charitable and voluntary organisations, while mothers were forced to become adept at finding financial aid and maintaining the home to the best of their abilities and means. Before independence, while males may have been tried for non-indictable offences, what is significant about the higher female prosecutions in the Assizes and Quarter Sessions is that the majority would have resulted in a prison sentence or incarceration in the State Inebriate Reformatory. In keeping with this differentiation, in 1882 the House of Commons Criminal and Judicial Statistics for Ireland stated: 'amongst the classes prosecuted for offences for which summary convictions take place, men are generally better able to pay fines than women, and so more likely to escape imprisonment.'[4]

From 1924, with changes to the law after independence, there were changes in the offences prosecuted. Non-indictable offences against children were amalgamated into one category – 'cruelty to or neglect of children', while the indictable offence of 'cruelty to children' covered all the more serious offences. This was an interesting development, as it grouped all offences against children into two. No longer would begging, exposure and ill-treatment receive different treatment; 'cruelty to children', an offence brought into the public domain by the NSPCC, was now the legal term used to describe child abuse. With regard to the gender of perpetrators, as Table 6.5 demonstrates in convictions for the indictable offence of 'cruelty to children', in contrast to the period 1880 to 1920, men represented the largest proportion of 'offenders'.

Furthermore, as Table 6.6 illustrates, the situation was the same for those proceeded against for the non-indictable offence of 'cruelty to or neglect of children'.

There are a number of reasons for this shift. As the Poor Law had been abolished, men who had previously been prosecuted for 'neglect to main-

Table 6.5 Number of persons convicted on indictable offence of cruelty to children, 1924–49

Year	Male	Female
1924	39	16
1925	49	15
1926	36	12
1927	26	6
1928	18	9
1929	43	15
1930	19	6
1931	24	6
1932	25	5
1933	22	8
1934	27	10
1935	29	3
1936	16	1
1937	7	2
1938	22	3
1939	11	5
1940	11	4
1941	9	6
1942	18	5
1943	23	4
1944	15	4
1945	37	16
1946	47	9
1947	35	3
1948	32	7
1949	37	3
Total	677	183

tain family' were now charged with cruelty to children. Also, in the period after independence, desertion became an issue frequently addressed by the NSPCC. For this reason, some cases of cruelty to children also included a claim for maintenance for desertion. The following is an example of such a case.

In Green Street Courthouse in 1925, Paul Mahon was indicted for bigamy and cruelty to children. He had married Jane Molloy in 1901 and another woman in 1915. He admitted: '[she] was not aware I was a married man at the time, I represented myself as a single man'. The following is the statement from his first wife:

> My husband left me in September 1914, three months before Mary was born. On that occasion he said he was going to England. In the beginning

Table 6.6 Number of persons committed on conviction for the non-indictable offence of cruelty to or neglect of children, 1927–40

Year	Male	Female
1927	—	—
1928	—	59
1929	100	70
1930	87	34
1931	61	25
1932	75	25
1933	88	21
1934	144	36
1935	114	26
1936	87	16
1937	63	16
1938	70	34
1939	75	19
1940	25	19
Total	989	400

of 1915 I heard from him. He was then in Cork and wrote care of P.O. Haulbowline. I got an address that my husband left after him: 26, Castle Street, Cork. I wrote there and received an answer from a Miss O'Leary asking me was my husband married. Before I had time to answer this letter my husband wired and asked me not to answer it. I did not do so. From that time until June 1922 my husband sent me varying sums of 10/- and 5/- but never more than 10/- per week. Before Christmas 1922 I wrote to a Clergyman to know did my husband live at 26, Castle Street, Cork. After some correspondence the Clergyman asked me to have my husband home again. I agreed to this and he came home early in January but he was rather unsettled. He left again in February and pretended he was joining the Army. The N.S.P.C.C. looked him up and found out he had returned to Cork. My husband is a carpenter by trade. I had to go to work to keep myself and the children [as] the money he sent would not keep us in food. I now charge my said husband Timothy Doheny with neglect of his children in a manner likely to cause them unnecessary suffering and injury to her health and I pray a warrant for his arrest.[5]

This statement is interesting because, firstly, the reason why the woman did not pursue her husband earlier was probably due to the fact that they had agreed to separate, and only when the money was stopped did she decide to involve the NSPCC and the police. Secondly, the actions of the priest in trying to repair the first marriage demonstrate the Church's wish to restore the 'lawful' marriage. After independence, cases of neglect addressed by the courts often involved situations in which fathers were not maintaining their families. This form of neglect revolved around notions of domesticity, male supremacy, and a father's responsibility to support their family without financial assistance from other members of the family or the State. It was also directly related to fears surrounding the State's finances, as can be seen from the Oireachtas debates. Even though mothers were viewed as responsible for the physical neglect of children and of the home by the NSPCC, from the 1920s it was fathers who were most commonly prosecuted. In cases of school non-attendance, of the 111,615 people proceeded against from 1927 to 1940, 94,080 were men, 84 per cent of the total number. In fact, there were more people proceeded against for not sending their children to school than any other parental offence. As addressed in Chapter 4, in 1926 the School Attendance Act enforced compulsory schooling for all children between the ages of six and fourteen, and parents whose children were found to be absent from school were visited by school-attendance officers, gardaí or the NSPCC, and served with a formal warning. If the situation remained unchanged they would be issued with a court summons. Tony Fahey, in his examination of compulsory schooling, estimates that the legislation resulted in 15 to 20 per cent of all parents being visited, and as Table 6.6 demonstrates, many thousands were prosecuted.[6]

Deserted wives

In the records of the NSPCC – both the annual reports and the case files – it is seen that desertion, or specifically deserted wives, became a major aspect of the Society's work from the mid-1920s. The reasons why will be addressed throughout this section, but in short, it was a mixture of the social effects of the First World War, the War of Independence and the Civil War; the constitutional ban on divorce and expense of separation; the State's reluctance to introduce welfare reform; and the subordinate economic and legal position of most women. Many men who left (and a small number of women) remarried. Yet their first marriage could literally haunt them for years as they evaded arrest for the offence of bigamy. The cases therefore provide a glimpse into individual relationships, tactics people used to leave marriages and the effects of emigration on many married women in Ireland.

For the Irish State, fears of becoming a welfare state, as well as an emphasis on the male breadwinner generally, meant it did not help women who had been deserted in any substantive way – although some lip-service was paid. When cases came to the courts, maintenance was agreed but usually not paid for long. Yet the State would not introduce an allowance as it had done for widows in 1935. With divorce constitutionally banned, women could not remarry, so economically those in the poorer classes were reduced to living on charity. For the NSPCC and the SVDP, reuniting the first marriage – irrelevant of any subsequent marriages – remained the goal, as the following cases and analysis will address.

The cases

Except for the Irish Society for the Prevention of Cruelty to Children (which as its name implies, must be a last resort) nothing has been done to help these people. Governments anywhere are not concerned with human suffering unless the victims are organised and vocal.[7]

It would be an awful state of affairs if a man could clear off from his family and rear another family with another woman in another country just because his tea was not hot enough. (District Judge, Bunclody, Co. Wexford, 22 December 1936)

The first quotation above is taken from a series of articles in the *Evening Press* on wife-beating and desertion. It is unlikely the series would have appeared prior to the late 1960s in Ireland, as not only did it highlight emigration, desertion and domestic violence, but most importantly it questioned the State's treatment of women and families from independence. Speaking on the violence her father inflicted on her mother, her siblings and herself before deserting them, one woman observed: 'in some rural districts, a male's manliness is too often judged by the scorn he displays for women and how often he beats his wife'.[8] In another case in the series, a woman whose husband had deserted her and her fourteen-month-old baby before Christmas in 1936 described how after the child contracted meningitis and died; the NSPCC could no longer help her. As she could not trace his death certificate over the years, she could not receive a widow's pension and, as late as 1959, could not remarry as the Church would not allow it. While the NSPCC and the child protection movement began to acknowledge the situation of battered wives in Ireland from the 1920s, its treatment of desertion was far more aggressive and consistent. In the annual reports from this period, sample cases regularly dealt with the issue of desertion, as the Society actively lobbied the State to implement legislation to punish deserting husbands. Although the focus remained on the role of husband as breadwinner, and the responsibility of fathers to provide for their children, the actions of the Society did enable many women to pursue husbands for maintenance. In this instance, the Irish branches' position under the umbrella of the British Society offered inspectors resources and manpower in Britain to chase deserting husbands.

In the United States, desertion was seen as an escalating and urgent social problem from the turn of the twentieth century. In Ireland it was increasingly reported in the newspapers and the NSPCC files from the mid-1920s, and particularly in the 1930s. In general, desertion was framed as a father's 'weak and cowardly evasion of masculine responsibility',[9] and both the NSPCC and the State were moralistic and punitive in their response. The policy was to force deserting husbands to pay, as opposed to seek aid for single mothers. In February 1944, Michael Moran (FF) asked the Minister for Justice if he was aware that, since Section 2 of the Vagrancy (Ireland) Act, 1847, was repealed by the Public Assistance Act, 1939,

> ... the courts of this State have no power to make amenable to justice citizens of Éire who have deserted their wives and families and who are resident out of the jurisdiction of the State, and that no machinery is now provided for their apprehension; and if he will take immediate steps to have legislation introduced in Dáil Eireann to remedy this defect in the law.

In response, Minister Boland stated:

> The position created by the repeal of Section 2 of the Vagrancy (Ireland) Act, 1847, by the Public Assistance Act, 1939, is not exactly as stated in the question. The courts, it is true, are no longer able to utilise the power to issue warrants for arrest which was conferred by the 1847 Act. So far as the Dublin Metropolitan Area is concerned, however, the justices of the District Court still have, and exercise in cases arising under the 1939 Act, the power to issue warrants conferred on them by the Dublin Police Act, 1842. As regards the country generally, resort can be had in certain cases to the provisions of Section 12 of the Children Act, 1908, to secure the issue of a warrant for arrest. The position, however, is not entirely satisfactory and the matter has been under consideration in my Department with a view to remedying the defect in the law either by rule of court or, if necessary, by legislation.

It would be almost 40 years before the situation for deserted wives was actually addressed. The following are an example of two cases from the NSPCC's files. In 1938, a wife and mother of two children made a complaint to the NSPCC inspector about her husband who was working in London. The correspondence between the two is revealing:

> My darling, just got your lovely letter. I have only one fault to find with you that is you don't write often enough ... I wouldn't like to rear children in this hole. I would like to give them a memory of Ireland until they reach about 12 so my dear when you are coming over, if you do you'll have to leave one behind.

After the woman had not received any money from her husband, she visited the NSPCC inspector. The following letter was sent from her husband after a visit from an English inspector:

> Received your threat which hasn't had any effect on me as you know yourself neither you nor the Cruelty man can do anything to me. I have offered you a home here and you have refused thereby putting yourself in a position that favours me in not maintaining you.

Not only does the letter contrast starkly with the first, it shows the arrogance of the man and his disregard for his wife. In the final letter, the husband's words were equally bitter: 'Better people than you have lived in one room'.[10]

As previously mentioned, in many cases women were victims of both wife-beating and desertion. In 1929, a mother of one in Enniscorthy approached the NSPCC inspector for advice. She had married her husband in 1927, and although she had the child before marriage she claimed: 'he has never denied paternity'. While they were living with his family and he was unemployed, she asked to him to apply for relief. He refused and so she applied instead and received four shillings per week. Although she initially told the inspector she had come for advice on how to apply for maintenance, she began to describe the violence she had endured. The following is the extract from the inspector's notebook:

> Woman describes first assault in August 1928, after which she called the Civic Guard. Husband replied – 'there is no place for you here now after you have gone to the Guards you can go where you like'. Husband bound to the peace and told to maintain his child. Woman lived with neighbours. While pregnant at the end of 1929 he again assaulted her, stating 'go and get a hold of yourself and go to the County Home where you were best used to'. When he began working she went to him and asked him his plan for the children to which he replied – 'No. I have no plan for you or the children. The County Home is your place and get back to it before night. I have no place for you here.' She has not received money from him, she says 'she is living on the charity of friends and neighbours'.

When approached by the Inspector for money in 1929 the man responded: 'I can do gaol on my ear'. In a final report, after twenty-two visits from the inspector between November 1928 and 1930, the case file states: 'Visited with Dr. Cadigan who gave certificate. Found family sleeping on floor. Peter (3yrs.) weighs 25lbs. Joseph (7months) 13lbs.'[11]

While acknowledging that wife-beating and desertion are two very different issues, in a discussion of the family and the State, they have a number of commonalities. Both were issues brought to the attention of the NSPCC by mothers from the 1920s; both involved married women, the majority of whom were economically dependent on their husbands; and both were highlighted and ignored by the state and its agencies throughout the period. After independence, desertion was framed in the context of 'public morality', with husbands and fathers representing the focus of the State and the NSPCC, while wife-beating was explicitly not dealt with and remained a phenomenon that occurred within the private sphere of the home. One represented a financial issue for the State, the other an accepted practice. Yet both concerned women's position in society, economically and socially, and notions of masculinity, responsibility and the expectations wives and husbands had of one another.

There are a number of observations that can be made with regard to the files. First, almost all cases in the press involve mention of the NSPCC or the SVDP. In 1924, the *Irish Times* recorded a case in which a labourer, Mr Taylor, was charged by the Society for neglecting to maintain his wife and two children. The man's wife claimed he had left three and a half years previously and had not contributed to the family. The Society proceeded to trace Mr Taylor, and he was found in the SVDP Shelter in Dublin. In an unusual insight into the couple's relationship, the prosecutor stated that Mr Taylor had sent his wife a photograph of himself on a postcard, in which he addressed her by her maiden name and signed himself 'D. Freeman', meaning that he was a 'free man'. This received laughs from the court, but the man was sentenced to three months' imprisonment with hard labour and ordered to pay £10 to his wife. In most case where a sentence was imposed, the norm appears to have been three months of hard labour. In the 1920s, there were also a number of cases involving British soldiers charged with child neglect. In 1926, a case came to the courts in which the woman had not seen her husband since 1919. The man, who was English, and very much identified as such, was given a six-month sentence. This longer sentence appears to have been due to the fact that he had remarried, and there was also a suggestion that he had used this woman while in Ireland and then went to England when the War of Independence began.

Again, at times, the cases can provide interesting insights into marriage and individual choices in Ireland – details that are often difficult to obtain from other sources. Many men remarried quite soon after leaving their wives, and it is in the bigamy cases that we see the most severe sentences being imposed. Yet men continued over the years to leave and get remarried, demonstrating that they felt it was worth the risk of a prison sentence to start a new life or leave an existing situation. Many wives also appear to have waited for years before taking a case to the authorities. The reasons are not always clear, but in some instances it could be ascertained that the separation was a mutual decision. Finally, when we look at the State's role, it appears its two primary concerns were cost and divorce. Divorce was not an option (although separations could be achieved with money or in a different location), but the development of a welfare state was also rejected vehemently. If men could not or would not pay maintenance after a court order, a wife's only option was to go and ask for home assistance. This was a meagre sum and was not always granted. However, in 1945 the Galway County Manager estimated that the budget for home assistance would need to be increased from £12,000 to £15,400 to deal with the demands 'occasioned by men who are working in England abandoning their wives and families', demonstrating such assistance was being given out.

In 1970, prior to the introduction of the deserted wives allowances, Michael Viney wrote an article in the *Irish Times* entitled 'The broken marriage, desertion – who pays?' He began by quoting a passage from the British Committee on the Enforcement of Debts: 'Citizens in 1969 do not think of failure to discharge matrimonial obligations as criminal behaviour, and to treat it as such by imprisoning offenders in the absence of supporting public sentiment damages the law and degrades marriage'. He continued: 'We can only guess at what Irish citizens think, the point has so rarely arisen. As long as the husband can skip to England – if he's not there already – an Irish court maintenance order has been scarcely worth making, let alone pressing to the point of jailing the defaulting husband. There are no available figures for the total orders in force, but the number of new ones in 1969 was 38'. Viney goes on to highlight the problems with the new legislation, primarily the six-month waiting period. He also runs through what kind of people the wives and husbands are – young men mostly – stating: 'it's a story of inadequacy rather than viciousness'. He concludes with a paragraph on the wife, whom he claims is 'far more defenceless and lonely than people would think'. Who pays – the title of the article – is shown to be the State in cases where the man is unable or unwilling to give maintenance. But he addresses further issues: 'divorce Irish Style', as one judge called it, and the economic position of women in Irish society. Overall, what an examination of deserted and battered wives shows is the bind for married women in a system characterised by an unsympathetic judiciary, legislature and, often, Church. Once married, women's rights were severely hampered, as Mick O'Brien recorded of his experiences of growing up in Dublin in the 1930s: 'Basically, the woman was there for her husband. He had his rights and that was it. The husband was the boss, his word was law. The woman had no say. The priest would just say "grin and bear it". It was wrong'. While this may appear to be a stereotypical view of the life of a working-class married woman in Ireland at the time, the situation for deserted wives shows that their choices were severely limited, and it would take more adjustments than the allowances to change this, although they were a long-awaited start.

'The Society for wives and children'[12]: wife-beating and the NSPCC

As Liz Steiner-Scott has shown, wife-beating was a regular occurrence for women in nineteenth-century Ireland and one that appeared frequently in the courts and in the press. Over the last thirty years, Linda Gordon and other feminist writers have argued that the basis of wife-beating is male dominance, a dominance built on social, economic, political and psychological power. In order to examine why wife-beating occurred and was accepted in nineteenth- and twentieth-century Ireland, these powers need to be addressed. Defining wife-beating as a social problem, not something that occurs in the privacy of certain homes, remains one of the greatest achievements of second-wave feminism, but understanding its occurrence historically involves placing it in the context of the time.

On the whole, an examination of wife-beating and desertion reveals the State's reluctance to support women outside of the family, or risk undermining the breadwinner structure and responsibility of families to support themselves. In Britain from 1880 to 1950, legislation was enacted regarding women's succession rights, mothers' parental rights, access to divorce, maintenance and family welfare. In contrast, many women in Ireland, revered as mothers in literature and song, were placed in intolerable situations. Integral to this examination is the economic dependence of wives; the societal expectations of mothers, wives, husbands and fathers; class difference between women; and the subordinate position of women in Ireland in the period. As previously addressed, from 1920–40, wife-beating featured very infrequently in both the press and the courts. It was at this stage, when the

State was ignoring the issue of wife-beating, that wives began to approach the NSPCC. This was due both to their lack of recourse to the courts and to their awareness of the NSPCC's newly-defined role as advisory agency. However, as with women's use of religious organisations in order to gain material aid, wives began to use their roles as mothers to align their plight with the plight of their children, as the following case demonstrates:

> On Friday noon I asked my husband to go down to the fields for some bushes – he had a sore shoulder – he said he couldn't do it as his shoulder was paining him. He kicked the fire off the hearth and started arguing and fighting and caught me by the throat and said only he didn't feel like it right now [and] he'd bash in my head with his stick which he had in his hand. I said, 'You'd better not do anything like that'. He calmed down after some time and went to bed. Then about 5 or 6 o'clock when he had gone down to bed I baked a cake and got ready the tea. I told him his tea was ready, but he did not get up to it. After tea I put the child to bed in a cot in the same room as the father was in. About 8 o'clock my husband got up and came in to the kitchen where I was washing some baby clothes [and] he said, 'Pour out that tea for me!' I said, 'Couldn't you pour it out yourself while I finished the washing?' He then picked up the teapot from the hearth where it was standing and threw it across the floor. It is an enamel teapot and is now leaking. At the same time he used the expression, 'F you, you dirty little bitch.' My husband then left the house and returned in a short time, he asked for water to wash his shoulder. I said it will be boiled in a few minutes, [but] he kicked the saucepan off the fire. He left the house and remained out until 11.45 Saturday morning, when he came in he made a lot of noise. I said 'Don't wake the child.' [He said] 'To hell with you and the child.' Saturday morning at noon he struck me in the face with his hand open; this happened in the hallway. I went to the Barracks at 1.30pm [and] my husband came with me. I made a complaint to the Sergeant at Killarin. He said I should take a summons. I then went to Fr. O'Byrne and made a complaint to him. He advised me to leave him when I couldn't live with him. My husband was not present at this ... in the last attack he said – 'I'll take your bloody life the night and will not leave you able to be telling tales.'[13]

The statement was given to the NSPCC inspector in Wexford in 1934. Without the presence of the child in this story, the case would never have been recorded, at least not by the NSPCC. Unsurprisingly, the inspector's book ends with a note that the child was left with both parents, as although both the gardaí and the clergy feature in this woman's ordeal, neither offered any practical advice as to how she would survive if she did leave her husband. Economically dependent with a young child to support, the options for women in situations of domestic violence[14] were limited. Entering domestic service would have meant giving up the child; emigration threw up similar economic and child-care problems, and as divorce was not an option, remarriage certainly would not have been a choice. In this instance, leaving her husband would almost certainly have guaranteed that she lost her child. There was therefore little or no path of recourse.

In the early years of the NSPCC, wife-beating was rarely discussed in official reports. As the case files have not survived, it is not possible to comment on whether individual inspectors recorded instances of wife-beating, but the emphasis of inspectors appears to have been on intemperance and the inadequacy of mothers, not her susceptibility to violence in the home. But with the changing structure of social work, and the redefinition and professionalisation of the NSPCC, this situation changed. From the 1930s, cases of wife-beating began to feature regularly in the sample cases of the Society's annual reports, as it began to connect the situations of mothers and children in violent homes. The following was recorded in the 1933 Dublin branch report:

> A young mother came to the Local Office with her child, aged one year and a half. She complained that her husband was continually brutally beating her and the child. The inspector examined the child and found her badly marked. This was confirmed by a certificate form the Society's doctor. When the man was interviewed by the inspector he admitted beating the child and his wife in a fit of rage. He also admitted continually frightening the child to make it scream. He was brought before the judge, who had him medically examined. He was certified sane, and sentenced to six months' imprisonment.[15]

What the case demonstrates is the Society's willingness to associate the abuse of mother and child. It is also representative of a period in which women had begun to use the Society to protect themselves and their children from violence. In contrast to earlier years, from the 1930s mothers and wives were coming directly to the NSPCC with complaints of domestic violence, as well as instances of non-support and desertion. Whether women came to the Society first, or the Society had decided to acknowledge desertion and wife-beating, is difficult to assess. It was more likely a change in Society policy. As prosecutions for cruelty to children and child neglect were now primarily being taken against men, women must also have felt they could use the NSPCC (now promoting itself as an advisory agency) to a much greater degree.

The following cases were all recorded in one inspector's book from January to October 1935, and overall in the book, one-third of cases involved wife-beating. In the first, the parents of five children were investigated for neglect, but the situation described was also one of wife-beating: 'Row between husband and wife as he would not give back some of the money so she could buy meat. Struck wife ... girl (5 years) was present when mother was assaulted and terrified. After childbirth was in mental home with both girl (5) and boy (8 years).'[16] This is typical of many cases of wife-beating in which disputes emerged over wages and the money needed to maintain the home. Many men resisted the idea that (as one man put it) 'so much' was needed, yet they would get equally annoyed when food and hygiene standards were not up to their expectations. The economic dependence of women is again fundamental. In Kearns's study of mothers in working-class Dublin, he highlights how, to have a husband who handed over all his wages 'was envied by women and respected by men'.[17] Similarly, Lindsey Earner-Byrne's study of mothers in Dublin demonstrates how women ate last, feeding the breadwinner and children first. Not only were many women negotiating resources with different charities and voluntary organisations, they were stretching the resources as far as they could within the home. For the inspectors, cases of wife-beating needed to be addressed in reference to the effects on children. The following entry was emblematic of many cases involving wife-beating in the 1920s and 1930s: '____ (37), 3 children, 13–17 years. He assaults wife – children are terrified by father's violent outbursts. Left with parents.'

In another case in 1938, a father of five was investigated for ill-treatment and assault. He was forty-one years old, an army pensioner and described by the inspector as 'lazy and useless, fond of drink and gambling, [with a] violent temper'. His 44-year-old wife had 'sober tendencies'. That this woman was seen to be 'good and industrious' was important to the inspector's perception of the situation. The five children were all aged between seven and thirteen years, and one instance in particular was recorded:

> Father returned home late on night of 30th April 1938 and was the worse for drink. He assaulted his boy ... [but] the boy got away and went to his room. Later the father broke the kitchen windows and a flower pot. ____ states she is afraid of her husband. The matter was reported to the police. Children left with parents.[18]

The case is typical of many recorded, for both the father's drunkenness and the presence of the children during the assault. The involvement of the police was also quite common, as although wives made domestic violence known to inspectors, the Society then had to deal with the case by reporting it to the police. But many wives were aware that if the case went to court, the inspector could be called on to plead the wife's case, and also to obtain relief if the husband was imprisoned. In another case of ill-treatment and assault in 1938, the inspector describes the wife as 'in delicate health', while the husband is depicted as 'bad tempered and violent, [and] fond of drink'. In one particular incident the inspector records that 'the man threw a knife at his son and assaulted his wife'.

In general, in order to receive relief and assistance from the NSPCC, wives needed to be seen as vulnerable, innocent and weak. In this regard, the Victorian image of the docile wife was still prevalent. If a woman was viewed as provoking an assault, the inspector would be less sympathetic, as the following case in 1939 outlines: 'Both parents are ... difficult. The man is hot-tempered and his wife continues to nag him which he resents.' 'Nagging' was a term that began to be used more frequently from the 1930s as an explanation for domestic violence. In this instance, the inspector viewed wife-beating as violence between equal combatants, and in which the woman had provoked much of the abuse.

Wife-beating in the nineteenth-century

In the mid-to-late nineteenth century, as with incest and cruelty to children, wife-beating was portrayed by temperance advocates and social reformers as a working-class problem in which working-class men were 'barbaric' individuals, whose 'pathetic' wives needed protection from the State. In 1853 the Aggravated Assaults on Women and Children Act was introduced to address the issue. Unsurprisingly, very few women were willing to prosecute their husbands under the act, due to 'their economic dependency, fear of reprisals, and distrust of the law'.[19] Throughout the 1880s wives declined to prosecute husbands, or refused to substantiate charges made.[20] The following case is typical of many that came to court but were not prosecuted:

> A man named ____ , a labourer living at 134 Great Britain Street was charged in the Northern Divisional Police Court, Dublin before Mr O'Donal with having assaulted his wife. When the case was called, the complainant, a respectably-dressed woman, refused to prosecute ... The Complainant said that if her husband was sent to jail she and her children would starve. Mr. O'Donal said they could go to the poorhouse, and the woman still declining to prosecute, his worship discharged the prisoner.[21]

In the context of a discussion of the family, the woman's consideration of the economic position that both she and her children would be left in if her husband had been imprisoned is significant. Had she been childless she may have chosen to leave her husband and live a separate life (although this was very rarely the case), but factoring in the dependence of her children placed her in an impossible situation. Offered the choice of the workhouse or a violent husband, she considered that staying with the latter would disrupt her and her children's lives the least. At the same sessions, a man received two months' imprisonment for an assault on his wife which had been witnessed by a police constable. The woman had retrieved the constable after an initial assault, and upon entering the room he 'jumped up and swearing he would take her life struck her in the face'. The woman stated that her husband had previously 'knocked her off a stool on which she had been sitting by a kick in the jaw, and then while she was on the floor he attempted to choke her'. In the court, the husband stated that 'he was sorry he had not done more'.[22] What the cases demonstrate is that unless women feared for their lives, they were very reluctant to prosecute husbands. The 1853 Act did legislate for wife-beating, but it did nothing to deal with the structural inequalities that enabled husbands to beat their wives without fear of reprimand. Even in the cases that were prosecuted, the economic dependence of wives and economic independence of men remained an issue, as men were able to pay the fines given by judges in the courts. For those cases that made it to court, but in which women refused to prosecute, most women told the judge they would forgive their husband hoping that a warning would effect change for even a short period of time.[23]

In general, if a woman married a 'bad' husband, she learned to live with the consequences. Whereas middle-class women could afford to pay solicitors to help them separate from abusive husbands, or arrange maintenance payments with regard to supporting children, this was not the case for poor women. As an examination of the court records reveals, class not only limited the freedom with which women could resist abusive and non-supporting husbands; it was critical to what women believed was acceptable behaviour. Steiner-Scott argues that although cases were commonly recorded in the press and dealt with in the courts, there was no sustained movement against wife-beating in Ireland. In contrast to Britain and the United States, where feminists campaigned against wife-beating, battered wives had little attention focused on them and little recourse.[24] Although some temperance campaigners did address the issue peripherally, it was in the context of highlighting the positive aspects of sobriety as opposed to the repression of women. Even in the *Irish Citizen*, wife-beating was rarely addressed. While cases were reported in the press in the first forty years of this examination, from 1920 to the late 1960s wife-beating was rarely discussed in the press, in the Oireachtas, by the legal and medical professions or by women's organisations. Internationally, this was a common phenomenon in the period, but as the NSPCC set up Women's Groups in Britain in the 1940s and in the United States feminists and social work agencies connected the situations of women and children in violent homes, in Ireland battered wives received little recognition.

Why did the feminist movement in Ireland not address the issue of wife-beating? Was there an acknowledgement that if suffrage was achieved structural changes could be implemented that would improve the situation for all women? Or was it the case that as middle-class feminists could afford to separate or live independently in situations of domestic violence, the situation for working-class and poor women was not paramount? Economic dependence is central to this debate. In 1882, the House of Commons Judicial and Criminal Statistics for Ireland stated:

> In the English table, the number of women of no occupation and presumably in poverty is only 28.3 per cent of the whole. In Ireland this class reaches 44 per cent of the whole, 5522 out of every 12359, indicating the greater pressure of distress on women in Ireland than in England.[25]

If, as Steiner-Scott and other scholars have demonstrated, economic dependence limits the opportunities for recourse for battered wives, the above statistic reveals that the situation for women in Ireland in 1881 was more severe than for those in England. However, from 1890 the economic independence of women further deteriorated. In 1881, there were 814,600 women designated as employed. By 1911, this figure was 430,100 and from 1890 to 1914, female labour in Ireland came to be dominated by housework. In fact, in the first forty years of independence, women who performed household work in their own houses constituted the largest block of adult women,²⁶ making it more difficult for women in situations of violence to leave.

Aside from the lack of attention to wife-beating by feminists, Liz Steiner-Scott argues that in many cases wives wanted their husbands not to be prosecuted, but merely warned by magistrates in the hope that this would improve the situation in the future. In her sample of cases from 1853 to 1920, the average length of sentence was three months, and twenty-two per cent of those petitioning received a sentence of six months with hard labour. She describes the rate of recidivism as 'relatively high'.²⁷ As the courts in Ireland were to a large extent focused on land and property in the period, many defendants attempted to establish provocation, and Steiner-Scott demonstrates how many assaults emerged from the expectations which husbands and wives had of one another – that she would be sober and compliant and that he would hand over the wages and support the family. This assertion is backed up in Joanna Bourke's work, which demonstrates that many assaults took place due to accusations of poor housework.²⁸ In many cases, if a man could demonstrate that his wife had 'provoked' the attack, the courts (which consisted of male jurors, male judiciaries and male solicitors) applied leniency in sentencing.

The notion of women as equal combatants in cases of wife-beating has been addressed differently by scholars. In contrast to Liz Steiner-Scott, Carolyn Conley argues that in the courts, 'domestic violence was more often perceived in the same manner as recreational violence – brawls between willing participants whose inhibitions had been loosened by passion and alcohol.'²⁹ Although many defendants did claim they had been provoked, Conley's analysis does not question why women fought back, or take into account economic or structural issues in society that prevented many women from taking cases to the court. Similarly not addressed in the analysis are the leniency with which wife-beating was treated in sentencing and the fact that many men could afford to pay fines often offered as recognisance.

In general, most men who came before the court did not receive long sentences, although the assaults may have been very severe. The following provide a brief example of the type of cases and sentences applied: In June 1894, ____ received five weeks with hard labour for each of the three counts of assaulting his wife, at Green Street Court in Dublin. In August 1896, ____ received one calendar month for the assault of his wife, also at Green Street Court.³⁰ In 1897 ____ received twelve calendar months for beating, wounding and ill-treating his wife. While this represents a more substantial sentence, ____ had not only beaten his wife on a number of occasions, he had tried 'to push her over the parapet of a certain bridge'.³¹ At the same sessions, ____ received twelve months for three counts of assault on his wife.³² Again, the sentence was due to severity of the assaults, and his wife's fear that he would kill her the next time he beat her. In October 1897, ____ was bound to the court on a recognizance of £50 for assaulting, beating and wounding his wife.³³ Although the evidence against the prisoner was irrefutable, the judge had chosen to give the man a recognisance as he felt it better for the family's own situation. That he had the £50 shows how men's role as breadwinner secured them double protection in the eyes of the court. Fines also appear to have been decided upon in the light of what a man could afford, as in a similar case in December ____ received a recognisance of £10 for assaulting his wife.

In order to examine the most severe cases of wife-beating and murder prosecuted by the courts, a sample of sixty cases from the convict reference files (CRF) of the assault or murder of wives from 1880 to 1920 was compiled. The severity of the crimes can be seen in the average sentence for assault or malicious wounding, which was eighteen months. With regard to wife-murder, most men were 'found to be insane' and transferred to Dundrum Lunatic Asylum, or received death sentences (often reduced to penal servitude for life). Insanity was often used as a defence by the prosecution. Similarly, many judges declared men who had killed their wives to be insane. As a source, the nature of the convict reference files must be taken into consideration here. As they represented petitions to the Crown for release, prisoners who were serving shorter sentences would not have appealed as the process would have taken longer than the sentence. Before looking at cases of wife-murder, severe assaults will be addressed.

In 1899, a sixty-year-old farmer was tried at Sligo Assizes for assaulting his wife and sentenced to twelve months of hard labour. The longer sentence was given due to the man's use of a weapon in the assault, and the presence of witnesses. After a dispute on the morning of the 11 February 1899, the defendant had gone into the kitchen, picked up an iron bar two feet long and proceeded to beat his wife with it. Following this, he chased her outside where the neighbours witnessed him beat her numerous times. The assault was so severe that in the course of the trial it emerged that he thought he had killed her. He was a widower when the couple had married in May 1897 and she was twenty-seven years of age. In his petition for release, the man stated:

> If I am discharged from custody I am intended to reside with a friend of mine who has the grass of portion of my farm. I will live with him, pending a settlement to allow my wife a yearly allowance to reside away from me. I also intend to consult a lawyer on the matter, as it would be useless for me to go back to my own house, as long as my wife and her brothers live there.

He was released on £50 recognisance to keep the peace for three years.[34] The file states that the man was believed to frequently beat his wife, but as with many cases the assaults were not prosecuted until they were regarded as being 'too severe'.

Poisoning also appears frequently in the files. In December 1883, ____ was sentenced to penal servitude for life at the Cavan Assizes 'for administering poison with intent to kill his wife'. He was thirty years of age on conviction, and received a life sentence. The deposition from the prisoner's wife describes how he poisoned her over a number of days – first with whisky and wine, then with bread and water and how each tasted 'tart and bitter'. After experiencing vomiting, she found a bottle with red liquid in it and also observed her husband putting white powder on a lemon. She was later admitted to the Monaghan Lunatic Asylum after their only child died while she was sick. This may also have contributed to the judge's decision to give the man a life sentence. In 1897, a petition was included with the man's request for release. It was signed by the Bishop of Kilmore, twelve magistrates, seven Roman Catholic clergymen, four Church of Ireland clergymen, the chairman of the Cavan Town Commissioners, the vice-chairman and seven members of the Cavan Board of Guardians and the dispensary doctor of the District. Even with this petition, however, the man's sentence was only commuted to twenty-three years' penal servitude.[35]

In one of the few cases involving women as the perpetrators, _____ was convicted of murdering her husband by poisoning him with arsenic in July 1885. She received a death sentence which was commuted to life. During the trial she argued that her children had also been involved in the crime. What the case demonstrates is that when it came to sentencing, the courts viewed women and men equally in cases of murder. While the case does not mention why she murdered her husband, in many instances the motive was desperation due to abuse inflicted by husbands. In 1893, another woman was convicted of attempting to poison her husband at the Cork Winter Assizes. In December 1892 she had written a letter to the local doctor complaining that her husband was robbing her and the children. The letter stated: 'if you send me or give me a little dose of something to give that would not act sudden but would linger for 3 or 4 days before it would prove fatal I will pay you whatever amount you ask'. The doctor reported the woman to the police, after which she was arrested and prosecuted. In her petition for release she explained the circumstances surrounding her request and the situation in the home:

> I was driven to desperation from him being a bad head to me and squandering all my means and running myself and children to beggary. He is a terrible drunkard ... I would feel grateful if Your Excellency would take a few months off my time as I have a helpless young family and no one to look after them but strangers, my husband not being the best to them. I am the mother of 14 children and in my very delicate health ... I had neither solicitor or councillor to plead my case for me, one of my children has died since I came in here and I am sure a good many other things have gone to loss.

In response to the petition the judge stated:

> The conclusion I arrived at, after reading the deposition, was that her husband had behaved badly to her – possibly very badly, and that she

had deliberately formed her design to poison him, and had taken steps, in order to carry her design with effect by applying to a doctor to supply her with poison for the purpose. She appeared to be a frail, worn woman. I passed what I thought a very lenient sentence upon her, viz. twelve calendar months imprisonment, and, unless continued imprisonment, under such prison regulations as are applicable to her case, will involve the right of permanent injury to her health, I am unable to recommend any mitigation of her sentence.

From the judge's statement it is apparent that in certain cases, judges understood the violence many women and children were exposed to and the measures they would employ in desperation to escape. In this instance, the woman was released after twelve years upon the understanding that she would move to America to live with her eldest son. Both cases are significant as they involve children. In over ninety per cent of the cases examined, the women involved were mothers, and explanations for prosecuting husbands regularly centred on fears for the safety and survival of their children. Although an examination of wife-beating may appear to be outside the context of an examination of children and the State, in ignoring the situation for wives, the NSPCC, the State and philanthropists failed to connect the effects of violence in the home to the welfare of children. As with attitudes to corporal punishment and conditions in institutions, this demonstrates that the 'rights of the child' espoused by reformers were far more limited than they were willing to address.

Aside from cases of severe assault, the CRF contain a number of cases involving wife-murder. As previously mentioned, the difference in the treatment of wife-beaters and that of wife-murderers is noteworthy. It appears it was socially and legally acceptable to keep a wife 'in line', but to murder a wife, particularly a mother, held different ramifications. The following statements indicate the length of sentences given to men in cases of murder or attempted murder. In 1894, ____ received ten years' penal servitude for the murder of his wife.[36] On 3 August 1904, ____ was convicted of the murder of his wife and received a death sentence. After petitioning the crown, the sentence was commuted to penal servitude for life.[37] In April 1905, ____ received three years' penal servitude for the manslaughter of his wife.[38] In 1903, a man received twelve years' penal servitude for the manslaughter of his wife at Green Street court house in Dublin.[39] In October, ____ received five years' penal servitude for the murder of his wife.[40] In October 1901, ____ received ten years' penal servitude for the manslaughter of his wife.[41] In April 1902, ____ received twelve calendar months for the manslaughter of his wife.[42] While the above all received sentences of penal servitude and imprisonment, in many cases insanity was chosen as a defence by the defendant's lawyer. Even when this was not the situation, many judges declared men who had murdered their wives insane, and ordered their transfer to Dundrum Lunatic Asylum, as will now be addressed.

Insanity and 'murdering one's wife'

of the entire number of lunatics in England and Wales in 1880, only 3 out of 848 had been committed by Justices as dangerous, as contrasted with 1386 out of 1489 committed to asylums in a single year in Ireland as dangerous, or 232 times as many ... This is possibly the most striking contrast in this volume between Irish and English statistics.[43]

In her study of violence in post-famine Ireland, Carolyn Conley points to the fact that while thirty-three per cent of Irish female homicide victims were killed by their husbands, the Irish press and Irish judges frequently argued that killing a wife was rare in Ireland',[44] and that in many of the cases of wife-murder insanity was proffered as an explanation.[45] In reference to the statistics from the House of Commons Report in 1882, did Irish courts view wife-murder as an 'insane' offence, or was the use of asylums yet another example of the over-reliance of the Irish courts and the State on institutions? The different treatment of wife-beaters and wife-murderers by the courts was an interesting phenomenon, and one that has similarities with the issue of cruelty to children and corporal punishment. While a certain measure of violence against women and children was deemed acceptable – particularly in instances in which women and children needed to be 'disciplined' in the home and in the classroom – the killing of a wife permanently removed the mother from the family. Or was it perhaps that judges were reluctant to take a chance when it came to 'dangerous lunatics'? In 1902 a petition was received from a man in Dundrum Lunatic Asylum. He had been convicted of the murder of his wife in July 1872, but 'was found insane and unfit to plea'. He was ordered to be kept in custody and later received a twenty-year sentence. Upon committal in 1872 he attempted to commit suicide and was described as 'violently insane' and suffering from 'mania'. All petitions up to 1902 were rejected, but what is interesting about the cases is the different reports from inspectors in the asylum over the period. While one inspector described the man as 'violently insane', another argued that he did not believe the prisoner was insane.

In July 1898, ____ was convicted of the murder of his wife at the Cork Assizes. After petitioning the court, the sentence of death was commuted to that of penal servitude for life. The judge's report outlined the details of the case:

> the defence was that he was insane, so as not to be responsible for his acts at the time. The evidence that he killed his wife was clear. He married her about 23 years ago in Kanturk. In about a year afterwards they went to New Zealand where he appears to have been employed looking after sheep. After about 6 years they came back to Kanturk. They lived there for some years and he then went to America and she followed him there in 1894 ... there was a dispute in America over his sister's money, [and] his wife came back and lived with her mother and their son. On the date of the murder the husband came to the mother's house and shot her with a revolver in the sitting room.

He elaborates on the defence of insanity:

> the opinion of both the medical men, however, was that he was and had been quite able to know what he was doing when he fired at and shot his wife, and that he knew he was doing wrong and they were not shaken in this opinion upon cross-examination of the prisoner's counsel, although in reply to a juror Dr. Woods stated that he did not think that any man with a patch of softening in his brain could be perfectly sane ... Although I think the jury were warranted in believing that he could discriminate between right and wrong when he fired on his wife, I believe his mental capacity to discriminate was considerably impaired, and that his act stands in a different light from the act of a perfectly sane man. Where sanity is to any extent impaired it is, in my opinion, almost impossible to justly estimate its effect on a man's acts and I regard this as a case in which although the verdict according to the evidence and the laws ... I do not think the case demands the execution of the prisoner and I submit it to the consideration of His Excellency.[46]

There were some instances in which the courts demonstrated leniency in wife-murder cases, usually based on the man's circumstances. In 1915, the *Irish Citizen* recorded two cases of wife-murder prosecuted by the same judge and reported in the *Irish Times*. A comparison of the two cases demonstrates the disparity in the treatment of wife-beating and wife-murder in many instances:

> His Lordship (Mr. Justice Dodd) said that the man appeared to have gone straight except on this occasion, and it cost him his wife. It was a serious thing for a husband to stab his wife with a penknife. If he gave the accused penal servitude he would lose his pension, and that would not be fair remembering his services to his country. He would sentence him to nine months in the second division, the sentence to run from the date of his committal at end of August. (*Irish Times*, 4th December) The following day the same paper reported the trial of another soldier, who was found guilty before Mr. justice Gibson in Dublin for murdering his wife by drowning her in the Royal Canal in Kilcock, 'The Judge, addressing the prisoner, said he had been sentenced on the clearest evidence: His Lordship then having said that he would forward at once to His Excellency the recommendation to mercy, pronounced sentence of death'.[47]

As mentioned previously, up to 1920, the press regularly reported cases of wife-beating, although sometimes in a light-hearted manner. In 1920, the *Irish Independent* recorded a case in the United States in which: 'A man who was arrested for wife-beating ... fled the country when he found that he was to be tried by a jury of women'.[48] In 1907, the *Irish Independent* claimed:

> In Dublin, the late Recorder, who was as merciful a man as ever occupied the position of criminal judge, put down a very common crime some years ago, that of wife-beating, by imposing severe sentences, and no doubt to the hardened criminal a little corporal punishment seldom fails to have a salutary effect.[49]

Conclusion

I never thought a Corkman would beat his wife.[50]

Throughout the nineteenth century, both the press and the courts regularly recorded and dealt with cases of wife-beating. Contrary to Royal Magistrate Hodder's comment above, its occurrence was known and accepted. Provocation when established by husbands could result in them escaping a sentence, and in a few desperate situations women murdered or attempted to murder their husbands to escape. For most working-class and poor women, however, marriage and economic dependence locked them into abusive relationships. With fewer women employed after 1920 than previously, this dependence increased, and the silence surrounding wife-beating from the 1920s to the emergence of second-wave feminism created unbearable conditions for many. This silence was both upheld and enforced by the Church, which frequently told battered wives to remain in the home – 'the family' was the most important factor. Some, however, realised that the fear of violence to their children could allow them to approach the NSPCC and seek some relief. In conjunction with many deserted wives, from the late-1920s women began to approach the Society and plead for material assistance, which many received. By connecting their own violent situation with that of their children in the home, they were using the child-protection agenda to the best of their means. For deserted wives, this was often more successful as both the British and Irish NSPCC inspectors would pursue husbands for maintenance. Overall, however, the situation for both battered and deserted women remained flawed in a system characterised by an unsympathetic judiciary, legislature and Church.

In this examination of the treatment of mothers and fathers by the NSPCC and the State, gender inequality can be seen in a number of areas – from welfare provision to the courts. For working-class mothers particularly, the amount of attention that was directed at them through social and medical campaigns during and after the First World War was extensive. Yet aside from better maternity provision and widows' and orphans' pensions, mothers were rarely supported. For this reason, they were forced, out of necessity, to become adept at negotiating the services and charities available to them. This they did, as the increase in advice sought cases investigated by the NSPCC from 1922 demonstrates. The differentiation between deserving and undeserving mothers can also be identified in the period. While the Society dealt with many unmarried mothers, support to retain their children was not offered in most instances; and for widows, an illegitimate child would cancel the little support the State was providing. For fathers, the State continued to view their role as that of provider, and they would be prosecuted if this role was not fulfilled. While the NSPCC attempted to help deserted wives, the extent to which they were successful is questionable. For battered wives, it appears the Society could only offer to listen and provide a small State subsidy if a woman chose to leave her husband, which most rarely did.

If gender inequality was a feature of welfare initiatives, it was an even greater feature of many households visited by the NSPCC. Situations of wife-beating can be seen in the earliest entries by the Society, and as Liz Steiner-Scott has shown, wife-beating was a common feature of the courts and the press from the mid-nineteenth-century to 1921.[51] Yet in comparison to the position of deserted wives, women suffering from domestic abuse were ignored by the State, and from 1922 to 1960, by the press. Although only wives who were also mothers could approach the NSPCC for help, in this instance the situation of mothers and children were intertwined. As one judge stated, 'the Society for Wives and Children' was one of the few avenues for battered wives.[52]

Notes

1 For a theoretical discussion of cleanliness and order, see Mary Douglas, *Purity and Danger: An analysis of the concepts of purity and taboo* (Routledge 1966), pp. 2, 5, 43–7, 199.
2 Prior to the 1894 and 1908 acts, persons thought to be ill-treating their children could be prosecuted for abandonment, ill-treatment, exposure or begging, each carrying varying sentences, some as long as two years.
3 This was under Acts 10 & 11 Vic., section 2, of the Poor Law. Prior to 1895, the offence was 'deserting or neglecting to support family'.
4 Ibid., p. 32.
5 Indictment no. 22, 3 June 1925, Green Street, Dublin (NAI, Dublin). Punctuation edited for clarity.
6 Tony Fahey, 'State, family and *compulsory* schooling in *Ireland*'. *Economic and Social Review,* 23:4 (1992), 369–95.
7 'Deserted wives', *Evening Press,* 4 April 1967.
8 Ibid.
9 CF #33 (ISPCC, Limerick).
10 CF/38/003 (NAI, Dublin).
11 Inspector Book for Wexford District Branch NSPCC, 7 August 1930 to 22 August 1930 (ISPCC, Limerick).
12 Statement made by a Quarter Sessions Judge during a child neglect case.
13 Mary Powers, 23 March 1934, 2.4, Inspector Book from 3 April 1934 to 19 November 1934. Punctuation edited for clarity.
14 'Domestic violence' is a modern term, but it will be used in this context to describe the situation of women subjected to violence in the home.
15 AR Dublin District Branch NSPCC, 1932–33 (ISPCC, Limerick), p. 6.
16 Inspector Book for Wexford District Branch NSPCC, 5 January 1935 to 11 October 1935 (ISPCC, Limerick).
17 Kearns, *Dublin's Lost Heroines,* p. 176.
18 CF/38/014 (NAI, Dublin).
19 Elizabeth Steiner-Scott, '"To bounce a boot off her now and then...": Domestic violence in post-famine Ireland', in M. Valiulis and M. O'Dowd, *Women and Irish History* (Attic Press,1997), pp. 125–43. See also in the context of London, Ellen Ross, '"Fierce questions and taunts": Married life in working-class

London, 1870–1914', *Feminist Studies*, 8:3 (Autumn 1982), pp. 575–602.
20   Steiner-Scott, 'To bounce a boot off her now and then', p. 126.
21   'Wife-beating', *Irish Times*, 6 March 1880.
22   Ibid.
23   'Wife-beating', *Irish Times*, 20 March 1880.
24   A few temperance campaigners did attempt to raise public awareness of the issue, but their emphasis was on the benefits that sobriety would bring to the family, rather than on the gross violation that individual women and children suffered as a result of abusive husbands and fathers.
25   *Criminal and Judicial Statistics for Ireland 1882* (C3355) 75:243, p. 37.
26   Caitríona Clear, *Women of the House: Women's Household Work in Ireland 1922–1961: Discourses, Experiences, Memories.* (Irish Academic Press, 2000), p. 1.
27   Ibid., p. 133.
28   Joanna Bourke, *Husbandry to Housewifery Women, Economic Change, and Housework in Ireland 1890–1914* (Oxford, 1993).
29   Ibid., p. 70.
30   Bill 8, August 1896, 1C-28-7 (NAI, Dublin).
31   Bills 43 and 44, April 1897, 1C-28-7 (NAI, Dublin).
32   Bill 14, 1C-28-7 (NAI, Dublin).
33   Bill 5, October 1897, 1C-28-7 (NAI, Dublin)
34   CRF/1900/J4 (NAI, Dublin).
35   CRF/1900/S28 (NAI, Dublin).
36   Bills 25 and 26, December 1894, 1C-28-7 (NAI, Dublin).
37   Bill 1, 1C-28-9 (NAI, Dublin).
38   Bill 6, April 1905, CC Crown Books Dublin, 1C-28-9 (NAI, Dublin)
39   Bill 3, June 1903, CC Crown Books Dublin, 1C-28-8 (NAI, Dublin).
40   Bills 19 and 20, October 1903, CC Crown Books Dublin, 1C-28-8 (NAI, Dublin).
41   Bills 13 and 37, October 1901.
42   Bills 14, 15 and 16, 10 April 1902.
43   Criminal and Judicial Statistics for Ireland 1882 (C3355), p. 37.
44   Carolyn Conley, *Melancholy Accidents: The Meaning of Violence in Post-Famine Ireland* (Lexington Books, 1999) p. 61.
45   For a discussion of suicide and insanity in Ireland, see Georgina Laragy, 'Suicide in Ireland, 1831–1921: a social and cultural study', Ph.D. thesis (NUI Maynooth, 2005). Laragy connects the treatment of suicide and insanity in Ireland with modernity, arguing that with regard to asylums, the colonial relationship between landlord and tenant was replicated through the asylum.
46   CRF/1907/B33 (NAI, Dublin).
47   *Irish Citizen*, 11 December 1915.
48   *Irish Independent*, 24 December 1920.
49   'A whipping judge', *Irish Independent*, 4 April 1908.
50   Comment of Mr Hodder, R.M., during a wife-beating case, 18 October 1907. CRF/1909/A32 (NAI, Dublin).
51   Steiner-Scott, 'To bounce a boot off her now and then', pp. 125–43.
52   CRF/1895/M67.

Conclusion

Train up the child in the way he should go, And when he is old he will not depart from it.[1]

The above quote, taken from the first Irish NSPCC report and reprinted in 1939 in the Society's Golden Jubilee booklet, encapsulates the attitude of the NSPCC to children and childhood from its foundation. The message is clear – children are future citizens, and all can be helped and reformed. Although the Society in 1939 claimed that its work could now be categorised as involving 'sensibility without sentimentality',[2] it could be argued that neither were a part of its actual work for families, only its rhetoric. Aside from its role as an advisory agency after independence, in which the Society obtained material relief for destitute families, investigating and prosecuting parents, removing children to industrial schools and policing families represented the bulk of its work. In the 1880s, when the NSPCC in Britain and Ireland began its public campaign to raise awareness of cruelty to children, the concept was not a new phenomenon. What was new was how it was used to control families through legislation and surveillance. Children had been subjected to cruelty before 1908 and would continue to be after that date. Had the NSPCC not approached its work by seeking to 'treat' poverty with punitive measures, its role could have been more positive. The State followed the lead of philanthropy and voluntary charity, and continued to rely on the services of such organisations in Ireland well into the twentieth century, instead of developing a proper public welfare system. By continuing to rely on voluntarism over State welfare for provision of social services, the State ensured that the NSPCC's role continued to be significant.

In contrast to the period after independence, from 1880 to 1921, the NSPCC was explicit in its condemnation of parents, and particularly mothers, who constituted the majority of those prosecuted for offences of cruelty to children and committals to Ennis State Inebriate Reformatory. All sample cases cited in the earlier reports involved drunkenness or intemperance. Yet as the case-study of the convict reference files and the connection between 'being a habitual drunkard' and child neglect addressed, poverty was the overarching *raison d'être* for the neglect the NSPCC was investigating. In fact, until 1921, 'neglect and starvation' was the primary form of neglect investigated by the Society. After this, the expansion and recategorisation of neglect focused attention on 'putative fathers', 'juvenile delinquents', nurse-children and 'illegitimate' children. Neglect's all-encompassing mandate implied unlimited jurisdiction, authorised through legislative change. While the 1908 Children Act would be scrutinised and reformed in Britain with regard to institutionalisation, juvenile delinquency and school non-attendance in the 1920s, Irish legislation further penalised parents and offered no more protection to children. The 1908 Punishment of Incest Act remained unchanged; the 1926 School Attendance Act in conjunction with the 1929 Children Act would be used to institutionalise thousands of children; and the 1927 Public Safety Act placed responsibility on parents for the petty crimes for which 'juvenile delinquents' were charged. In general, the period after independence further eroded parental rights yet provided no more protection to children or the family. Neither the rights of children as espoused in the 1919 Democratic Programme nor the 'sanctity of the family' advocated in the 1937 Constitution represented reality for poor families. In relation to education, health, institutionalisation and welfare, financial and religious concerns superseded the welfare of families. Only after the horrific social and economic conditions for working-class families came to the fore during the Emergency period did the State consider providing a meagre financial sum to support large families. Yet even this measure was limited by concerns over State interference in the family.

For the State, the reluctance to tackle the social or economic problems facing families in poverty, not to mention the underlying causes, is sharply contrasted with its concerns about sexuality and financial solvency. While various scholars have addressed the effects of draconian policies introduced by the State from the 1920s to the 1940s, the distress that families endured as a result of those policies deserves greater attention. This book has hopefully provided a glimpse into the situations for single mothers, widowers, families in poverty and children placed in the myriad of institutions. The investigation of the industrial schools revealed that Catholic fears of Protestant proselytism and the capitation fee system for industrial schools created a situation in which 'saving the souls' of children was an active 'spiritual' and material endeavour. The continuation of this policy of institutionalisation by the State ignored the socio-economic reality for families, as institutionalisation was used as a poor alternative to welfare in the first instance, and the promotion of a just and equal society in the broadest sense, where all of the nation's children were cherished. That officially members of parliament were aware of the conditions in many schools only adds to the argument that the children placed there were seen as disposable.

With reference to gender bias in the treatment of mothers and fathers by the NSPCC, and gender inequality in welfare, Chapter 6 demonstrated that working-class women and men were penalised by both the NSPCC and the State for different 'crimes' over the period. With regard to the obstacles faced by mothers in poverty in maintaining their children, the examination of wife-beating and desertion has exemplified the State's disregard for poor vulnerable women. Had the cases investigated not involved children, there would have been no place for wives to turn. For the NSPCC, the discourse on desertion emerged from its need to keep families intact where at all possible. By tracing husbands for maintenance, for example, as opposed to lobbying for sufficient welfare for single mothers, the Society was ensuring it did not rock the Church/State boat. In highlighting families in poverty and facilitating the removal of children to industrial schools, the Society had moved far from its policy of protecting children within the home. Although it did address social problems in official reports, its position as a voluntary charity ensured it would compromise where needed. Yet, perhaps the most at fault was the State, which provided neither the resources nor the political will to change the lives of many families. Unfortunately, it was most often vulnerable children who suffered the most from this apathy and disregard.

Looking at history of child welfare from 1956 to the present time, the narrative could be viewed as one of progress and continued negligence by the State and its agencies. Progress can be seen in the development of social work from the 1970s, the introduction of welfare payments for single-parent families, increased educational opportunities for minority groups and women, and legislation in regard to incest and child protection. On the other hand, today, social work stands at a crossroads – on one path increased managerialism and marketisation, on the other, the opportunity to be guided by social justice. With regard to legislation, the children's rights amendment has been lauded as the missing piece with regard to the protection of children in care – in reality, as this book has hopefully demonstrated, without the resources and political will to improve the lives of families in poverty and vulnerable children, this is but a change to the constitution. For those still in care, 5,000–6,000 on average each year, life can still be hazardous, as the issue of child deaths has highlighted. This is a critique not of the services or those working in the services but of a system that needs improvement and increased resources. In reference to the political climate, in a period of austerity and crisis, the State is again ignoring the relationship between welfare, the distribution of wealth and the health of its citizens. While the majority of the families addressed in this book were from the working-class and rural poor, today, many families struggling financially are in the middle class, as the gap between the richest and poorest in our society continues to widen. With regard to minority groups – such as immigrants and those in the travelling community – much work also needs to be done. As with other issues, hopefully any gains made in previous years will not be reversed. Finally, while conceptions of childhood have evolved beyond recognition from what they were in the nineteenth century, today, children face new challenges and threats.

As the introduction addressed, today's debates concern issues that are rooted in the historical record. These debates emerged from the mid-nineteenth century at a time when the State became actively involved in the family unit. If we are to understand how to tackle the problems in families and those facing children today, we must look to the past and implement real change, such was envisioned in the 1919 Democratic Programme, and today in the very real ideas surrounding social justice and the State. Without this change, the history of child welfare and the State in the years to come may again be one of negligence and apathy.

Notes

1   NSPCC Golden Jubilee Commemorative Booklet, 1939 (ISPCC, Limerick), p. 10.
2   Ibid., p. 4.

Appendix A

NSPCC annual branch reports

1889–1932

Athlone: 1898–1902.
Cahir and Templemore Districts: 1906–1908.
Carlow: 1898–99, 1902–1910.
Clonmel: 1898–1914 (excl. 1906–7) and 1926–1932.
Cork and District: 1891–98 (excl. 1892, 1894) and 1902–32 (excl. 1909, 1912, 1916, 1919–20, 1922).
Dublin: 1890–1932 (excl. 1892).
Dundalk District Committee: 1898.
Dungarvan Aid Committee: 1898–99.
Dungarvan and District: 1926–32.
Galway: 1926–32.
Kerry: 1928–32.
Kerry and North Cork: 1912–15 (excl. 1914, 1926–27).
Kilkenny and District: 1898–1911 (excl. 1907).
Kilkenny, Carlow and Queen's County: 1912–32 (excl. 1916–18, 1920–22).
Kingstown: 1909–19.
Limerick and District: 1904–11 (excl. 1905).
Limerick, Clare and District: 1911–1932 (excl. 1914, 1918–19, 1921–22, 1926, 1928, 1932).
Mayo: 1931–32.
Meath, Louth and District: 1904–9.
Meath, South Louth and District: 1910–1932 (excl. 1912, 1917–18, 1920, 1922) (excl. 1914, 1918–19, 1921–22, 1926, 1928, 1932).
North Louth and Monaghan: 1914–32 (excl. 1916, 1918–20, 1924–26).
Sligo and Leitrim: 1924–32.
Templemore District: 1906.
Waterford and District: 1898–1938 (1898 missing);
Waterford and District: 1926–32 (excl. 1929).
Waterford, Dungarvan, Carrick-on-Suir and Lismore: 1899–1906.
West Meath, King's County and District: 1903–32 (excl. 1918, 1923).
Wexford and District: 1900–32.

Appendix A

1933–55

Clonmel and District: 1933–55 (excl. 1948 and 1949).
Cork and District: 1933–55 (excl. 1941, 1949).
Galway and District: 1933–55 (excl. 1940, 1947, 1949, 1953–54).
Kerry: 1933–55 (excl. 1935–36, 1941–42). Many of the reports incorporate two years.
Kilkenny, Carlow and Queen's County (Leix from 1937): 1933–55 (excl. 1943, 1949–50, 1955).
Limerick, Clare and District: 1933–55 (excl. 1935, 1941, 1946, 1948, 1949, 1950, 1951, 1952, 1953, 1954).
Mayo: 1933–55 (excl. 1934, 1940–41, 1943).
Meath, South Louth and District: 1933–55.
Waterford and District: 1933–55 (excl. 1937, 1941).
Westmeath, King's County and District: 1933–55 (1937, Westmeath, Offaly and District; 1952, Midlands Counties).
Wexford and District: 1933–55.

Appendix B

Sample NSPCC assessment form

FORM IV.   PLAINT NO:

THE NATIONAL SOCIETY FOR THE PREVENTION OF CRUELTY TO CHILDREN
Central Office: – VICTORY HOUSE, LEICESTER SQUARE, LONDON, W.C.2

Date of Complaint: Branch:
Date of Inquiry:

CHILDREN – Names, Ages and Address

Children's religion?	Are they insured?
Relationship to accused?	For how much?
Are parents living?	In what Society?
Are children illegitimate?	Parents' income?

ALLEGATION —	**AGAINST —**
Nature of:	Name:
Time of:	Address:
Locality:	Family/Occupation:

Name and addresses of witnesses:

INSPECTOR'S REPORT

Dates and
Times of Visits

Condition of
Children

Condition of
Home, and
rent paid

Appendix B

INSPECTOR'S REPORT — Continued

**Character of
Parents, and
if previously
under notice**

**Parents'
Explanation**

**General
Remarks**

Action taken

Result

**How children
Dealt with**

Inspector

Date   **REPORTS OF SUPERVISION VISITS**

Select bibliography

Primary sources

Archive of the National Society for the Prevention of Cruelty to Children (NSPCC; ISPCC, Limerick)

National Archives of Ireland (NAI, Dublin)
- Chief Secretary's Office, Registered Papers.

Convict Reference Files (CRF)
- Index books for convict reference files, 1880–1920.
- Available convict reference files from 1880–1920 relating to offences surrounding cruelty to children or child neglect, wife-beating, incest and violence within the extended family. In total, approximately 250 files. Roughly half of the files recalled were available, but the remainder were no longer extant.

Crown and Peace Office Files
- Index books for Assizes and Quarter Sessions, and Crown Files for Cork, Dublin (City and County Commissions), Kerry, Mayo and Monaghan, 1880–1920.
- Files, Crown Courts, Cork, Dublin, Kerry, Mayo and Monaghan, 1880–1920.

Department of Justice
- Files, Central Criminal Court, Dublin, 1924–40.
- Files, Central Criminal Court, Kerry, 1924–40.
- Files, Central Criminal Court, Mayo, 1923–40.
- Files, Central Criminal Court, Monaghan, 1924–40.
- State books, Circuit Court, Dublin (City and County), 1924–40.
- State books, Circuit Court, Kerry, 1924–40.
- State books, Circuit Court, Mayo, 1924–40.
- State books, Circuit Court, Monaghan, 1924–40.
- State files, Circuit Court, Dublin (City and County), 1924–40.
- State files, Circuit Court, Kerry, 1924–40.
- State files, Circuit Court, Mayo, 1924–40.
- State files, Circuit Court, Monaghan, 1924–40.
- Trial record books, Central Criminal Court, 1924–40.
- Committee on Evil Literature, File Jus/7/2/9.
- Committee on Evil Literature, File Jus/7/2/14.

- Criminal Law Amendment Act, correspondence, File Jus/8/20/1.
- Criminal Statistics, 1926–43, File Jus/72/53, part 1.
- Memorandum on Crime, 1936, File Jus/8/451.
- Minutes of Evidence, the Carrigan Committee, File Jus/90/4.

Department of the Taoiseach
- File s2804, Criminal Law Amendment Acts, 1932–4.
- File s2864, Criminal Law Amendment Acts, 1932–4.
- File s4183, Venereal Disease in the Irish Free State, 1924–7.
- File s5998, Criminal Law Amendment Bill, 1929–34.
- File s6489 Criminal Law Amendment Bill, 1934.
- File s6489A, Criminal Law Amendment Act, 1935.
- File s10815A, General File on Adoption of Children.
- File d13290A1, Kennedy Report, 1970.
- File s121117A & B, Files on Family Allowances.
- File s11109B.
- File s13186.
- File s5698.
- File s9278.
- File s14103A.

Joint Committee of Women's Societies and Social Workers (JCWSSW)
- File 98/14/5/1, Minute Book 1935–39.
- File 98/14/5/2, Minute Book 1939–48.

Official sources

Criminal and Judicial Statistics for Ireland 1880–1921.
Dáil Éireann, Debates, 1922–50.
Seanad Éireann, Debates, 1922–50.

Reports of governmental organisations

Annual Report of the Registrar-General for Saorstát Éireann (Dublin, 1924).
Report of the Commission on the Relief of the Sick and Destitute Poor, Including the Insane Poor (Dublin, 1928).
Report of the Committee to Inquire into the Reformatory and Industrial School System (Dublin, 1936).
Reports of the Committee of Inquiry into Widows' and Orphans' Pensions (Dublin, 1933).
Report of the Criminal Law Amendment Acts (1880–85) and Juvenile Prostitution (Dublin, 1931).
Report of the Interdepartmental Committee of Inquiry regarding Venereal Disease (Dublin, 1926).
Royal Commission on Venereal Diseases, Reports and Minutes of Evidence, House of Commons (Cd7475) xlix, 1914; 1916 (Cd8189) xvi; 1916 (Cd8190) xvi.
Statistical Abstracts of Ireland, 1927–40 (Dublin, 1927–41).

Reports of non-governmental organisations

Catholic Protection and Rescue Society, 15th Annual Report of Catholic Protection and Rescue Society, 1928 (Dublin, n.d.).
Society of St Vincent de Paul, *Annual Report of the Society of St Vincent de Paul, 1928–40* (Dublin).
Society of St Vincent de Paul, *Reports of the Catholic Male Discharged Prisoners' Aid Committee, 1928–40*.
Society of St Vincent de Paul, *Reports of the Council of Ireland, 1929–40*.
Williams, G.D., *Dublin Charities: Being a Handbook of Dublin Philanthropic Organisations and Charities* (Dublin, 1902).

Contemporary newspapers, journals and magazines

- *Catholic Bulletin*
- *Child's Guardian*
- *Cork Examiner*
- *Hermanthena*
- *Inspector's Directory*
- *Irish Citizen*
- *Irish Ecclesiastical Record*
- *Irish Independent*
- *Irish Law Times and Solicitors' Journal*
- *Irish Press*
- *Irish Times*
- *Journal of the Statistical and Social Inquiry Society of Ireland*
- *Lancet*
- *Studies*

Secondary sources

Articles and chapters

Bailey, V., and S. Blackburn, 'The Punishment of Incest Act, 1908: A case study of criminal law creation', *Criminal Law Review*, 685–744 (November 1979), 708–18.
Beaumont, C., 'Women and the politics of equality: The Irish women's movement 1930–1943', in M. Valiulis and M. O'Dowd (eds), *Women and Irish History*, pp. 173–88.
Bourke, Joanna, 'Avoiding poverty: Strategies for women in rural Ireland, 1880–1914', in Richard Wall and John Henderson (eds), *Poor Women and Children in the European Past* (Routledge, 1994), pp. 292–311.
Bourke, Joanna, 'The health caravan: Female labour and domestic education in rural Ireland, 1890–1914', *Eire-Ireland*, 24:4 (Winter 1989), 21–38.
Breathnach, C., 'The CDB and the changing role of Irish women in the rural economy 1891–1921', *New Hibernia Review* (Spring 2004), 80–92.
Bretherton, G., 'Irish inebriate reformatories, 1899–1920', in I. O'Donnell and F. McAuley (eds) *Criminal Justice History: Themes and Controversies from Pre-independence Ireland* (Four Courts Press, 2003).
Buckley, S.A., 'Child neglect, poverty and class: The NSPCC in Ireland, 1889–1938

– a case study', *Saothar: Journal of Irish Labour History*, 33 (2008), 57–72.

Buckley, S.A., 'Family and power: Incest in Ireland, 1880–1950', in *Power in History: From Medieval Ireland to the Post-Modern World. Historical Studies XXVII* (Irish Academic Press, 2011).

Buckley, S.A., '"Found in a dying condition": Nurse children in Ireland 1872–1952', in Elaine Farrell (ed.),*'She said she was in a family way': Pregnancy and Infancy in Modern Ireland* (Institute of Historical Research, 2012).

Buckley, S.A., 'The problem is not one of criminal tendencies but poverty': The NSPCC, John Byrne and the industrial school system in Ireland', *Locked Out: A Century of Irish Working Class Life* (Irish Academic Press, 2013).

Buckley, S.A., '"Saver of the children": The National Society for the Prevention of Cruelty to Children in Ireland, 1889–1900', *Conference Proceedings from the 2010 Nineteenth-Century Ireland Conference on Philanthropy* (Four Courts Press, forthcoming).

Clark, A., 'Wild workhouse girls and the liberal imperial State in the mid-nineteenth century Ireland', *Journal of Social History*, 39 (2005), 389–409.

Clark, A., 'Orphans and the Poor Law: Rage against the machine', in V. Crossman and P. Gray (eds), *Poverty and Welfare in Ireland, 1838–1948* (Irish Academic Press, 2011).

Clear, C., 'Walls within walls: Nuns in nineteenth-century Ireland', in C. Curtin (ed.) *Gender in Irish Society* (Galway University Press, 1987), pp. 134–51.

Clear, C., 'The limits of female autonomy: Nuns in nineteenth-century Ireland', in M. Luddy and C. Murphy (eds), *Women Surviving: Studies in Irish Women's History in the 19th and 20th Centuries* (Poolpeg, 1990), pp. 15–50.

Clear, C., '"The women cannot be blamed": The commission on vocational organisation, feminism and "home makers" in Independent Ireland in the 1930s and '40s', in M. O'Dowd and S. Wichert (eds), *Chattel, Servant or Citizen: Women's Status in Church, State and Society* (Institute of Irish Studies, 1995), pp. 179–86.

Clear, C., 'Women in de Valera's Ireland, 1932–48: A reappraisal', in G. Doherty and D. Keogh (eds), *De Valera's Irelands* (Mercier Press, 2003), pp. 104–14.

Coakley, A., 'Mothers and poverty', in P. Kennedy (ed.), *Motherhood in Ireland: Creation and Context* (Mercier Press, 2004), pp. 207–17.

Conroy, P., 'Maternity confined – the struggle for fertility control', in P. Kennedy (ed.), *Motherhood in Ireland: Creation and Context* (Mercier Press, 2004), pp. 127–38.

Cousins, M., 'The introduction of children's allowances in Ireland, 1939–1944', *Irish Economic and Social History*, 27 (November 1999), 35–55.

Crossman, V., 'Viewing family and sexuality through the prism of the Irish poor laws', *Women's History Review*, 15 (2006), 541–50.

Crossman, V., 'Cribbed, contained and confined? The care of children under the Irish Poor Law', *Éire-Ireland*, 44:1–2 (Spring/Summer 2009), 37–61.

Daly, M.E., 'Social structure of the Dublin working class, 1871–1911', *Irish Historical Studies*, 23:100 (November, 1982), pp. 159–94.

Daly, M.E., '"Turn on the tap": The State, Irish women and running water', in M. Valiulis and M. O'Dowd (eds), *Women and Irish History: Essays in Honour of Margaret McCurtain* (Wolfhound Press, 1997), pp. 206–19.

Daly, M.E., 'The Irish family since the Famine', *Irish Journal of Feminist Studies*, 3:2 (Autumn, 1999), 1–21.

Daly, M.E., '"The primary and natural educator"?: The role of parents in the education of their children in independent Ireland', *Éire-Ireland*, 44:1–2 (Spring/Summer, 2009), 194–217.

D'Cruze, S., 'Women and the family', in J. Purvis (ed.), *Women's History in Britain, 1850–1945* (St Martin's Press, 1995), pp. 51–76.

Deeny, J., 'Poverty as a cause of ill-health', *Journal of the Statistical and Social Inquiry Society of Ireland*, 16 (1944), 75–84.

Devane, Revd R.S., SJ, 'The unmarried mother: Some legal aspects of the problem', *Irish Ecclesiastical Record*, 23 (1924), 55–68.

Devane, Revd R.S., SJ, 'The unmarried mother and the Poor Law Commission', *Irish Ecclesiastical Record*, 31 (1928), 561–82.

Devane, Revd R.S., SJ, 'The legal protection of girls', *Irish Ecclesiastical Record*, 37 (1931), 20–40.

Digby, A., 'Poverty, health and the politics of gender in Britain, 1870–1948', in A. Digby and J. Stewart (eds), *Gender, Health and Welfare* (Routledge, 1996), pp. 67–90.

Dillon, T.W.T., 'The social services in Éire', *Studies*, 34 (September 1945), 331.

Dunne, E., 'Action and reaction: Catholic lay organisations in Dublin in the 1920s and 1930s', *Archivium Hibernicum*, 48 (1994), 107–18.

Earner-Byrne, L., 'The boat to England: An analysis of the official reactions to the emigration of single expectant Irishwomen to Britain, 1922–72', *Irish Economic and Social History*, 30 (November 2003), 57.

Earner-Byrne, L., '"Moral repatriation": The response to Irish unmarried mothers in Britain, 1920s–1960s', in Patrick J. Duffy (ed.), *To and From Ireland: Planned Migration Schemes c. 1600–2000* (Geography Publications, 2004), pp. 155–73.

Earner-Byrne, L., '"Managing motherhood": Negotiating a maternity service for Catholic mothers in Dublin, 1930–54', *Social History of Medicine*, 20:2 (August 2006), 261–77.

Ferguson, H., 'Cleveland in history: The abused child and child protection, 1880–1914', in R. Cooter (ed.) *In the Name of the Child: Health and Welfare 1880–1914* (London, 1992), pp. 146–73.

Finnane, M., 'The Carrigan Committee of 1930–31 and the "moral condition" of the Saorstát', *Irish Historical Studies*, 32 (2001), 519–36.

Fitzpatrick, D., 'The disappearance of the Irish agricultural babourer', *Irish Economic and Social History*, 7 (1980), 66–92.

Fitzpatrick, D., 'Irish farming families before the First World War', *Comparative Studies in History and Society*, 25 (1984), 339–74.

Garrett, P.M., 'The abnormal flight: The migration and repatriation of unmarried mothers', *Social History*, 25 (2000), 330–43.

Guinnane, T., 'Coming of age in rural Ireland at the turn of the twentieth century', *Continuity and Change*, 5:3 (1990) 443–72.

Guinnane, T., 'Rethinking the Western European marriage pattern: The decision to marry in Ireland at the turn of the twentieth century', *Journal of Family History*, 16:1 (1991), 47–64.

Guinnane, T., 'Inter-generational transfers, emigration and the rural Irish household system', *Explorations in Economic History*, 29:4 (1992), 456–76.

Homrighaus, R., 'Baby farming: The care of illegitimate children in England, 1860–1943' (unpublished PhD thesis, University of Carolina at Chapel Hill, 2003).

Kennedy, F., 'The suppression of the Carrigan Report: A historical perspective on child abuse', *Studies*, 89 (2000), 354–62.

Koven, S., and S. Michel, 'Womanly duties: Maternalist politics and the origins of welfare states in France, Germany, Great Britain, and the United States, 1880–1920', *American History Review*, 95:4–5 (1990), 1076–108.

Leane, M., "Female sexuality in Ireland 1920 to 1940: Construction and regulation", Unpublished PhD thesis (University College Cork, 1999).

Luddy, M., 'Irish women and the Contagious Disease Acts 1864–1886', *History Ireland*, 1 (1993), 32–4.

Luddy, M., '"Abandoned women and bad characters": Prostitution in nineteenth-century Ireland', *Women's History Review*, 6 (1997), 485–503.

Luddy, M., 'Moral rescue and unmarried mothers in Ireland in the 1920s', *Women's Studies*, 30 (2001), 797–817.

Luddy, M., 'The early years of the NSPCC in Ireland', *Éire-Ireland*, 44:1–2 (Spring/Summer 2009), 62–90.

McAvoy, S. L., 'The regulation of sexuality in the Irish Free State, 1929–1935', in Greta Jones and Elizabeth Malcolm (eds), *Medicine, Disease and the State in Ireland, 1650–1940* (Mercier Press, 1999), pp. 253–66.

McAvoy, S. L., 'Before Cadden: Abortion in mid-twentieth-century Ireland', in D. Keogh, F. O'Shea and C. Quinlan (eds), *The Lost Decade: Ireland in the 1950s* (Mercier Press, 2004), pp. 147–63.

McAvoy, S. L., 'Sexual crime and Irish women's campaign for a Criminal Law Amendment Act, 1912–35', in Maryann Gialanna Valiulis *Gender and Power in Modern Ireland* (Irish Academic Press, 2009), pp. 84–99.

McLoughlin, D., 'Women and sexuality in nineteenth-century Ireland', *Irish Journal of Psychology*, 15 (1994), 266–75.

Macnicol, J., 'Welfare, wages and the family: Child endowment in comparative perspective, 1900–1950', in R. Cooter (ed.), *In the Name of the Child: Health and Welfare 1880–1940* (Routledge 1992), pp. 224–75.

Maguire, M., 'Foreign adoptions and the evolution of Irish adoption policy, 1945–52', *Journal of Social History*, 36: 2 (Winter 2002), 387–404.

Maguire, M., and Seámus Ó'Cinnéide, '"A good beating never hurt anyone": The punishment and abuse of children in twentieth century Ireland', *Journal of Social History*, 38:3 (Spring 2005), 635–52.

Malcolm, E., '"Ireland's crowded madhouses": The institutional confinement of the insane in nineteenth- and twentieth-century Ireland', in Roy Porter and David Wright (eds), *The Confinement of the Insane: International Perspectives, 1800–1965* (Cambridge University Press, 2003), pp. 315–33.

Meehan, N., 'Church and State and the Bethany Home', *History Ireland*, 18:5 (2010).

Ó Cinneide, S., 'The development of the Home Assistance Service', *Administration*, 17 (1969), 248–308.

Ó Gráda, C., '"The greatest blessing of all": The old age pension', *Past and Present*, 175 (May, 2002), pp. 124–61.

O hOgartaigh, M., 'Dr Dorothy Price and the elimination of childhood tuberculosis', in J. Augusteijn (ed.), *Ireland in the 1930s: New Perspectives* (Four Courts Press, 1999), pp. 67–82.

O'Sullivan, E. 'Restored to virtue, to society and to God': Juvenile justice and the regulation of the poor, *Irish Criminal Law Journal*, 17:2 (1997), 171–94.

O'Sullivan, E., 'This otherwise delicate subject': Child abuse in early twentieth-century Ireland', in Paul O'Mahony (ed.), *Criminal Justice in Ireland* (Institute

of Public Administration, 2002), pp. 172–202.
Rattigan, C., '"Crimes of passion of the worst character": Abortion cases and gender in Ireland, 1925–50', in M. Valiulis (ed.), *Gender and Power in Irish History* (Irish Academic Press, 2008), pp. 115–40.
Reidy, C., 'Borstal boys: The institution at Clonmel: 1906–1914,' *History Studies* (University of Limerick), 6 (2005), 64–78.
Sacco, L., 'Sanitized for your protection: Medical discourse and the denial of incest in the United States, 1890–1940,' *Journal of Women's History*, 14:3 (Autumn 2002), 80–104.
Smart, C., 'Reconsidering the recent history of child sexual abuse, 1910–1960', *Journal of Social Policy*, 29 (2000), 55–71.
Smith, J., 'The politics of sexual knowledge: The origins of Ireland's containment culture and the Carrigan Report (1931)', *Journal of the History of Sexuality*,13:2 (April 2004), 208–33.
Steiner-Scott, E., '"To bounce a boot off her now and then...'': Domestic violence in post-famine Ireland', in M. Valiulis and M. O'Dowd (eds), *Women and Irish History: Essays in Honour of Margaret McCurtain* (Wolfhound Press, 1997), pp. 125–43.
Stewart, J., 'Children, parents and the State: The Children Act, 1908', *Children & Society*, 9:1 (1995), 90–9.
Valiulis, M., 'Neither feminist nor flapper: The ecclesiastical construction of the Ideal Irish woman', in M. O'Dowd and S. Wichert (eds), *Chattell, Servant or Citizen: Women's Status in Church, State and Society* (Institute of Irish Studies, 1995), pp. 168–78.

Books

Abrams, L., *The Orphan Country: Children of Scotland's Broken Homes From 1845 to the Present Day* (John Donald, 1998).
Anderson, M., *Approaches to the History of the Western Family 1500–1914* (Macmillan, 1980).
Arensberg, C.M., and S.T. Kimball, *Family and Community in Ireland*, 2nd edn (Harvard University Press, 1968).
Aries, P., *Centuries of Childhood* (Harmondsworth, 1960).
Augusteijn, J. (ed.), *Ireland in the 1930s: New Perspectives* (Mercier University Press, 1986).
Backus, M., *The Gothic Family Romance: Heterosexuality, Child Sacrifice, and the Anglo-Irish Colonial Order* (Duke University Press, 1999).
Barnes, J., *Irish Industrial Schools, 1868–1908: Origins and Development* (Irish Academic Press, 1984).
Barrington, R., *Health, Medicine and Politics in Ireland 1900–1970* (Dublin, 1987).
Beale, J., *Women in Ireland: Voices of Change* (Gill and Macmillan,1986).
Behlmer, G.K., *Child Abuse and Moral Reform in England, 1870–1908* (Stanford University Press, 1982).
Behlmer, G.K., *Friends of the Family: The English Home and Its Guardians, 1850–1940* (Stanford University Press, 1998).
Bock, G., and P. Thane (eds), *Maternity and Gender Policies: Women and the Rise of European Welfare States, 1880–1950* (Routledge, 1991).
Bourke, J., *Husbandry to Housewifery: Women, Economic Change, and Housework*

in Ireland 1890–1914 (Oxford University Press, 1993).
Bourke, J., *Working-Class Cultures in Britain, 1890–1960: Gender, Class and Ethnicity* (Routledge, 1993).
Breathnach, C., *The Congested Districts Board of Ireland, 1891–1923: Poverty and Development in the West of Ireland* (Four Courts Press, 2005).
Bremmer, R.H., *Children and Youth in America 1866–1932, Vol. 2, Parts 7–8* (Harvard University Press, 1971).
Brown, M.R. (ed.), *Picturing Children: Constructions of Childhood Between Rousseau and Freud* (Ashgate, 2002).
Brown, T. *Ireland: A Social and Cultural History, 1922–1985* (Cornell, 1985).
Clear, C., *Nuns in Nineteenth-Century Ireland* (Gill and Macmillan, 1987).
Clear, C., *Women of the House: Women's Household Work in Ireland 1922-1961: Discourses, Experiences, Memories* (Irish Academic Press, 2000).
Connolly, L., *The Women's Movement: From Revolution to Devolution* (Palgrave Macmillan, 2002).
Conley, C., *Melancholy Accidents: The Meaning of Violence in Post-Famine Ireland* (Lexington Books, 1999).
Conrad, Kathryn A., *Locked in the Family Cell: Gender, Sexuality and Political Agency in Irish Nationalist Discourse* (University of Wisconsin Press, 2004).
Cooter, R. (ed.), *In the Name of the Child: Health and Welfare 1880–1940* (Routledge, 1992).
Corish, O., *The Irish Catholic Experience: A Historical Survey* (Gill and Macmillan, 1985).
Creighton, S., *Trends in Child Abuse* (NSPCC, 1984).
Cullen Owens, R., *Louie Bennett: A Biography* (Cork University Press, 2001).
Cunningham, H., *The Children of the Poor: Representations of Childhood since the Seventeenth Century* (Blackwell, 1991).
Cunningham, H., *Children and Childhood in Western Society Since 1500* (Blackwell, 1995; 2005).
Davin, A., *Growing Up Poor Home, School and Street in London 1870–1914* (Rivers Oram Press, 1996).
DeMause, L. (ed.), *The History of Childhood* (Harper and Row, 1974; 1976).
Dingwall, R., J. Eekelaa and T. Murray, *The Protection of Children: State Intervention and Family Life* (Blackwell, 1983).
Donzelot, J., *The Policing of Families*, 3rd edn (John Hopkins University Press, 1997).
Doyle, Paddy, *The God Squad* (Corgi, 1989.)
Dwork, D., *War is Good for Babies and Other Young Children: A History of the Infant and Child Welfare Movement in England, 1891–1918* (Tavistock Publications, 1987).
Earner-Byrne, L., *Mother and Child: Maternity and Child Welfare in Dublin, 1922–60* (Manchester University Press, 2007).
Elias, N., *The Civilizing Process, Volume 1: The History of Manners* (Pantheon, 1978).
Fallon, B., *An Age of Innocence: Irish Culture 1930–1960* (Gill and Macmillan, 1998).
Fanning, R., *Independent Ireland* (Helicon, 1998).
Farrell, E. (ed.), *'She said she was in a family way': Pregnancy and Infancy in Modern Ireland* (Institute of Historical Research, 2012).

Farrell, E., 'A Most Diabolical Deed': Infanticide and Irish Society (Manchester University Press, 2013).
Feeney, J., John Charles McQuaid: The Man and the Mask (Mercier Press, 1974).
Ferriter, D., The Transformation of Ireland, 1900–2000 (Overlook Press, 2004)
Ferriter, D., Occasions of Sin: Sex and Society in Modern Ireland (Profile Books, 2009).
Ferriter, D., Mothers, Maidens and Myths: A History of the ICA (n.d.).
Foucault, M., Discipline and Punish: The Birth of the Prison, translated by Alan Sheridan (Knopf Doubleday, 1979).
Foucault, M., The History of Sexuality, Vol. 1, translated by Robert Hurley (Pantheon, 1978; Vintage Book, 1990).
Finnegan, F., Do Penance or Perish: Magdalen Asylums in Ireland (Oxford University Press, 2001).
Fletcher, A., and S. Hussey (eds), Childhood in Question: Children, Parents and the State (Manchester University Press, 1999).
Foster, R.F., Modern Ireland, 1600–1972 (Oxford University Press, 1988).
Fuller, L., Irish Catholicism Since 1950: The Undoing of a Culture (Gill and Macmillan, 2004).
Gillis, J.R., L.A. Tilly and D. Levine, The European Experience of Declining Fertility 1850–1970: A Quiet Revolution 1850–1970 (Blackwell, 1992).
Gordon, L., Heroes of Their Own Lives (Virago, 1989).
Gordon, L., Pitied but not Entitled: Single Mothers and the Origins of Welfare (Free Press, 1994).
Gray, T., The Lost Years: The Emergency Years in Ireland, 1939–45 (Little Brown, 1997).
Hall, L., Sex, Gender and Social Change in Britain since 1880 (Palgrave Macmillan, 2000).
Hendrick, H. Child Welfare: Historical Dimensions, Contemporary Debate (Polity Press, 2003).
Heywood, C., Childhood in Nineteenth-Century France: Work, Health and Education Among the 'Classes Populaires' (Cambridge University Press, 1988).
Higonnet, A., Pictures of Innocence: The History and Crisis of Ideal Childhood (Thames and Hudson, 1998).
Hill, M., Women in Ireland: A Century of Change (Blackstaff, 2003).
Hug, C., The Politics of Sexual Morality in Ireland (Macmillan, 1999).
Humphrey, J.A., New Dubliners: Urbanization and the Irish Family (Routledge, 1966).
Humphries, S., Hooligans or Rebels? An Oral History of Working–Class Childhood and Youth, 1889–1939 (Basil Blackwell, 1981).
Inglis, T., Moral Monopoly: The Catholic Church in Modern Irish Society (University College Dublin Press, 1987).
Jackson, L.A., Child Sexual Abuse in Victorian England (Routledge, 2000).
Jackson, M. (ed.), Infanticide: Historical Perspectives on Child Murder and Concealment, 1550–2000 (Aldershot: Ashgate, 2002).
Jones, G., 'Captain of All These Men of Death': The History of Tuberculosis in Nineteenth and Twentieth Century Ireland (Rodopi, 2001).
Kearns, K.C., Dublin Tenement Life: An Oral History (Gill and Macmillan, 1994).
Kearns, K.C., Dublin's Lost Heroines: Mammies and Grannies in a Vanished City (Gill and Macmillan, 2004).

Kennedy, F., *Cottage to Creche: Family Change in Ireland* (Institute of Public Administration, 2001).
Kennedy, P. (ed.), *Motherhood in Ireland: Creation and Context* (Mercier Press, 2004).
Kenny, M., *Goodbye to Catholic Ireland* (Templegate, 2000).
Keogh, D., *Twentieth-Century Ireland: Nation and State* (Gill and Macmillan, 1994).
Keogh, D., F. O'Shea and C. Quinlan (eds), *The Lost Decade: Ireland in the 1950s* (Mercier Press, 2004).
Kunzel, R.G., *Fallen Women, Problem Girls: Unmarried Mothers and the Professionalization of Social Work, 1890–1945* (Yale University Press, 1993).
Lasch, C., *Haven in a Heartless World: The Family Besieged* (Basic Books, 1977).
Lee, J.J., *The Modernization of Irish Society 1848–1918* (Gill and Macmillan, 1973).
Lee, J.J., *Ireland, 1912–1985: Politics and Society* (Cambridge University Press, 1989).
Lewis, J., *The Politics of Motherhood: Child and Maternal Welfare in England, 1900–1939* (Croom Helm, 1980).
Luddy, M., *Women and Philanthropy in Nineteenth-Century Ireland* (Cambridge University Press, 1995).
Luddy, M., *Prostitution and Irish Society: 1800-1940* (Cambridge University Press, 2007).
Luddy, M., and C. Murphy (eds), *Women Surviving: Studies in Irish Women's History in the 19th and 20th Centuries* (Poolbeg Press, 1990).
MacCurtain, M., and D. Ó Corrain (eds), *Women in Irish Society: The Historical Dimension* (Connecticut Press, 1978).
McGarry, F., *Eoin O'Duffy: A Self-Made Hero* (Oxford University Press, 2005).
Maguire, M., *Precarious Childhood in Post-independence Ireland* (Manchester University Press, 2009).
Mahood, L., *Policing Gender, Class and Family: Britain 1850–1940* (University College London Press, 1995).
Malcolm, E., and G. Jones, *'Ireland Sober, Ireland Free': Drink and Temperance in Nineteenth-Century Ireland* (Gill and Macmillan, 1986).
Malcolm, E., and G. Jones, *Medicine, Disease and the State in Ireland, 1650–1940* (Cork University Press, 1999).
Milotte, M., *Banished Babies: The Secret History of Ireland's Baby Export Business* (New Island Books, 1997).
Mort, F., *Dangerous Sexualities: Medico-moral Politics in England since 1830* (Routledge and Kegan Paul, 1988).
Oakley, A., *Women Confined: Towards a Sociology of Childbirth* (Martin Robertson, 1980).
Ó Broin, L., *Frank Duff: A Biography* (Gill and Macmillan, 1982).
O'Donnell, I., O'Sullivan, E. and Hughes, N., *Sourcebook of Irish Criminal Justice Statistics* (Institute of Public Administration, 2005).
O'Dowd, M., and S., Wichert (eds), *Chattell, Servant or Citizen: Women's Status in Church, State and Society* (Queens University Press, 1995).
Ó'Drisceoil, D., *Censorship in Ireland 1939–1945: Neutrality, Politics and Society* (Cork University Press, 1996).
Ó'Drisceoil, D., and Fintan Lane, *Politics and the Irish Working Class, 1830–1945* (Palgrave, 2005).

Ó Gráda, C., *Ireland: A New Economic History 1780–1939* (Oxford University Press, 1994).
Ó hÓgartaigh, M., *Kathleen Lynn, Irishwoman, Patriot, Doctor* (Irish Academic Press, 2006).
Platt, A.M., *The Child Savers: The Invention of Delinquency* (University of Chicago Press, 1969; 1977).
Pederson, S., *Family, Dependence, and the Origins of the Welfare State: Britain and France, 1914–1945* (Cambridge University Press, 1993).
Pollock, L., *Forgotten Children: Parent–Child Relations from 1500 to 1900* (Cambridge University Press, 1983).
Powell, F., *The Politics of Social Work* (Sage, 2001).
Powell, F., and Guerin, D., *Civil Society and Social Policy: Voluntarism in Ireland* (Pavilion Publishing, 1997).
Prunty, J., *Dublin Slums 1800–1925: A Study in Urban Geography* (Irish Academic Press, 1998).
Raftery, M., and E. O'Sullivan, *Suffer the Little Children: The Inside Story of Ireland's Industrial Schools* (New Island Books, 1999).
Rattigan, C., *'What else could I do?' Single Mothers and Infanticide in Ireland, 1900–1950* (Irish Academic Press, 2011).
Reidy, C., *Ireland's 'Moral Hospital': The Irish Borstal System, 1906–1956* (Irish Academic Press, 2009).
Robins, J. *The Lost Children: A Study of Charity Children in Ireland 1700–1900* (Institute of Public Administration, 1980).
Ross, E., *Love and Toil: Motherhood in Outcast London, 1870–1918* (Oxford University Press, 1993).
Shorter, E., *A History of Women's Bodies* (Viking, 1983).
Skehill, C., *History of the Present: Child Protection and Welfare Social Work in Ireland* (Edwin Mellen Press, 2004).
Steedman, C., *Strange Dislocations: Childhood and the Idea of Human Interiority, 1780–1930* (Harvard University Press, 1995).
Tosh, J., *A Man's Place: Masculinity and the Middle-Class Home in Victorian England* (Yale University Press, 1999).
Tweedy, H., *A Link in the Chain: The Story of the Irish Housewives Association 1942–1992* (Attic Press, 1992).
Tyrrell, P. *Founded on Fear: Letterfrack Industrial School, War and Exile*, edited by Diarmuid Whelan (Irish Academic Press, 2006).
Valiulis, M.G., and M. O'Dowd (eds), *Women and Irish History: Essays in Honour of Margaret McCurtain* (Wolfhound Press, 1997).
Ward, M., *The Missing Sex: Putting Women into Irish History* (Attic Press, 1991).
Weeks, J., *Sex, Politics and Society: The Regulation of Sexuality Since 1800* (Longman, 1981).
Whelan, B. (ed.) *Women and Paid Work in Ireland 1500–1931* (Four Courts Press, 2000).
Whyte, J.H., *Church and State in Modern Ireland 1923–1979* (Gill Macmillan, 1980).

Index

8 Uhr Blatt (newspaper, Germany) 34
1913 strike and lockout 23–4

Abercorn, Duke of 48
abortion 29, 103, 147, 174
adoption 28, 31–6, 72, 78, 84, 87, 90, 103, 106, 110, 134
Adoption Society of Ireland 32–3
adultery 74
alcohol intemperance 22, 54, 56–63, 75–6, 84, 86, 142, 163, 165, 187–8, 190, 199n24, 200
Anthony, Richard 126–8
approved schools 114, 124
Aries, Phillipe 2
Arnold, Bruce 111, 121, 131

Babies' Clubs 22
'baby-farming' 16–17, 20, 42n23, 43n29
Bailey, Victor 154
Barnes, Jane 144
Barrett, Fr Cecil 35
Beauchamp, Richard Hawkins 49, 66n10
begging 76, 78, 83, 87, 120, 122, 172, 198n2
Behlmer, George K. 3, 57
Beresford, Jim 144
Beveridge Report (Inter-Departmental Committee on Social Insurance and Allied Services, 1942) 39, 41, 103
bigamy 178, 180, 184
birth concealment 17, 172
Blackburn, Sheila 154
boarding-out/fostering 11–15, 18, 33, 42n8, 90, 110, 115, 121, 124, 126, 134, 142
Board of Health 21
Boland, Gerald 182
borstals 6, 113, 116–18, 121, 129, 131–2
   Clonmel 117
Bourke, Joanna 191

Bretherton, George 60
British Medical Journal (BMJ) 16
Browne, Bishop Robert 55
Brunker, A.A. 38
Buckley, Christine 110
Bunreacht na hÉireann (Irish Constitution, 1937) 27, 29, 41, 79, 104, 110, 134, 201
   children's rights (31st) amendment to Constitution 1, 202
Businessmen's Party 80
Byrne, Alfred 125
Byrne, Archbishop Edward 98, 100–1

Campaign for the Care of Deprived Children (CARE) 146
Cannon, Revd P.L. 117
Carrigan Committee (Committee on the Criminal Law Amendment Acts, 1931) 30, 159, 161, 163, 170n42
   report 157, 159–60
Carrigan, William 159
Casey, Charles 33–4
Casti Connubii (papal encyclical, 1930) 29–30
Catholic Action 71
Catholic Church 7, 28–30, 34, 40, 64, 70, 79, 82, 84, 104–5, 110–11, 126, 128, 133, 147, 153, 179, 181, 197
   and child welfare 6, 13, 28, 32–3, 35, 75, 105, 136–40, 147
   opposes Provision of School Meals Act (1906) 22
   opposition to socialism 11, 24
   politicisation of child welfare 12
   provider of social/medical services 71, 105
Catholic Male Discharged Prisoners' Aid Committee 98–100
Catholic Rescue and Protection Society of Ireland 36, 99, 123

Cavanan, Joseph E. 121
censorship 35–6, 106, 165
charitable/voluntary organisations 4–5, 10–12, 19, 22, 29, 38–40, 47–8, 65, 70–1, 97, 103–5, 112, 118, 124, 128, 132, 134, 156, 171–2, 177, 188, 200
child/children
    abandonment 53, 83, 146, 172, 174, 198n2
    abuse of/cruelty to 47, 55–8, 62–3, 76, 82–3, 87, 90, 102, 112, 124, 143–4, 146, 156, 163, 171–5, 178–9, 187, 200, 202
    as 'assets' 10, 140
    family allowances 39–41, 105
    labour 26, 36, 88
    'of the nation' 10, 74
    neglect 19–20, 55–7, 60–2, 72–6, 85–8, 90–3, 105, 114–15, 124, 134, 144, 165, 171–5, 179–80, 184, 187, 200–1
    sexual abuse 1, 35–6, 133–4, 146, 153, 155–6, 160–1, 164–5, 167–8
    undernourishment/starvation 56, 73–4, 83, 85, 200
    unemployment 27–8
    welfare, financial considerations of 6, 15–22, 50, 87, 90, 116–17, 122, 124–30, 134, 136–7, 139–40, 143, 180, 201
    welfare, nationalist movement's politicisation of 10–12, 23–4
    welfare, religious influence on provisions for 11, 23
    welfare and the courts 5–6, 20, 22–3, 25–8, 51, 53, 62–4, 69n62, 75, 77, 81–2, 84, 90, 95, 122, 128, 134, 137–40, 144, 153–6, 162–4, 167, 169nn20–2, 171–86, 188–98
    welfare and local authorities 15, 18
    welfare movement, international emergence of 51–2
    welfare officers 85
    welfare and philanthropists 12–14, 17–18, 36, 47, 51–3, 58, 60, 65, 70, 194, 200
    welfare and police 6, 22, 25–6, 50, 92, 131, 134, 138–9, 155, 159, 162–4, 166, 170n42, 180, 186
    see also Catholic Church
childhood death see infant mortality
Child Study Movement 21
Christian Brothers 97, 122–3, 143
Church Missions Homes 33
Clark, Anna 12

Clear, Caitríona 39–40
Commission on the Relief of the Sick and Destitute Poor, Including the Insane Poor (1927) 28, 30–1
Commission on Youth Unemployment (1943–51) 28
Committee on Reformatory and Industrial Schools (1970) 28
Committee on the Enforcement of Debts (UK) 184
Conley, Carolyn 191, 195
contraception/birth control 29, 33, 103, 106
Coombe Hospital (Dublin) 20
Cork Constitution 49
Cork Examiner 49
Cork Herald 49
corporal punishment 25, 27, 58, 75, 81, 88, 121, 124, 130, 145, 194–6
Cosgrave, William J. 115
Cottage Home (Dun Laoghaire) 19–20
county homes 31, 95, 122, 140–1.
    see also workhouses
courts
    children's 74, 113, 115–16, 123, 145–6, 167
    juvenile 114–15
Cousins, Mel 39–40
Criminal Law Amendment Bill and Sexual Offences Bill (1918), report on the 157
Criminal Law Amendment Bills (1&2), report on the 157
Crossman, Virginia 3, 12–13, 110, 119
Cullen, Cardinal Paul 98
Cumann na nGaedheal 28
Cunningham, Hugh 2
Curtis Committee report (1948) 115
Cussen, George 87, 123
Cussen Report (Commission of Inquiry into the Reformatory and Industrial School System, 1934–36) 28, 115–16, 119, 123, 125, 131

Daly, Mary 3, 25, 79, 82
Davin, Anna 25, 27
Dear Daughter (RTÉ) 110
Democratic Programme (First Dáil) 70, 106n1, 201, 203
Departmental Committee on Sexual Offences against Young Persons, report on (1925; UK) 157
Departmental Committee on the Treatment of Young Offenders (1925) 114
Department of Defence 158

Department of Education 79, 81, 116, 123, 137
Department of External Affairs 36
Department of Finance 37, 39, 81, 116
Department of Foreign Affairs 34
Department of Health 138
Department of Justice 36, 123, 129, 131, 158–9
Department of Local Government and Public Health 13, 31, 123, 158
Derrig, Tomás 129–30
desertion (family) 7, 11, 31, 49–50, 77, 88–9, 103, 105, 120, 178–85, 197, 201–2
de Valera, Eamon 29, 36, 39
Devane, R.S. 117, 161, 170n42
Dickie, Marie 14–15
Dillon, James M. 115–16, 125, 129
Dillon, T.W. 38
divorce 106, 180, 184
Dublin Board of Assistance 31
Dublin Chamber of Commerce 38
Dublin Corporation 123
Dublin Trades Council 123
Duff, Frank 100–1, 138, 158
Duff, John 158
Duggan, M.E. 156
Dunne, Revd P. 98

Earner-Byrne, Lindsey 1, 3, 11, 21, 79, 89, 97, 156, 188
Easons and Sons Schoolboys' Strike 24
Education, Department of 116
Emergency, the (1939–46) 36–9, 103, 201
Ennis State Inebriate Reformatory 57, 60–1, 172, 200
Episcopal Committee 35
Eucharistic Congress (1932) 29
Evening Herald 49
Evening Press 181

Fahey, Tony 180
Fahy, Edward 100, 131–2
Falkiner, F. 55
Farmers' Party 80
Farrell, Elaine 17
female sexuality 29–30, 71
Ferguson, Harry 2–3, 47
Ferriter, Diarmaid 7
Fianna Fáil 29, 39
Fitzgerald-Kenney, James 155
fostering *see* boarding-out/fostering
Foucault, Michel 134
Frankfurt School 9n4

Freeman's Journal 24
free medical aid 22
Garrett, Paul 79
Gleeson, Dermot 159
Glynn, John A. 98
Gonne, Maud 22–3
Good, John 80
Gordon, Linda 51–2, 72–3, 185
Gormanston, Viscountess 59
Gray, Peter 3
Grimshaw, Cecil Thomas Wrigley 48, 66n5

Hackett, Mary 123
Hanna, Joseph 123
Hart, Ernest 16
Heffernan, Michael 80
Hendrick, Harry 2, 4, 21, 27, 53, 55, 57–8, 72, 112, 114–15, 144
Heron, Archie 128
Higgins, Col. Thomas 158
home assistance/poor relief 30, 72, 74, 77–8, 121, 125, 157, 184

illegitimacy/illegitimate children 15–17, 31–2, 35, 73, 75, 77–9, 82–6, 92, 103, 105, 118, 120, 122, 133, 197
'immorality'/moral neglect 7, 29, 35, 74, 76, 83, 88, 93, 103, 133, 136, 139, 152–62, 164–5, 168
'improper' guardianship 74
incest 7, 68n31, 72, 115, 152–68
Industrial School Managers Association 123
industrial schools 11, 16, 23, 31, 36, 52, 57, 60, 64, 75, 81–2, 87, 90–3, 101, 105–6, 110–47, 147n2, 148n16, 161, 165, 168, 200–2
  Artane (Dublin) 131, 135, 144–5
  Carriglea (Dun Laoghaire, Co. Dublin) 136
  Clonakility 144
  Glencree (Co. Wicklow) 73, 117
  Goldenbridge (Dublin) 110–11
  Greenmount (Cork) 128
  Letterfrack (Co. Galway) 143
  Salthill (Co. Galway) 143
  Sandymount (Dublin) 112
  St Aidan's (New Ross, Co. Wexford) 50, 135, 137, 140–1
  St Kylan (Rathdrum, Dublin) 135
  St Michael's (Cappoquin, Co. Waterford) 135, 137
  St Michael's (Wexford) 135–8
infanticide 16–17, 20, 29, 79, 87, 163–5, 172–3

infant life protection 22
infant mortality 10, 13, 17, 19–21, 27, 29, 53, 85
Ingram, John K. 13
inquests 19
inspections/supervision/registration/accreditation/oversight of child-welfare workers/facilities/foster homes 14–15, 18–21, 23, 33–4, 122, 124, 127, 130
institutionalisation 2–3, 5–6, 17, 32, 40, 60, 70, 74, 87, 106, 110–13, 118, 121, 132, 135, 145, 147n3, 148n13, 163, 165, 167, 201
Irish Citizen 27, 30, 94, 190, 196
Irish Independent 24, 59, 90, 117, 144, 196
Irish Labour Defence League 131
Irish Society for the Prevention of Cruelty to Children (ISPCC) 47, 146, 181
  see also National Society for the Prevention of Cruelty to Children (NSPCC)
Irish Times 16, 19–20, 75, 117, 145, 183–4, 196
Irish Women Citizens' and Local Government Association 123
Irish Women's Temperance Union 60
Irish Worker 24

Jackson, Louise A. 133, 161
Johnson, Thomas 125
juvenile delinquency/offenders 1, 22, 74–5, 103, 106, 111, 113–18, 132, 145, 201
Juvenile Liaison Officer Scheme (1962) 28
juvenile smoking 22

Kavanagh, Florrie 34
Kavanagh, Michael 34
Kavanagh, Tommy 34
Kearns, Kevin 79, 96, 101, 187
Kennedy, Eileen 28
Kennedy, Finola 39–40
Kennedy Report (Reformatory and Industrial Schools System Report, 1970) 10, 124–5, 145–6
Kettle, Mary 117

Labour Party 38
Ladies' School Dinner Committee 22
Larkin, James 24
Lasch, Christopher 114
League of Nations 29, 70
Leane, Máire 30
Lee, J.J. 39
Legion of Mary 100–2, 105, 137–8

legislation 28, 71, 153
  Adoption Act (1952) 33–5
  Aggravated Assaults on Women and Children Act (1853) 189
  Child Care Act (1991) 122
  child labour laws 53
  Children Act (1908) 11, 17–18, 20, 22–3, 26, 84–5, 114, 122, 128, 162, 165, 167–8, 172, 182, 201
  Children Act (1934) 28
  Children Act (1991) 23
  Children and Young Persons Act (1933) 114–15
  Children's Act (1929) 26, 81, 121–2, 129, 201
  Children's Allowances Act (1944) 40
  County Boards of Health (Assistance) Order (1924) 12
  Courts of Justice Act (1924) 28, 77
  Criminal Law Amendment (CLA) Acts 30, 85, 156–7, 122, 159–61
    CLA Act (1880) 30, 85
    CLA Act (1885) 30, 85, 160
    CLA Act (1935) 30, 160–1
  Criminal Law (Incest Proceedings) Act (1995) 154
  Dublin Police Act (1842) 182
  Education (Provision of Meals) (Ireland) Act (1914) 22
  Elementary Education Acts (1870–93) 26, 82
  Health Act (1953) 28
  Illegitimate Affiliation Order Bill in Ireland (1930) 155
  Illegitimate Children (Affiliation Orders) Act (1930) 78
  Industrial Schools Amendment Act (1880) 148n14
  Industrial Schools (Ireland) Act (1868) 11, 112–13, 148n14
  Inebriates Act (1898) 59–60
  Infant Life Protection Act (1872) 16, 19–20, 84
  Infant Life Protection Amendment Act (1897) 18–19
  Irish Education Act (1892) 25
  Irish Poor Law Amendment Act (1862) 11–12
  Local Government (Temporary Provision) Act (1923) 30
  Married Women Maintenance in Cases of Desertion Act (1886) 78
  Midwives (Ireland) Act (1918) 22
  Notification of Births Act (1907) 21

Notification of Births (Ireland) Act (1915) 21
Pauper Children Act (1898) 11
Poor Law Amendment Act (1834) 17
Poor Law (Ireland) Act (1838) 10–13
Poor Laws (general) 18, 21, 30, 47, 119, 122, 172, 175
Prevention of Crimes Act (1871) 148n14
Prevention of Cruelty to Children Act (1889) 21, 48, 64, 172
  amendment (1894) 22
Prevention of Cruelty to Children Act (1904) 19, 23
Probation of Offenders Act (1907) 11
Provision of School Meals Act (1906) 22
Public Assistance Act (1939) 12, 181–2
Public Safety Act (1927) 115, 201
Punishment of Incest Act (1908; amended 1922, 1995) 6, 72, 153–4, 201
Reformatory Schools (Ireland) Act, (1858) 11
School Attendance Act (1926) 28, 79–80, 82, 121–2, 180, 201
Summary Jurisdiction over Children Act (1884) 11
Vagrancy (Ireland) Act (1847) 181–2
Widow's and Orphan's Pension Act (1931) 91
Lemass, Seán 39
Letchworth, W.P. 65
Little, Patrick 126–7
Local Government Board for Ireland 13–15, 55
Lodge, The (Belfast) 60
Luddy, Maria 2–3, 11, 51, 54, 57–8, 79
lunatic asylums 121, 199n45
  Dundrum (Dublin) 125, 192, 194–5
  Monaghan 193
  Mullingar 63
Lynn, Kathleen 22

MacCarvill, Patrick 123
MacEntee, Seán 39, 128
Magdalene laundries 1, 32, 101, 121, 140, 147, 164–6
  Good Shepherd Convent (Cork) 109n87, 165
Maguire, Moira 1, 3, 7, 32, 72, 79
Maher, Mary 145
Mahood, Linda 134
McArdle, Revd Joseph 123
McAvoy, Sandra 160
McCafferty, Nell 146

McDonnell, Percy 158
McGowan, Gerrard 116
McNulty, Revd J. 163
McQuaid, Archbishop John Charles 33, 35, 138
Meade, Bishop Edward 55
medical neglect 73–5, 83, 125
medical profession 29
mixed marriages 35, 100–1
Montefiore, Dora 24
Moore, Séamus 125–8
Moorhead, Dr 158
Moran, Michael 181
mother-and-baby homes 31, 33, 35, 64, 91, 142
  Bessboro House (Cork) 31–2
  Pelletstown (Dublin) 31
mother and child scheme (1951) 33, 75, 104
mother's payments 87
Murphy, Francis 66n8

National Council of Women of Ireland 160
National Society for the Prevention of Cruelty to Children (NSPCC)
  addresses Commission to Inquire into the Reformatory and Industrial School System (1934) 123
  'advice sought' (investigations) 72, 76, 83, 103, 171, 197
  advisory agency 186–7
  and 'immorality' 161
  bequests in favour of 49, 66
  branches 47, 66n3
    Cork 49, 52, 54–5, 6/n17, 84, 161–2
    Dublin 59, 67n17, 75–7, 84, 86, 141–2, 161–2, 187
    Limerick/Clare 162
    Liverpool 51, 105
    London 21
    North Louth, Monaghan and Cavan 102
    Waterford 135
    Wexford 53, 55, 79, 81–4, 93, 104, 134
  case loads 49
  Charter 54
  Children's League of Pity 49
  Child's Guardian 52
  class consciousness/bias 3, 47, 51–2, 56–8, 65, 83, 139, 171, 201
  collaboration with the State 6, 81, 104, 106, 111, 136, 147
  corporal punishment 81
  'Cruelty Man' 103, 138, 182
  Dublin Aid Committee 46, 48, 175
  early development 47–9, 51–2, 64

ethos/aims 2, 46, 48, 55, 59–60, 63, 65, 72, 88, 102
foundation 46
funding 49, 52, 54, 64, 71, 104
gender bias 18, 51, 83, 139, 171, 188, 197–8, 201
Golden Jubilee 102, 128, 200
industrial schools, attitude towards/ collaboration with 64, 104–5, 110, 132–8, 141, 161, 165, 200, 202
Infant Protection Visitor 85
inspections of private homes 18, 20, 53, 56–7, 61, 63, 65, 73, 84–5, 95
inspectors 18, 25, 49–51, 56–7, 60–3, 68n34, 71–2, 74, 76–7, 81, 84–7, 89–91, 93, 95, 104–5, 118, 121–2, 128, 134–42, 147, 166, 171, 181–3, 186–8, 197
Inspector's Directory 51, 56, 171
Inspectors' Quarterly 50
Ladies' Committee 107n31
lobbyist/campaigner for legislation/ reform 6, 21–3, 31, 47, 51–2, 59, 71, 78, 84, 94, 105, 115, 181
membership composition 48, 52, 54, 65
membership subscriptions 48–9, 64
on deserted families 7
on incest 6–7
on voluntary agencies 103
professionalisation 71
prosecutorial activities 19, 47–9, 51, 53, 58, 60, 64, 71, 73, 76, 83, 104–6, 118, 122, 144, 147, 168, 188, 200
relationship with British branch 47, 52–4, 59, 103–4, 181, 197
renamed ISPCC (1956) 104
reports 2, 5, 14, 46, 48–9, 52–9, 64, 67n17, 72, 77–8, 82, 84, 86, 90, 94, 102–4, 106n17, 133–4, 137, 140, 161, 165, 171, 180–1, 187, 200
'The whole work of the Society' 53
salaried staff 49
shelter (20 Molesworth Street, Dublin) 64
subtitle (1939): National Society for the Protection and Care of Children 102
surveillance of families 26
Women Visitors Scheme 103
see also Irish Society for the Prevention of Cruelty to Children (ISPCC)
National Vigilance Association (NVA) 6, 154
nurse children 13, 15–18, 20, 75, 82–7, 90

Oblate Fathers 148n15

O'Brien, Mick 185
O'Connell, Thomas 126
O'Duffy, Eoin 84, 159, 163, 170n42
O'Farrell, Seamus 123
Ó hÓgartaigh, Margaret 22
O'Leary, Fr Jerome 105
Order of Charity 122–3
O'Reilly, Thomas 61
orphanages 11, 47, 52–3, 64, 90–1, 96, 98–9, 101, 167
orphaned children 11, 31, 52, 122
O'Sullivan, Eoin 1, 6, 111, 113, 119, 138, 140, 160–1
O'Sullivan, John Marcus 81, 125–7, 130
Ó Tighearnaigh, Prionsias 123
overcrowding 72, 74, 93–5, 103

Parr, Robert J. 52, 54, 58, 67n23, 137
Parson, Talcott 8n4
Penal Reform League 114
Pius XI, Pope 30
Platt, Anthony 114
Poor Clares 123
Poor Law boards of guardians 13, 15, 17, 21, 30–1, 58, 60, 62, 90, 110, 174, 193
poor relief 103
poverty 13, 15, 22, 27–8, 31–2, 37–9, 49, 55, 57–9, 75, 77, 79, 85, 97, 105, 120–1, 125–6, 141–2, 200–2
Powell, Fred 39, 105
Presentation Brothers 122
Presentation Order, Sisters of 123
probation service 11, 100, 131–2
professionalisation of childcare/education/ medical care 9n4
pronatalism 39
proselytism 10–11, 24, 32–3, 35, 50, 53–4, 60, 65, 70, 89, 96–100, 201
prostitution 30, 36, 79, 88, 156–7, 159, 161
Protestant Churches 40
Prunty, Jacinta 96

Raftery, Mary 1, 6, 111, 119, 140
'ragged schools' 11, 52
Rattigan, Clíona 79
reformatories 11–12, 22–3, 28, 36, 53, 58–60, 62–4, 75, 87, 93, 110, 112–14, 116–26, 129, 131–2, 134, 141, 146, 148n15, 177
  Daingean (Co. Wicklow) 129, 132, 145
  Glencree (Co. Wicklow) 148
  St Brigid's (Waterford) 60
  St Patrick's (Wexford) 60

Index

refuges 53
Reidy, Conor 117
Relief of the Poor and Destitute Poor, Report into the (1927) 121
reporting (alleged wrongdoing) 50, 91–2
Robin, Joseph 2
Ross, E.A. 8n4
Royal College of Surgeons 48
Royal Commission on Housing of the Working Classes (1884–85) 55, 67n31, 154
Royal Commission on Venereal Disease (1916) 157, 159
    report 158
Russell, Angela 123
Russell, Jane 33–4
Ryan Report (Report of the Commission to Inquire into Child Abuse in Ireland, 2009) 6, 111, 121, 124, 128–9, 134, 138

Salvation Army 102
schooling 10, 25–8, 53, 79–82, 93, 106, 120–1
Scott, Sir John H. 55
sectarianism (religious) 54, 60, 65, 70
Sexual Offences Against Young Persons (1925), report on the 157
Sexual Offences Bill (1920), report on the 157
Sheehy-Skeffington, Hanna 131, 169n20
Sherrington, Christine Anne 5, 55, 57
Sherrington, Sue 72, 103
single mothers 17, 30, 70, 74, 77, 79, 84, 88–9, 91, 93, 105–6, 143–4, 165, 181, 201–2
Sisters of Charity, Irish 123, 137
Sisters of Charity of the St Vincent de Paul 123
Sisters of Mercy 123
Sisters of Our Lady of Refuge 123
Sisters of Saint Louis 123
Sisters of the Good Shepherd 123, 148n15
Skehill, Caroline 1, 3
Skibbereen Eagle 49
Smith, Samuel 51, 58
social control 8n4
social engineering 37, 39
Society of Friends 117
Society of St Vincent de Paul (SVDP) 6, 82, 96–102, 105, 109n87, 118, 123, 137–8, 180, 183
    Orphanage of St Vincent de Paul 96, 108n70

States of Fear (RTÉ) 6, 111, 130
Statistical and Social Inquiry Society of Ireland 13, 119
Staunton, Bishop J. 33
Steiner-Scott, Liz 185, 190–1, 198
St John of God (religious order, Waterford) 60
Suffer the Little Children (Raftery & O'Sullivan) 6, 111

Thunder, Br Francis P. 97
Tillet, Ben 24
Tuairim Report (Some of Our Children) (1966) 28
Tyrrell, Peter 143–4

unemployment 26–8, 38, 96
United Council of Christian Churches and Religious Communions in Ireland 160
unmarried mothers 17, 29, 31–3, 41, 74, 79, 84, 86–90, 143, 155, 160, 167, 197

Valiulis, Maryann 29
venereal disease 156–9, 168
    report on (1926) 157
    see also Royal Commission on Venereal Disease (1916)
Viney, Michael 145, 184

Walsh, Archbishop Dermot 24, 67n25
Wartime Economy Committee 37
Watching the Courts Committee 156, 169nn20–2
Waugh, Benjamin 52, 67n25
Webb, Mary Anne 71
welfare *see* child/children
Wexford County Board of Health 104
Whelan, Diarmuid 143
widows/widowers 5, 31, 74, 83, 85, 89, 91–3, 142, 165, 180
wife-beating/domestic violence 7, 154, 163, 167, 171–2, 181–3, 185–98, 201
Women's Cooperative Guild 41n3
Women's International League for Peace and Freedom 115
Women's National Health Association (WNHA) 11, 21, 41n3
Workers' Action 38–9
workhouses 12–13, 15–16, 30, 79, 95, 112–13, 119, 121–2, 189
    see also county homes
Wyse Power, Jane 155

youth unemployment 27–8

EU authorised representative for GPSR:
Easy Access System Europe, Mustamäe tee 50,
10621 Tallinn, Estonia
gpsr.requests@easproject.com

www.ingramcontent.com/pod-product-compliance
Lightning Source LLC
Chambersburg PA
CBHW071407300426
44114CB00016B/2216